LIVING IN TWO WORLDS

A Gwich'in Woman Shares her story

A NATIVE OF THE NORTHWEST TERRITORIES

Therese Remy-Sawyer

TERRY AT DIFFERENT AGES

Order this book online at www.trafford.com
or email orders@trafford.com

Most Trafford titles are also available at major online book retailers.

Printed in Victoria, BC, Canada.

ISBN: 978-1-4269-1126-2 (soft)
ISBN: 978-1-4269-1219-1 (ebook)

*Our mission is to efficiently provide the world's finest, most comprehensive
book publishing service, enabling every author to experience success.
To find out how to publish your book, your way, and have it available
worldwide, visit us online at www.trafford.com*

Trafford rev. 10/5/2009

 www.trafford.com

North America & international
toll-free: 1 888 232 4444 (USA & Canada)
phone: 250 383 6864 ♦ fax: 812 355 4082

Contents

Preface

These days it seems the bad news gets around so quickly! So when something positive happens it is a pleasure to hear of good news for a change. One of the recent items sure to receive a warm welcome is that Therese Remi- Sawyer born on an Arctic trap line near Arctic Red River deep in the Canadian North, has written her recollections of life in her region.

Canadians crowding to make homes on the 200 mile- wide corridor along the 49th parallel have been slow to take the vast and distinctive North to their hearts; too many of them have not seen the northern half of their country. If there are false views about our North being a cheerless land of perpetual winter, it is unfortunate and certainly underlies the importance of the story that this author brings.

No one is better qualified than Terry to tell about spring moving in on the heels of a long winter or the rush of birds returning to nest in the North. She can tell us about the appearance, as if by magic, of a million fresh water lakes; the glory of sub-Arctic flowers; the unbelievable reality of the midnight sun and the abundance of the Northern Arctic berries.

Canada has an urgent need for people who can explain the spell of the North. We welcome Therese Norwegian (Sawyer) a genuine daughter of the North, to the unique band of authors who give us their personal and profound perspective.

Grant Mac Ewan
Calgary, Alberta
(In memory of)

Foreword

Therese Remi- Sawyer was born on the trap line near the Arctic Red River and spent her childhood along the lower Mackenzie River. Raised by her grandparents, she learned from an early age how to live on the land, to dry meat and smoke and dry fish, to tan animal hides, to snare rabbits and sew hide garments. As Terry recounts her childhood, we learn the hardships and joys of these traditional Gwichya Gwich'in ways. We learn too of her grandparents' spiritual teachings and life values they taught her to respect.

Terry tells of significant events in Gwich'in history. The election of the first chief, her paternal grandfather Paul Niditchie; dealings with missionaries, Hudson's Bay Company traders and the RCMP, and the signing of Treaty 11 are all presented from the Gwich'in perspective.

Though rooted in traditional upbringing, Terry's story is also that of an aboriginal woman making her way in the non-aboriginal world. A skilled artisan and storyteller, her life as addictions counselor, Dene spokesperson and single mother has been remarkable, given her early challenges. Life at the residential school, racism, extended hospitalization and a series of poorly -paid jobs put Terry's spirit to the test. Most devastating of all was her first marriage to an abusive husband. Terry's description of this relationship is unflinchingly honest. Her account of her escape from this marriage and its legacy of helplessness and fear resonate with the determination of one who will survive and become and individual in her own right.

When she was a young girl, Terry's family hoped that she would become a messenger for her people, a bridge between the Gwichya Gwich'in and the outside world. With the publication of "Living in Two Worlds," Terry fulfills those early dreams. The message that she delivers is one of resilience, caring and respect. It comes from the teachings of the Gwich'in elders. Its power and wisdom speak to us all.

Thank you, (Ma'sii) Terry.
Susan Berry
Provincial Museum of Alberta Edmonton, Alberta

Introduction

Why am I writing my story? Like my Gwich'in ancestors, I believe that people should share stories. Stories help us understand one another and communicate without fear. For many years, I have dreamed about sharing my culture with others. Our culture gives us our identity, strength which in turn strengthens our self confidence. Let us hope that this will create a better understanding of who we are and where we come from. Though at times the road was rough on my journey of understanding, I continue to travel with hope and faith. Somewhere ahead the road will eventually become smooth. One time, someone asked me, "As an only child, were you ever lonely living alone out on the land? I laughed and said, "Never!" I did not know what the word alone meant. I had the land, nature, birds, animals; I was never lonely, or felt alone.

Dadda and Mamma were always there for me; they gave me love and I felt secure. I grew up amongst elders, stories and nature. Our culture comes alive through stories. "Because of our stories you know who you are, my elders would say. In the Gwich'in traditional way, the grandparent or parent give each child the gift of many stories, creating an unbreakable bond.

How could I ever feel alone? My father's parent's traditionally adopted me as an infant. Once Mama and Dadda took me in their arms, they never gave me back to my parents. Mama and Dadda said they were going to teach me the Gwich'in traditional culture, so I could also pass it on to future generations. Years later, as a young adult, I sadly wavered from these teachings. Maybe this happened because people taught the western way in residential school and in the workplace. Nevertheless, like a shadow, it followed me throughout my life, and I never forgot my Mamma and my Dadda's words. The urge to teach my Gwich'in history to our younger generation was like an unhealed wound.

I had to pay attention to it, but had no idea how or where to begin. Documenting my stories on tape would mean people might edit and change them, losing much meaning. Thinking of putting them down on paper made me realize how I longed for my culture. I wanted it to be a part of my life again, without shame or remorse. I wanted to embrace and live it! I know now that with my traditional early life and my western teachings" I can indeed live in two worlds. This realization changed my life, my thinking and my direction.

To bring balance to my life I had to embrace my cultural teachings and reconcile them with everything that I had learned in residential school. Rather than feel guilty for what I did and who I was, I needed to integrate the loving elements of the Christian faith with my heritage.

Until I was able to do this, I lived a life of fear and guilt. The horrifying experiences I had in my first relationship continue to haunt me. When I see physical abuse or hear abusive words, it awakens my fear and anger. I pray daily to my Creator and my Holy Mother to help me. I pray for strength to banish negativity from my heart. By telling my story I hope to heal and give hope to those who have found themselves in similar situations, especially where children are involved. . In my language, the elders would say, "(If you are an adult, act like one. Give your children love and protection; do not make them afraid. Fear will make them hate)."

All people have the ability to overcome adversity and life experiences that scar the human spirit. My hope and faith in my Creator, and my strength came from people who supported and encouraged me.

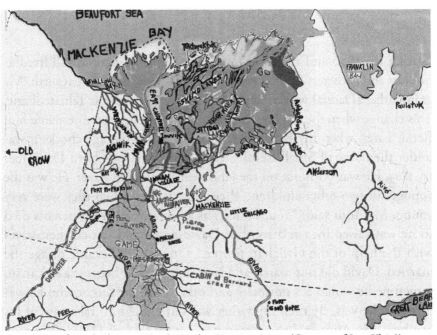

(Map of North Showing Terry's Families Hunting Area   (Courtesy of Joey Klein))

Profile of My Grandfather and Grandmother

During the 1800 and the early 1900, The Gwich'in people still lived as hunters and gatherers. Indian names were given to the infant at birth. My grandfather (Dadda) was known to the Gwich'in people as Tehiatedhzzie. This change when the missionary priest baptized him. They, re-name him Remi. Later, when my father began to receive his old age checks it was under the name of Small Remi. Remi, my father was born December 17, 1883. He was born out on the land near Arctic Red River. He was the younger of two other children. Their parents died when they were very young. My Aunt said, "Your father was an infant when his parents died so he was raised by a relative, but David and Aajill, raised themselves with the help of the Gwich'in people. Once Aajill became of age she married. David did not marry, and later in his life he became a sick man, sometime he would act normally and other times he forgot who he was or where he was. By then my father was old enough to take care of his brother. My Aunt said she remember a story told of David. The missionaries realized David was a very sick man, somehow they found a way to sent him South to a hospital, he was never heard of again. My family thinks he died in some hospital in the South and got buried there.

My grandmother (Mamma) Tsugunna was born January 25, 1884. Her baptism was Marie, but was known to the Gwich'in people as Tsugunna. She was an only child. Her mother taught her to become a very skilled and knowledgeable Gwich'in woman. In 1905 she married Tehiatedhizzie. (Small Remi) As an only child my great grandmother devoted teaching her all the traditional skills and stories. Dadda and Mamma prayed to the Creator to give them a child. They also ask the missionary priest to pray for them. There prayers were answered and in January 20th 1912 my father John Remi was born. As soon as John was old enough, he was sent to Fort Providence School. This place was far up the Mackenzie River, it took many days to get there. In those days commuting between villages was done by Traditional build moose skin boat. My Dadda said, "You're Mamma and I decided to send your father to the residential School in Fort Providence NWT. We wanted your father to become a missionary. They wanted my father to become a priest to work amongst his people. My father spends many years at this residential school.

The Bishop finally brought him home to visit his parents when he was in his teens. This was supposed to be his last visit before they took him further South to enter a place where they taught you to be a priest. Once my father was home he changed his mind. He was going to stay home and look after his parents. Many times Dadda talked about how hurt he felt. He felt he had broken his promise to the Creator but accepted my father decision. Because my father went to residential School when he was little, he now has to learn his language and culture. My father became a very good hunter. He learned to respect land and animals and in return he would always have plenty of food. The next few years were spent with father and son hunting and trapping. My father was now a man. His parents decided it was time for my father to marry. They had to find a young woman who was a good worker. Good traditional sewer, and was knowledgeable in all traditional skills. My mother Liza Niditchie was chosen. She was the daughter of Chief Paul and Camilla Niditchie. My grandparents said, "She will make a good wife for our son, a good mother for our grand children. John Remy and Liza Niditchie were married July 4th 1934. It was a double wedding; Otto Natsie and Bernadette Moses also got married. They said there was a big celebration with a big feast and a dance because the only son of Remi and Marie Tsugunna and the daughter of Chief Paul and Camilla Niditchie were wed. The celebration went for days until everyone was tired.

My grandparents on my mother side were Didii (grandfather) Paul and Didoo (grandmother) Camilla Niditchie. Didii Paul came over from Fort Yukon, Alaska,

As a young man, he married a Gwichya Gwich'in woman from Tsiigehtchic. They had a son and soon afterwards she pass away, So Didii Paul became a widow when he was still young. Didoo Camilla had been married also, but her husband also died. During her first marriage, Camilla and her husband adopted a boy, so now that she became a widow she had a son to raise. Some years had passed since Didii Paul and Camilla were widowed, they both married in 1916. My mother was born 1917 and my Aunt was born 1921. They also had a son who died when he was only about ten years old. They also had a little girl who died soon after birth. Some years later my Uncle Amos became a very special person in Dadda's and my lives. Uncle Amos became the son that Dadda had lost and Uncle Amos became the father I had lost.

MY DADDA (FACING)

MY MAMMA MARIE ETSUGUNA

TERRYS GRANDFATHER AND MARIE ETSUGUNNA
(CORTESY OF EMMA CLARK SHEURERE)

3

The Crown People

Didii Paul Niditchie became the first Chief of Arctic Red River (Tsiigehtchic) Village for 25 years. Chief for each community along the Mackenzie River was established in July of 1921. Prior to this time Elders govern their people. My Aunt said her parents told this story many times. The Crown people boat landed, they told the people the crown had sent them to make peace with the people who occupy the land of the far North. These people had been traveling down the Mackenzie River, that summer to make treaty with the people of the villages. These people said they brought messages from the Crown, they said they come in peace. Treaties were to be made with the people who occupy the land. They said "in the future your way of life would be protected; you will have stores which will carry necessary items which would make your trapping hunting, fishing much easier. Our medicine man will come live amongst you, to help you get well, when you are taken ill where your traditional medicine was not helping. Your children would also receive Educated. Fishing places would also be protected, and you will starve no more, because you will have white man store which will provide some of the food they may need. They would also be given 1 fishing net, 1box of rifle, 1shot gun shells and 1 box of 22 shells for their hunting. The Chief would also receive 35.00 dollars a year and 5.00 to every man, women, and child. In order for the promises to be kept, they too now must obey the crown. My Didii Paul Niditchie was chosen by the village. He was the first chief of Arctic Red River, Northwest Territories. Didii Paul Niditchie signed the treaty for the people in 1921 and he held this position for twenty five years.

PAUL NIDITCHIE'S FAMILY

CHAPTER 1

My Early Life on the Land

Big Rock, November 1935   Didii Paul and Didoo Camilla spent most of their life trapping in the winter and fishing in the summer. A place called Big Rock in the Mackenzie Delta was their bush camp. For the first two years of their married life my parents lived at Big Rock. It was at this bush-camp that I was born. My grandmother Camilla delivered me then gave me to my Aunt Annie to hold. She was so proud and said, "I was so tiny".

The Christmas of 35, when I was almost two months old my parents took me to Arctic Red River for Christmas holidays to meet my father's parents. My grandparents took one look at me, took me in their arms and never gave me back. They traditionally adopted me. As the first grandchild, they were to teach me the culture of our people so when it was my turn, I would teach the next generation.

In those days, if grandparents wanted to raise one or two of their grandchildren, it was on the mutual consent of both parties. The older generations still practice this custom, but not by the younger ones. Many customs have been lost. It is vital that the elders of today use their knowledge and wisdom to teach the younger generation. Elders, Grandparents, parents, Uncles, Aunts, older brothers and sisters had to teach what they have been taught to those who were younger of our traditional teachings, beliefs and survival skills, and above all else the law of RESPECT, It is the Law that gives direction to our people. It was taught to be followed by all life. It was the responsibility of each generation.

In this way, the traditional culture and language are preserved. When parents are too busy Parents raising the other siblings. Grandparents, aunts and uncles are there to help. I have wonderful memories of the years that my Dadda and Mamma raised me and nurtured me.

When I was two years old, we spent one winter at Travier Creek, 120 miles up the Mackenzie River. My Dadda worked and traded for the Hudson's Bay Company out on the land. Dadda spoke broken English. If he wanted to say," This is not good," he would say, "This one here no good here". "If you speak foolish," "Just here you talk crazy here." Nevertheless, the Bay man understood him.

He taught Dadda what and how many supplies a person should get for furs. He trapped and sold supplies to the people out on the land. For many, it was difficult to get to the trading post at the village.

A white man by the name of Billy Clark and his family also lived at Travier Creek. Billy's wife was a Gwichya-Gwich'in woman. Their daughters, Emma, Winnie, Beth and their son Dale lived nearby. Today Dale tells a story about me. He says I would cry for no reason, and that I always ran to my Mamma to tell her everything even if I had not hurt myself. I was a real crybaby. Dale said at times he wanted to shove my head in the snow; then I would cry for a reason.

Each September we packed our few belongings and winter supplies and leave for Bernard's Creek, my Dadda and Mama's bush camp. We spent the winter traveling the land towards the west as far as Snake River and east as far as Fish Lake. Our means of transportation was 5 or 6 sled dogs and a sled with a wrapper; they were used to transport our belongings. The adults had snowshoes and children, when they got old enough. We had a cabin at main camp but when we travel to trap throughout the winter we lived in tent, with spruce boughs for flooring. This keeps us warm from the cold frozen ground. Every winter season, families and their children lived out on the land. No one stayed in town.

Every two or three years we spent the winter somewhere else, either in the Mackenzie Delta or up the Mackenzie River. Everyone followed this same practice of shifting winter camp locations, allowing the land to rest and the earth to rejuvenate.

One winter two white men, young men Bill Cormack and his brother George spent the winter with my Dadda and Mamma. Dadda said that during their stay with us, I used to speak to them only in my Gwich'in language. I was told I chattered so much to Bill and George that by the time they left us they should have understood the Gwichya-Gwich'in language.

Some years later years, Bill piloted an old Norseman plane, (our first mail plane); he delivered mail to the isolated communities of the Mackenzie River. At first, it was monthly then later, in the Fifties, it became weekly. My Dadda always was happy to see Bill as Bill used to take him on occasional trips. It was Just to Bernard's Creek and Snake River, but they enjoyed the time together. My Dadda did not speak English very well, but all the white men that he met during his lifetime became his friends.

A pleasant surprise at Waldon Creek The year that my brother Pierre was born, Didii Paul and Didoo Camilla, along with my Aunt Annie who was not yet married, traveled with us. They left their bush camp in the delta, "Big Rock," to travel the country around Bernard's Creek and up around Snake River. My mother was pregnant with her second child, and my Didoo Camilla wanted to be close to her daughter when she gave birth. My Uncle Amos and his family also spent the winter with us. Sometimes the group would split up for awhile, and then gather again at Bernard's Creek.

It was late in October when our families decided to move to Waldon Creek about 15 miles further up the Red river from our main camp. At that time, I was unaware that my mother was expecting a child and that the family did not want to travel too far from our main camp until the baby was born.

One morning I woke up to find my father and mother with a baby. I asked them where the baby came from. My mamma explained that on the previous evening when all the children were sleeping but the adults were still up; someone heard sounds like a baby crying softly, so they all went out to see.

8

There, running around, was a baby. Mamma said, "Everyone chased, your father and mother were the lucky couple to catch the baby, so now the baby belongs to them." I thought about this during my morning meal and planned later to go outside and look for baby footprints. As soon as I finish eating, I asked Mamma if she would help me get dressed in my knitted rabbit skin snowsuit so I could go out to play. I searched all day for baby footprints, but found nothing. Finally, it was nightfall and I went home.

> *"She taught me to feel the energy of the land and the beauty of all the seasons. She taught me to listen to her and to her songs that others do not hear. I was to learn from her how to receive the messages nature that shares with us."*

Mamma asked," Where were you all day? Aren't you cold?" I said, Mamma "everyone was lying about chasing the baby because I could not find baby footprints," she chuckled and replied, "Come sit here and I will tell you why you cannot find footprints. "The baby is an angel before someone catches it, and only then that it becomes a baby. So how could you find the tracks of an angel?" I believed her.

I loved our camp at Waldon Creek because it was such a good place to snare rabbits. Every morning Mamma dressed me up warmly in my rabbit skin suit she had made for me; then we went to visit our snares. Mamma had so many snares it took us most of the day to visit them.

At that time, strings were still in use as there was no wire snare. It took some time to make the snare, and even longer to set it. I loved those times with Mamma because she let me take the rabbit off the snare and showed me how to reset it.

That year she taught me about feelings, about seeing and listening. This, she said, awakens our inner spirit for as long as our life lasts.

9

She taught me to feel the energy of the land and the beauty of all the seasons. She taught me to listen to her and to her songs that others do not hear. I was to learn from her how to receive the messages that nature shares with us.

Although I spent so much time alone with Mamma and Dadda during those years, I never felt alone or that I had missed out on anything. Once a person asked me if I was ever lonely and I replied that I did not know the word. I only discovered what it was like to be lonely after I lost my Mamma.

As a child growing up I went everywhere with her. I remember her loving ways and to this day tears come rushing when I think of her. I miss her so much and I am sure my life would have been different in many ways if she had lived with me into her elder years.

Before freeze-up, the men went hunting. When they killed a moose, the women got busy, drying the meat and smoking some of it, making pemmican and bone grease. Sometimes they added cranberries to the pemmican. When sugar became available from the traders, it was included to make a quick snack or treat. They especially appreciated this out on the trap lines when there was no time to cook.

Then, the women began to work with the hides so when they finish tanning, they made winter footwear. Men cut mounds of firewood to prepare for the many days that they would be away from home. When the lakes and rivers had frozen and trapping season opened (on November 1st), the men went to set their traps and the women stayed behind to look after the camp and the children.

> **"Once a person asked me if I was ever lonely and I replied that I didn't know the word. I only discovered what it was like to be lonely after I lost my Mamma."**

Bernard's Creek One day when we returned to our main camp at Bernard's Creek, we found that we had run out of dried fruit. There was a white trader named Harry Johnson lived about two miles down the river from our camp. Sometimes people from Fort Good Hope came over the mountains to buy supplies from him if they ran short of shells, tobacco, tea or sugar. My parents always tried to keep on hand a supply of dried prunes, raisins or dried apples, but on this occasion, we had none left. Although, I mentioned it, no one seemed to hear me, so I asked Mamma if I could walk to Mr. Johnson place, she said yes. I have to be responsible for walking there, get what I wanted, warm up and come right home. However, I had to wait until the next morning.

As soon as there was a bit of daylight, I was on my way to see Mr. Johnson. It took me almost half a day to get there. I had just turned three that fall and now I am astounded when I think about all the adventures that I had at such a young age.

Two miles is a very long distance for a little girl to walk. When I finally arrived, I walked in and showed Mr. Johnson my pack sack. He knew just what I wanted. First, he gave me hot cocoa, and then he took me to his stage (a cache of supplies kept safe from animals, high above the ground). Here I picked out all the dried fruit I wanted. He made sure it was not heavy as I had a long way to go.

Father plays a practical joke at Fish Lake I remember that year we stayed at Fish Lake, so my Dadda and father will hunt caribou and trap for animals. East of the Red River., Dadda, Mamma, and I shared one tent and my parents had another.

I remember so clearly the day I told Mamma I was going to set traps for weasel. I was so excited! I was going to do a big adult job.

I filled my pack sack with bait as I had seen Dadda and Mamma do many times. I put a bundle of traps all tied together a bait in my pack sack. As a three -year-old, I was very determined to do it by myself.

Away I went, following my Dadda's trail on the lake. When I looked back at the tent, all I could see was the smoke from the stovepipe, I thought, I walk far enough I should set my weasel trap about here... The trail was only a short distance away from the shoreline, what I sought was an ideal place to set a trap for a weasel. Even at my tender age I knew enough not to set it on the ice. I came to a place where the trail wasn't too far from the shoreline and decided to set my weasel trap.

I had to get to the shoreline to do this, I began to make my way from the trail but the snow was so deep. (About four feet depth), the snow off the trail was too much for my little legs so I crawled and tried to walk until I got to the shoreline.

I found a bunch of willows, made a nice bed of dry grass, tied my bait to the back and placed the trap. I was so happy that I had done all this by myself; it never entered my mind that I needed to open the traps to set them! (I was too small to have done this anyway). Early, every morning I visited my trap, nothing and feeling a bit disappointed, as I wanted to tell Dadda when he came home, I set trap and caught a weasel.

Mamma knew where I had gone, so when Dadda and my father came home from their trap line, she told them where I had set my weasel traps. One morning after my Dadda and father had returned from the trap line, I got up early and went to see my traps. Oh, I was so happy! There was a weasel in my trap!

There must have been about six traps, so I untied the one that had caught the weasel and dragged it home.

When I walked into the tent and showed Dadda and Mamma there was much excitement. I ran to my father and mother's tent and told them the news. When the excitement was over, I asked Dadda to take the weasel off the trap for me, and then returned to put the trap back with the rest.

The next morning the same thing happened. Again, the following morning there was another weasel in my trap. It was then I became suspicious because I noticed that there were no weasel tracks. I searched the area for weasel tracks but found none. Someone was playing a trick on me, trying to make me believe I was catching the weasels.

I was upset! When I got home, I marched right into the tent. My father was having tea with Dadda and Mamma, their morning ritual while they made the day's plans. As I was complaining to my Mamma that someone was playing a bad trick on me, making me think I caught the weasels myself I saw my father shaking. He had turned away from me, but I could see he was chuckling. Indignantly I stood in front of him and said "What kind of father would play a mean trick like this on his little girl?" My father answered, "Only a father who loves his little girl very much." I forgot my disappointment and gave him a big hug.

Story about Atatt-chi-u Kaaing Each evening Mamma told bedtime stories about our people. The stories were mostly about the Wolverine, Crow, Big Mosquito, Big Sky, a little girl by the name of Grey Wings and Grizzly Bear.

I loved the stories she told, especially the one about Atatt-chi-u kaaing, the "Man who paddles amongst all', she explained, before he came there was no orderly way of life. All the creatures lived, as they wanted. The Great Spirit knew all life needed a new way of life, and so he sent this man. Mamma said that long before he arrived, animals and people knew he was coming, but they wanted to continue to live as they were. They did not want any change.

One day someone shouted "Atatt-chiu-kaaing is coming soon. People, were excited but also very fearful. They went to find medicine man in the camp and ask him to find them a place to hide. He went to the river nearby and asked the loch fish to come in. Several loch fish swam to the shore of the river and the medicine man said, Oh, good fish of the Big River you have to help save my people, come ashore and open your mouth. As soon as the fish open its mouth, the medicine man told the people to go into the fish mouth; there they were to stay until it was safe to come out.

When Atatt-chiu- kaaing arrived at the camp, there were no people, only burning coals. The camp was deserted. Atatt-chi-u kaaing said, "What is going on? Every camp I come to is deserted. I mean no harm! My purpose for coming is to give order to a way of life. He continued to travel the rivers and land and when he would meet people he would tell them he meant no harm. He just wanted to give them a message to live a more orderly life, Animals to live their own way of life and also the people. He said to the wolverine, "you have caused much grief to all the living by stealing.

In the future, there will be just a few of you and you will have to hunt very hard for your survival

13

Nothing will come easy for you because of the grief you cause."
Then, he said to the people. "I will remain amongst you until you
hear me and I deliver a new way of life to all the living

HUNG FISH FOR WINTER USE FROM ICE FALL FISHING (COURTESY DON
HORROCKS) AND TSIIGEHTCHIC IN THE FOURTIES (COURTESY PRINCE OF
WHALES MUSEUM)

THE LEGEND OF THE
CROW AND THE GRISLY

AN EXPLANATION BY ELDERS OF THE CROW STORY

CROW AND GRISLEY

Stories of Ravens used as a lesson to listeners and told at bedtime. Long ago animals had many dealings with the Gwich'in people. The Raven narratives are used as bedtime stories.

Ravens are known to Gwich'in' in people as Black Crows. Long ago, the crow could change himself to a man when he wanted to and a crow when situations call for him to change to animal form. He was a man of knowledge and a bird of intelligence. If circumstances called for the help of a crow, he would help after much consideration. He always added some sense of humor to his help. He did this with a lesson to those who needed some life lesson. Sometimes his plan would backfire and he would be the one that lesson was taught to. Those story tellers said: Sometimes even the most knowledgeable are taught a lesson.

Long ago, a Grizzly Bear with Mrs. Grizzly and a young infant son lived at a Fishing place up the Big River (Mackenzie River). The fishing place was located at the bend of a long stretch. Down the river from their place at the other bend there were also some Gwich'in people fishing. The grizzly could see their camp from his camp. His son the little Grizzly was very spoiled, he would get whatever he asked of his father. One day the son was bored with all his playthings. Therefore, he began to cry. His father asked him, what he was crying for and he said I am tired of the things I play with; I want something different to play with. Then he began to cry again. Mr. and Mrs. Grizzly gave their son all things that might interest him but to no avail. He kept crying. Finally the father asked him "what do you want? The son said, "I want the moon ", now, now said his father if I take the moon for you, people will have no light to work with at night", the son began crying again, he cried and cried. Finally, when he could not stop crying the father

18

stretched out his arm into the sky and took the moon for his son to play with.

One day the son began to cry again, his father said ", son, what are you crying about this time". The son said, "I am tired of the moon, it is not bright enough. I need something brighter". The father said, "The sun is only the brightest, you cannot have this as we all need daylight to hunt and fish". Again, the son began to cry, he cried and he cried. Again, the father reached out into the sky and took the sun. Now the son was happy, as he had the brightest object in the world for his plaything.

The Land was in total darkness and, no one could hunt and fish. No one could work, the food was disappearing quickly and people began to worry. The people could see the Grizzly camp; it was the only brightest spot in the land. The only one they could seek help from was the Crow. They went to pay him a visit and said to the Crow, "can you help us? The big mean Grizzly took the moon and Sun from the sky for his spoiled son and now the people have no light and our food is going fast. We come to ask you for help". The Crow thought for a moment then he answered. "This is very serious, as people will starve if we don't have light soon. Leave it to me, I will think of a plan and I will deal with Mr. Grizzly". The people knew the Crow would do as he said; now they will go home and wait". One morning Mrs. grizzly woke up to find that she maybe pregnant, her belly was somewhat swollen and she thought, I have not felt sick which will indicate I may be pregnant, how could this be". Mr. Grizzly noticed this too and asked if she was and if she suspected this, why did she not tell him. She said, "I didn't know either but maybe I am.

The next morning she was much bigger, and now she had no doubt that she was pregnant. She said to Mr. Grizzly,

maybe our son or daughter will be born very quickly be-
cause he or she seems to be under the influence of a very
powerful medicine. Soon she bore another son and they
were very proud of this son. He grew very quickly and soon
began talking. They began to encourage the oldest son to
play with his brother. One day, as they were playing with
the Sun the baby let go of the sun and made sure it roll to
the entrance of the hut and gave it a good kick. The Sun
was kicked to the sky and there was daylight again, next
was the moon. As soon as he had done, what he wanted
to do the Crow gave one good cry and went his way. The
older brother began to cry, and his father, Mr. Grizzly was
very angry, the Crow had him fooled once more, the sun
has returned to the sky and he could never take it back for
his son. When the Crow returned to the people, there was
much rejoicing, now people could hunt and fish, again. This
story teaches us that no matter how powerful strength we
have, there is someone more powerful than we are, in dif-
ferent way. Therefore, we have to be always aware of this.
In addition, we have to be humble about the skills we have,
as they're maybe someone who can do better than we can.
Sometimes there were stories from Mamma's people. She
had learned these from her mother and grandmother. She
said that all these stories were passed to each of our gen-
erations. I would be responsible to tell them to the next
generation.

Gwaatrii In the fall of 1940, Dadda decided that we would give the land around Bernard's Creek a rest and spend the winter at Gwaatrii. This was about ten miles below Tree River, John Tsell and his wife Julianne bush camp. His son, Hyacinth, wife and children also lived there. They stayed at this bush camp in a log house they had built themselves. Once in awhile they would go to the village only to replenish their supplies. We never *owned the land; but each person* respected the other's bush camp and trap line. Out of respect, Dadda asked the family if we could spend the winter a few miles away from their camp at Gwaatrii. It was fine with them and Dadda said that, as we were just a short distance away we could visit them on Sundays. In those days, Sunday truly was a day of rest, gathering in one's home and saying the rosary. The women cooked and children played while the men told stories. I loved Gwaatrii from the beginning. It had a beautiful view of up and down the Mackenzie River. One day during the winter after I had eaten my morning meal, Mamma dressed me warmly to play outside with my puppy. I had just turned four that November. My puppy must have been about 3 months old because he was almost my height. I went to a hill behind our camp and began to slide down. Suddenly I heard my Mamma scream out my name, I ran home as fast as I could. Bursting through the flaps, I saw her sobbing; she cried out "your Dadda drank some bad medicine and is going to die".

My Dadda's was lying on their bed, on his back, his hand was folded on his chest, and he looked stiff and very white. I was too small to know what a dead person looked like, but he sure did not look good. Mamma said she would have to depend on me to get help.

I had to go to the Tree River people and ask them to help us. I said I would do it but she had to pray to our Creator to give us Dadda back. I was not afraid to go by myself. I had to go; it might save my Dadda's life.

Mamma dressed me up warmly and tied the string from my puppy collar to my mitt string.   I started down the hill. As I reached the bank of the Mackenzie River, I looked out at this huge river, for a moment I felt afraid, I said to myself, I will not looked at the river again. I would just follow the trail that would take me to the people of Tree River. Mamma said that they had moved across the Mackenzie River, so when I came to two trails along the way, I should take the left one that led across the river. The river was almost two miles wide; it was about or more seven miles from our place to my destination.

I started down the hill and once again I looked at the Mackenzie River, it appeared huge to me when I came to the two trails, and I took the one on my left side. Being right-handed, I knew left from right. The one I could do the least with was my left side! My elders taught this difference to me. I knew when it was noon by where the sun was. The sun also told me that it was way past noon when it began to go down. I tried to hurry, but I was very tired. I saw the shoreline and smoke and the smoke from the people's tent. I thought I must be close."

Don't these people ever come out of their tent and look out on the river?" I said to myself hopefully. My puppy was very good with me. He gave me no trouble and just walked alongside me. When I got close to the shore, someone came to meet me and carried me the rest of the way. Someone said they saw me about a quarter of a mile from the camp. They saw something on the river and thought it might be a fox. Did I look like a fox? Maybe, because I was wearing the rabbit skin suit.) They said to one another, "keep an eye on whatever it may be".

The Mackenzie River freezes rough in the fall and the ice caps at places were high. This made me disappear from sight now and then. Finally, I was not too far from the shore. As soon as the people knew it was a little child they rushed to meet me. They knew I was cold so someone carried me the rest of the way to the tent. I told them as best as I could what had happened and Mamma said to come quickly. A couple of men left with dog team and someone carried me to Dido Julianne tent. I was very cold so they gave me hot tea to drink.

I remember old Didoo Naatritt and someone who looked almost like her came into the tent. Didoo Naatritt greeted me and said," There is not another little girl who would do what you did". Then she said, "In the future, when you grow up you will be a very kind-hearted person and you will love people old people. Your ancestors gave you a special gift. You will not know of this until you are older. Someday you will do a great thing for your people. Your health will never be good, but you should try to ignore this, as you will live to a ripe old age. Here, I will give you a piece of my cane; this will be of help to you."

I can still remember how she looked. Her hair was so long, almost below her waist and it was a nice salt and pepper color and so shiny.

I was confused because Didoo Naatritt had very white hair and she always had it braided and tied with a string.

When I told the people that Didoo Naatritt was sitting beside me and was speaking to me, they replied that she could not have been. She was in the hospital in Aklavik. They said I had, had a vision. A grandmother from the past had paid me a visit and had given me a message! I should feel privileged.

There are people who are still alive who witnessed this incident. Diddoo Julian told her daughter Marca, "Therese is so silly, how someone who is never serious could do something for her people. I have kept an eye on her during my lifetime and she has done nothing. My time here is about to end, my daughter, please keeping an eye on her for me."

By the time, they brought me back to our camp, Dadda still looked very sick, but he was sitting up. I went right into his arms; he had tears in his eyes. I told him that he had to be very careful about what medicine he drinks the next time.

The people who came to rescue him said that he had drunk electric oil, a medicine to rub on sore joints. Dadda had thought it was Castor oil.

ANNIE AND LIZA

CLARA AND
JOANNE

TOP ANNIJE AND LIZA
BOTTOM CLARA AND JOYANNE

24

DOG BELL PREMONITION

During the winter of 41, there was a strange event. My parents lived at Gwaatrii, about 10 miles below Tree River. On Sundays, we visited John Tsell and his families bush camp. The adults along with their children said prayers in the morning, then the women cooked, the men shared stories. One day, Dadda said we were going to move to Tsaa vaa zhoo. This was a fish lake several miles inland, west of Mackenzie River.

The men wanted to hunt caribou and the women would snare rabbits. We began to prepare to leave our main camp. Tree River people would journey on their trail to this lake and we will take our own trail. Once the two parties met, they would choose a campsite and would settle to stay for the next month.

Every night before I went to bed, I went outside to the toilet. This particular evening I went out and during the time I was out there, I heard dog bells. Very faint, but I heard it. I remember it was a clear cold night; there was a bright moonlight, and the clear skies, filled with thousands of stars. On a cold clear day one can hear dog bells from far away. Running into our tent, I yelled to Dadda and Mama that I heard dog bells and I knew it was my father. He is coming to visit us. Dadda came outside, but could not hear it.

I said "Dadda I heard it". It was very faint but I heard dog bells, and I knew the sound of those bells. It was my father's dog bells. Dadda went out and listen, he looked towards where we had tied our dogs but they were sleeping, usually when dogs hear something their ears twitch, perk, then they begin to howl. However, this time they did not. When minutes pass by and he did not hear anything, he went back into the tent. I stayed outside. Finally, I went in to dress warmer and went back out to wait for my father to arrived, I knew was my father. I was getting cold and sleepy and no one came, I went in and got ready for bed. I asked Mama to wake me up when my father arrived. I woke up the next morning, re-membering the night before I asked my Mama if my father had arrived, softly she said no! I was disappointed.

That evening, it happened again, but by this time all the people at the camp knew about what I had heard the night before. I heard them talking, they said they hope I was not predicting bad news about mem-bers of families living elsewhere. Dadda and Mama told me not to say anymore because no one else heard it except me. Usually if children say something unusual, adults believed they may hear bad news, but I said that I had heard my father's dog bells and he was coming to visit us. The third evening it happened again. This time, I stayed outside, listened, and watched our dogs.

The dogs heard something; their ears began to twitch; and I yell to Dadda and Mama. Soon they began howling, and Dadda came outside and listened. He heard it to; he shouted at Mama ("some body is com-ing") as he heard the dog bells. Who would come in the middle of the winter as we lived so far away from people? I said to Dadda, "I know my father was coming". One can see if someone is coming by the light of the moon, which was bright and gave much light to travelers. The stranger approached and mushed his dog team by our tent; it was my father, John Remy. I was so happy to see him. Dadda help my father unhitch his dog, tied them up then fed them.

By this time, Mama had a hot meal prepared for him. Once he sat down to eat Dadda asked him what brought him so far away from home, which was (Big Rock) in the Delta, my father said he was worried about us and just wanted to know we were doing OK.

He began his journey three days ago; it was about the time when I began hearing his dog bells. Later Dadda said that as a child I had predicted many things. Some I remember, and some I do not.

"There is a Great Spirit who is stronger than all creation. Long time ago this Spirit made the land that we depend on for our survival, we should always respect her."

STORY

Long, long ago the Great Spirit made the land that; we live and depend on for our livelihood. When I was a child, Mama told me stories and explained why it was so important to respect the land and all life on it. We should never joke or make fun at another life on this land, wither it was animal or another human being. We should always show respect by our words and action to all times.

The stories were important to the younger generation because they gave direction, a path set by our ancestors for us to follow.

No matter how the world changed, our principles and values should never change. It is who we are. The law that governed our people was timeless. It is one word: RESPECT. Another story that mama told me is one that young people often enjoy and remember. This was the story of a young woman Tlin-na-go-vaa-jaa-a who had to learn a very hard lesson.

Tlin-na-go-vaa-jaa-a

Long, long ago there lived a girl by the name of Tlin-na-go-vaa-jaa-a. She lived with her parents amongst a group of Gwich'in people who traveled the land together. As soon as she became old enough her mother began teaching her how to become a good skilled sewer. The mother asked her to sew a pair of moccasins together and when she did this chore Tlin-na-go-vaa-jaa-a showed them to her mother. Her mother said, "Undo the sewing you just did, and do it all over again". This was because the stitches were not satisfactory to her mother. After several more attempts her mother was finally satisfied.

Once she began sewing to her mother's satisfaction, her mother made her sew several pairs of moccasins. When she finally finished the last pair, her mother said "Tlin-na-go-vaa-jaa-a there is another pair for you to sew" Tlin-na-go-vaa-jaa-a said, "oh no not again"! The tone of her voice and the way she answered was very disrespectful to her mother.

For this reason Tlin-na-go-vaa-jaa-a was not spoken to again, either from her father nor her mother. She had a friend who whispered to her one day there is talk about

moving camp and they are saying you will be left behind
She did not know when or their exact plans but if she hears
more, she will inform Tlin-na-go-vaa-jaa-a. One day her
friend whispered to her, she heard the people say, they
were going to prepare to move camp.

Her parents also began preparing themselves to leave,
one morning they began to take down their hut. Not a word
was said to her. She knew then the message, her friend
related to her was true. Before leaving, her friend came to
say goodbye and she gave Tlin-na-go-vaa-jaa-a a hug and
whispered, "my friend where I sleep behind some brush I
have left some burning coals and a bit of sinew".

Soon everyone had left. She went looking for the sinew
and found them where her friend said they were. She felt
so alone, her eyes began to fill with tears but quickly she
wiped them away. She had things to do if she wanted to
survive.

A Whiskey jack came and began searching for crumbs of
food at the now deserted camp. She had the coals, she had
to gather wood, Tlin-na-go-vaa-jaa-a busied herself gathering as much wood as she could, then sat down to the
warmth of the fire and began making snares to try to catch
the bird for food. Before nightfall, she caught a whiskey
jack, which she skinned carefully and cooked to the fire.
She ate a small piece and left some for morning.

Again, she cooked, ate, and was very careful in how she
skinned them, as she wanted to make a warm coat for herself. Each day she busied herself with gathering wood, and
by this time had built a good lean-to and had gather enough
spruce-boughs to have a good thick flooring. Each day she
caught several ravens, each time she skinned carefully,
drying the skin carefully for a warm coat. She also saved all

the sinew from the thighs, the sinew for snares and bones for maybe a fishhook and needle. She saved every part of this bird and a bone made into a tool. Several days had past and some of the skin had dried. Tlin-na-go-vaa-jaa-a began sewing this together for a warm coat. Finally, her coat was finished, the feathers to the inside, as it will keep her warm. She also had made several larger snares for rabbits. Now that she had something warm to wear, she went out to set rabbit snare. The rabbit she snared, she followed the same process, as she had done with the raven.

She had made a good fireplace and a place to sleep and sit, with spruce-boughs. Now that she had eaten, she decided to rest. She was very afraid not knowing what would happen to her. She said to herself." I will think only of this moment. I will put all the skills taught to me and think only of surviving. If I make it through this night then tomorrow I can plan what I will do". The night seemed so long but finally the traveling star told her that it was close to dawn, she got up and ate the small food that she saved the night before and went to gather wood. By the time it got daylight, she had enough wood and by this time, ravens came to invade and empty campsite. Now she can also set a few snares for the ravens. They were much bigger birds and had more meat. She caught some and now she set out to skin them.

She skinned it carefully. She dried the skin and saved every part of the rabbit for tools, needles, hooks and sinew for snares. She dried the skin and decided to knit a blanket and a wrap for the tipi, also more warm clothing.

Many days and many nights had past, new moon and full moon, the days began to get longer and finally the snow began to melt. She knew spring was here, she decided to move camp. Perhaps she would go to a river or a fish lake, or a good rabbit country. Tlin-na-go-vaa-jaa-a went walking everyday in search of a river or a lake. Finally, one day she came to a river. She knew the river had fish and the country looked good for rabbit, Tlin-na-go vaa-jaa-a began to prepare to move camp. She first went and looked for a good campsite, in the shelter of many trees. This would protect her from the cold winds, and her camp would be well hidden from strangers. Tlin-na-go-vaa-jaa-a once settled went out to set rabbit snares.

As the weather turned warm, she began to smoke and make dry the meat. The meat would spoil once it thawed, so she hard to preserve it. One day soon, when the ice from the river is gone she will set hooks then make a fish trap.

During this time, she was unaware of someone watching her. Two young men were hunting many days and nights away from their people's camp. One day while walking they thought that they saw something moving at a distance. Therefore, they hid, watched, and saw that it was a person. This person had on faded old gray rabbit skin clothing.

They did not know if it was a man or a woman. One day they followed her home. It was a young woman. They kept watching her and one day they said "it is time to introduce ourselves. They came out of hiding; she got so afraid when she saw them that she ran all the way home and disappeared into her hut. For several days they kept talking to her, they told her about themselves, what they were doing in that part of the country and that they meant her no harm.

As her fear lessens, she got brave enough to give them something to eat and drink. She was still afraid so she never invited them to her hut. They made a hut for themselves, lived close by and hunted for her. Tlin-na-go vaa-

jaa-a was happy to smoke and dry the meat; she did the same for fish they catch. One day, one of the young men said to her" I hope you trust us. We would like to take care of you.

We can be your men to protect and provide for you," she then answered, "I will think about it" Sometime had past, she said to them, I have thought of your offer and I have decided to say YES. I will permit, you to move into my hut and become my men, you have kept me well.

From that time on, they began hunting for her, Tlin-na-go-vaa-jaa-a prepared the meat, tan the hides and made clothing and footwear. She made dry meat, bone grease, pemmican, dried and smoke fish, made fancy leather garments and moccasins. She was grateful to the young men for taking good care of her.

One day the young men said,"Tlin-na-go-vaa-jaa-a, we have been gone for a long time from our people; we would like to know if all is well with them." Tlin-na-go-vaa-jaa-a said "Go and find your people, if you find them bring them back as we have plenty of food to share with them, they will not go hungry with us.

Many days, nights past, and she heard one of her man say from a distance, "We have found them, and aside from very low on food, they are well. Cook lots woman, we will feed them. People were arriving and her men were feeding the people, she was busy cooking, all at once, the flap of her hut open and there stood a young woman.

She looked familiar, Tlin–na-go-vaa-jaa-a said; you looked very familiar, "long ago I had a friend who looked very much like you. She saved my life, when everyone else abandoned me with nothing; she left me coals and sinew, with this I survived".

The young woman at the entrance said, "It is I my friend. For a moment, she stood still then with happy cries, they hug one another. Tlin na-go-vaa-jaa-a then said, "My friend I have a big hut, you will stay on the opposite side of me. Everything that I have, we will share I will also give you one of my men, they are very good hunters". Therefore, the two friends were happy they met again and they promise one another they will never again part.

In the summer of 1941, Mama got sick. In the 1940s if someone got sick, they never saw a Doctor. The trip to Aklavik to see a doctor took many days, so no one bothered. They would rather use traditional medicine from plants. If it did not work, they accepted death. I cannot remember if people were afraid to die, I just know that the people accepted this as part of life. People sometimes died out on the land and we just buried them. Only when we came to the village in June did we report their death to the police or missionary priest.

I remember that summer well. Although mama did not feel well, on her good days, she busied herself with making dried fish. The knife she had given me to help her was very dull. She warned me not to touch the sharp ones as I might hurt myself.

One day, she went to our tent to have a cup of hot tea and take a rest. I try to learn how to make dry fish but they always gave me a dull knife, I couldn't cut the fish. Mama never allowed me to have sharp knife as I may cut myself. As she disappeared out of sight I grabbed her sharp knife and began cutting the fish. I thought to myself, by the time took she nap I would finish making my dry fish; she would not know I had used her sharp knife. I took her knife and began cutting my fish. The knife slipped and I cut my arm badly. As soon as I saw the blood, I started to cry and ran to the tent. Mamma just looked at me and in a calm voice said, "This is the reason I told you not to touch the sharp knife."

She washed and bandaged my arm in flannelette's, then checked it every day to make sure it did not get was infected. I have a large scar on my left arm that reminds me of that time with my Mamma.

As summer went on Mamma was resting a lot and was doing less and less. She said that she could not understand what made her tire so easily. Mamma never got better and died in the tent sometime in late August.

I was heartbroken. How could someone who loved me so much leave me? I know my life would have been much different if she had lived. I probably would have never left home and would have become the spinster of Tsiigehtchic! I shed many tears. What was going to happen to my Dadda and me? We had no one but each other. My father said, "We all had to take care of one another;" Mamma would have wanted us too.

Jack fish Creek

Dadda and I went to Jack fish Creek in the fall and winter of 1942-43...
Dadda did not want to stay at Bernard's Creek because, "Many things
will bring memories of Mamma and it would make him sad. Dadda
told me that another family, Ernest and Mary and their children, would
come to stay with us at Jack fish Creek. They will looked after you during the time I am away to hunt and trap. That year I used to visit traps
with Dadda when the trail on his trap line was good and we used our
dog team. If he had to use snowshoes and went on foot; I stayed with the
Kendo's.

I remember one day a stench filled the air and we could not breathe
well. Mary said there was a huge wolverine that lived under ground a
few miles up the river from our camp. "This animal must have moved to
change positions and some of his smell must have escaped," Later on, I
smelled the same kind of rotten aroma. It came from a gas plant.

AKLAVIK (Courtesy of Prince of Whales

In June of 1943, Dadda took me to Aklavik to see a doctor because I had sore throat too often. The doctor said I had to have my tonsils out. I was afraid to be away from Dadda, but I had to be brave. I remember going into the operating room but nothing else until I woke up in my room and I began to cry. My throat was sore and I did not want to be there. I cried so hard I began to get sick. The more I cried the sicker I got.

Later when Dadda came to visit, they let him take me home.

The nurse told Dadda I could not eat solid food, only ice cream and soup. In Aklavik, there was a big house, where people went to eat whenever they were hungry.

They called it a restaurant; I did not know any English so this was all new to me. People called the proprietor Mrs. Kost and everyone liked her, because she was kind and friendly.

Dr. Livingston was also trying to farm at the edge of town. He had chickens and a few cows. That was the first time I saw cows and they scared me.

We stayed a couple of days, and then left for Arctic Red River. During our absence, Pierre's mother, (my biological mother) had a baby girl, my youngest sister Lizzy. This was in June of 1943.

Pierre's parents, John and Liza Remi had a bush camp at Pierre's Creek, 30 miles up the Mackenzie River. They spent their winter at Pierre's Creek. My father had built a cabin at the place so every winter; they stayed at this bush camp. In this region of the Mackenzie delta, there were three communities, Arctic Red River, Aklavik, and Fort McPherson. In 1954, Inuvik became the site for a new town, and building began in 1955. All the others I mention are family bush camps.

We left Arctic Red River in September. There was Dadda and I, Gabriel, Lucy and their daughter Mary. When we arrived at Jack fish Creek, we set up camp. Dadda and Gabriel decided to build a cabin before the weather got colder so they got busy as soon as we settled.

They worked tirelessly, cutting logs and pulling them to our camp with dog team. Within a month, we had a fair-sized log cabin. Now we were all going to stay warm for the winter. Sometime after Christmas Dadda said, "We were going overland to the Mackenzie River; we are going to pass spring with your father and mother at Pierre's Creek." I cannot remember how long it took us to get there, but there was no trail and Dadda, who was sixty-one years old, had to break trail all the way.

My parents were happy that Dadda and I had decided to spend the spring with them. We were all going to town (Artic Red River) for Easter. I was excited! As a little girl, I seldom went to town for Christmas or Easter. I think we went to Christmas twice and Easter only once. People left town with their families for their bush camps in September and did not return until the next June. We traveled by dog team in those days, and it took many days to cover even a short distance.

At Easter of 1944, we all arrived at Arctic Red River. There was much excitement as people went around visiting and catching up on one another's news. In addition, there was going to be a wedding.

John and Julian Andre's daughter Marca and Francois Coyen, son of Andre and Odella Coyen, were to be married. That week, I heard Dadda tell my father and mother that John Tsell was feeling sick. He hoped he will be feeling better by Sunday for his daughter's wedding.

I do not remember much about the wedding, but when everyone was leaving, the church and we were all outside congratulating the newly married couple. John did not attend his daughter's wedding as he was still sick. Someone said, "Everyone, quiet." The person who is taking care of John Tsell is waving; maybe he wants to say something to the people. Let him speak.

He said, "I have sad news to tell you. John Tsell passed away a few minutes ago." Dadda exclaimed," What happened? People just don't die from colds."

The laughter died and in its place came tears of disbelief. How could this happen? This man had been in good health a few days ago. Instead of joy, there was now sadness; the family had called off the happily planned feast.

Unbelievably, a few days later, the bridegroom also died, and everyone else was getting sick. Gil, our RCMP officer, and our Parish priest Father Colaas worked tirelessly among the sick, but each day we heard about another death.

My father John Remy and Andre Coyen did not get this deadly flu yet, so they dug graves for the dead every day. They only had an Axe and shovel and the ground solid frozen. One day they came home for tea and I remember my father saying, "Well my friend, we are just breaking our trail to heaven. I hope when we get there, this is in our favor and the Creator will forget all our wrongs in this world." With this they laughed.

I never forgot this incident because a few days later Andre Coyen took sick and he too passed away. Then my father became ill. It was spring and snow was melting. Those who have recovered from the flue, left town to go out on the land for the spring hunt. Dadda said we would move 20 miles up the Red River for the hunt and he would have to travel overland.

My father wanted to come with us but Dadda did not want him to go out on the land when he was still very ill. He wanted his son to stay in town where there was a police officer and priest. If his condition worsened, at least he would get help. The land was too rough to travel for someone who was not well. My father was stubborn. He had made up his mind to go out with his father.

Chi-cgho ju-aing. It was one sunny spring day we all packed the sleigh and started trekking overland to Chi-cgho ju-aing (Single Big Rock Place). Ernest Kendo and his family were also going to past the spring there. This was fortunate because my Dadda did not want my mother to stay alone with my father while he was sick. About 3 miles up the Red from where we were, also Father Colas was going to past spring at the mission wood camp. An old man by the name of Big Andrew also had a bush camp up river from us. Once Dadda had finished setting up camp for us and cut enough wood, he and Ernest left to hunt for beaver.

One morning, my mother and Ernest's wife Mary were at camp with my father and us children. We were all playing when my mother called me to put up the tent flaps so my father could enjoy the warmth of a beautiful spring day. I did this while my father lay on her lap. She then asked me to make a cup of tea for him, which I willingly did.

Back at play, it seemed like only seconds later when I heard my mother scream and saw her come out of the tent crying. Mary, who had been expecting this to happen, was at her side instantly. She held and comforted my mother as we gathered around them.   She said to us, "Our Creator has taken your father home".

I ran to the tent and tried to wake my father. He did not move. I tried to tell him there was the tea that he had not finished. I said that he could not leave us, as we were all too little. My mother, little brothers and sisters, Dadda and I needed him.

It was the morning of May 30, 1944. My sister Marie Alice was going to turn one year old on June 14. As young as I was, many things raced through my mind.

My father did not raise me but he was there when I needed him. I may have not lived with my parents but I was my father's little girl.

When we ate meals, we children had to be very quiet. We said grace and only answered when asked a question. I disliked egg yoke. I used to pass the yoke over to my father under the table and he would eat it for me, without my mother suspecting us. He was such a very special part of my life. I was special to my father and to my grandparents. I was the first grandchild, the firstborn. I was friendly, and had a compassionate heart for other people. I spoke my mind! My family hoped that I would become one of the traditional messengers and carry the traditional stories forward into the future.

My father was my special friend. He would tease me and play tricks on me, but he always told me that I was special to him. Now he, too, was gone. One night my Mama told me to say my prayers and gave me a kiss goodnight. The next morning she was dead. My father wanted to have fresh air and enjoy the beautiful spring day with a cup of tea and the next minute he was dead. The people I loved were all dying on me. I told my Creator that since he was taking the people I loved from me he had to take them into his heaven with no questions asked about their life on earth. Dadda and Ernest were still gone, so Mary took a rifle and started shooting, hoping old Andrew would hear the shots. He did and soon arrived.

When they told him news, Andrew said that he would get Father Colaas. While he was gone, Dadda came back; someone had told him about my father. He asked if they would leave him alone, so he could spend a few minutes with his son. I heard him cry; it was almost like a moan. I wanted to go to him and say, "Dadda, I am still here," but my mother would not let me.

She said my Dadda needed that time alone with my father, his son. My mother and Mary had already dressed my father so when Father Colaas came all we had to do was load up our canoe and head to town. Dadda told us that while he had been out hunting the night before, a voice had told him to go back to camp, because he was needed.

He knew then that my father was not going to live. He had rushed home because he wanted to hold his son in his arms. In my culture, it is important to receive the last words of a loved one.

We arrived at the village of Arctic Red River; I cannot remember my father's funeral too well except Dadda and me spending most of our time at the church with my father until the funeral. When everything was over my mother had set a tent down on the flats and moved there with the children. Dadda was disappointed. He felt that for now our family should be together.

I was upset with my mother, I felt she abandon us. We all needed to stay close supporting each other during this sad time.

I was eight years old, but already felt that it was my duty to remind everyone around me about his or her responsibilities to each other. The first time I felt anger was when Mamma died, and the second was when my mother moved out of our house to live by herself with my brothers and sisters.

Sometime that winter, Dadda received a letter from the south from a white man named Bill Knett. This man said that his late uncle had been a prospector around Bell River in the Yukon and before his death had given him a map showing where he might find gold which might be in some way connected to the gold deposits found in Dawson. The uncle had suggested that he search this area with some help from the native people, and so he had written to the white people in the region asking for advice.

He found out that an Indian man named Small Remy from Arctic Red River was just the man for him, as he knew the country well.

Dadda said that he was going with Bill across the mountains to Bell River and that I was to stay with my mother at Pierre's Creek, where she

42

was fishing for the summer. Dadda said that keeping busy was one way to deal with his grief and I understood.

Dadda was gone most of the summer. When he returned, he said Bill had found what he was looking for. He promised he would be in touch by Christmas to let Dadda know, his plans for the following summer. Bill said that because Dadda had played a big part in the success of the trip, he had also staked a claim for him. Dadda did not know what he meant; whatever Bill said was fine with him.

By Christmas, Dadda received a letter saying that there would be several men coming with Bill after spring break-up and asking Dadda to assist them on the trip to Bell River. Dadda was looking forward to a busy summer, but no one came.

CHAPTER 2

Residential School Days
Immaculate Conception School

1944. In the fall of 1944, my mother decided to send my brother Pierre to Immaculate Conception School, a Roman Catholic residential school in Aklavik. She could no longer look after all the children and he was the eldest of the four at home. He was of school age and since mother had attended the residential school, she felt it would be for the best.

Dadda said that it was too difficult for him to raise a little girl out on the land and since I was too young to stay at camp when he was out on his trap line, a safe and warm place with the nuns in Aklavik was the best solution for me, too. I did not want to go, but I knew that he was right. He did not know that I shed many tears dreading it when I was alone. Mother and Dadda said that they were depending on me to take care of my brother Pierre.

It was 9 pm. when we arrived at Aklavik. At the residence, the nuns immediately separated the boys and girls. They made us take all our clothes off and have a sponge bath, and then gave us a huge flannelette nightgown. I had always related flannelette to baby diapers or a granny shirt.

Before we left, Dadda and my mother had bought us new clothes and mother had made us a new pair of wrap-around moccasins decorated

44

with quill work. I was so proud of the new moccasins, which I thought were very pretty. The nuns took them away and I never saw them again. I never forgot this incident because this was the last pair of moccasins anyone ever made for me. I had to learn English quickly as the nuns did not want us to speak our traditional language. We were to speak only in English language. I wondered how my poor brother survived those months as he only spoke Gwich'in. I also spoke only Gwich'in, I was older and he was so little. I did not see Pierre again until a whole month later when we visited our brothers in the parlor. All the girls and boys sat across from each other in the tiny room. Sister stood at the door watching our every move so it was difficult to carry on any type of conversation. In addition, of course the conversation had to be in English! They would punish us if we spoke in our own language. They black marked us by be denying us some privileges that others were given.

No wonder many children forgot their Gwich'in language. As young as I was I wandered why the nuns can speak their language freely and we were not allowed to speak ours. Also when we ate they fed us in broken enamel plates and food that smells it made some us sick. But they forced us to eat all our food or we would get punished, so we were afraid to ever complain. The nuns and priest ate in their own dining room, and good food cooked differently then the children. I missed my food which was fresh all the time. Fresh fish, rabbit, and moose meat I had had all the time.

During the winter, I caught a cold and it did not seem to go away. I recall being in the dormitory and eating meals in bed, too sick to get up. Finally the nuns said that they had to admit me to the hospital where I would get the care I needed. I cannot recall the length of time I spent in hospital but I entered in winter and it as still winter when I was discharged. In a way I am glad that this happened because they made me room with two grannies from Arctic Red River. This was an honor, as grannies. Love to tell stories. The two elders were Didoo (granny) Naatritt and Didoo Philomene. I was glad of the chance to care for them. They needed rubbing with liniment and I was able to do this for them. I also combed and braided their hair, filled their basins with water each morning so they could wash, and emptied the basins when they had finished. Those two grannies were grateful for my help. They said, "You have shown good work to the elders and for this reason you will live a long life. Our time here will end soon and when our Creator takes us home we will be watching over you from up there. "My goodness, I was the grateful one! I have to listen to their stories, which made me happy, and I did not have to go to a classroom and listen to the grouchy nuns. I do not know what illness I had. Perhaps it was a touch of tuberculosis.

No Chance to Say Goodbye, In March, my mother arrived in Aklavik. To survive with 3 small children out on the land was too difficult for her, she decided she would find work at the hospital and she did. She made the trip alone from Arctic Red River with the three youngest children, using my father's sled and dog-team. She sold the dog team, sled, snowshoes, and probably the hunting rifles of my father. I never saw his personal effects again.

Mother put my sister Florence and brother Michell in school and kept my youngest sister Lizzy with her. Unfortunately, she ended up in the hospital herself, diagnosed with tuberculosis. I was the only one who went home that summer to Dadda. My maternal grandmother had passed away that year and I missed her as she used to send me a flour sack full of dried meat, pemmican and bone grease.

In the fall of 1946, I had returned reluctantly to the residential school. Sometime during the winter I felt sick again, it was like a bad cold that never went away. I was back in the hospital again. I was diagnosis with TB. There were two patients to a room so I went to room with mother. When I was, admitted, mother was walking around and only had to rest in the afternoon. She had gained weight and looked healthy. Mother said that she was looking forward to going home in the summer with the children. Mother did beautiful traditional craft work. She created beautiful piece-work on mitts, moccasin, gloves and many more. She sewed for many people from town so she could make few dollars. I thought, someday I will sew like her. I was worried about her, as she often complained of a headache. One evening each month there was a movie for patients, a Gene Autry or Roy Rogers black and white feature. This was a real treat. I asked mother to come see the Thursday picture show. When we were not resting, she sewed for her friends in town; this gave her the few dollars that she needed. The morning of the movie, mother was not feeling well and by late afternoon, she apologized and said that she was too sick to go. Later, when the movie was over and I return to my room, a nun told me I had to stay with the little girls as my mother's condition had worsened. She was very ill and they thought it best if she was alone. The nuns took turns sitting at her door in case my mother needed them. It was on Sunday, May 20, 1947 at about 4 am my mother knocked on the wall. I went out into the hall and told the nun my mother needed help. Shortly after returning to bed, I saw the nun rush by to go downstairs and thought that she must be going to get what mother needed.

The next morning I woke to a nun calling me, "Therese, wake up." I thought she is going to tell me mother was better and that I would be moving back to her room. Instead, I learned that my mother had died. I did not say a word and I did not cry; I acted like a zombie. I spoke only when I had to. My heart felt so heavy in my chest. I wanted to cry but no tears came, just a heavy lump that was stuck somewhere in my throat. To this day, I feel this way whenever my feelings are hurt. I had never called her Mother until then, always called her Liza or Pierre's mother. I was just beginning to know her

I asked if I could go to her funeral but the nuns said no. I hated them for that. I wanted to say goodbye to my mother but they would not let me. My mother's death affected me very much. What were the children to do? Who would care for them? I had Dadda, they had no one. I asked the Creator, Why have this happened?" I received no answer. I told our Creator that if He was not going to answer me I would ask His mother, the Blessed Virgin Mary. Maybe she would answer me. She was the one who wanted all people to love her Son above all things. She wanted to help bring people to Him. From that time on, I turned to her to intercede for me. I did not know what else to do. From the time I was a little girl my mama taught me to believe in our Creator, his love which he shows me daily throughout the land. It's beauty. The strength of her, in shapes and forms, colors throughout one season to season, the land has everything for our survival, we just have to have great love and respect for her and always are grateful and never forget to thank her for sharing her riches and beauty with us. My faith has carried me through so much sadness in my life. I believed that if I go through this one somewhere up the road there is joy. I learn very early in life to talk to my Creator, blessed Mother and the Angels and my ancestors, especially grandmothers. I said, "Your Son has called our mother back home. Now we are left motherless, you have to become our mother so we can be taken care of here on earth." I spoke to her as if she were standing next to me. My brothers and sisters did not go home that summer. Mary was only three years old so the nuns took care of her. They discharged me from the hospital in September of 1947 and I went back to school, promising myself that this would be my last year. I was determined to stay home next year because I spent most of my three years at the residential school in the hospital anyway.

Summer Days, In June 1948 the school, term was over and the mission boat Immaculata came to take the children home to Fort Good Hope and Arctic Red River. I felt sorry for all the children we left behind, the ones who never go home but stayed at this institution, year after year.

We children were excited as the boat made its first Stop at my hometown, Arctic Red River. It then continued its trip to Fort Good Hope, another 220 miles south up the Mackenzie River. Dadda was not in town when we arrived. He had gone to Aklavik to pick us up. My Aunt Annie took my sisters Florence and Marie Alice. My two brothers, Pierre and Michell, and I had to fend for ourselves. We had not seen Dadda when we were coming on the river so he must have taken another channel.

For a week, my brothers and I stayed by ourselves. With some help from Edward and his wife Joanne Nazon. After we settled in Dadda's house, we made a fire and cooked for ourselves. One of the first things that we had to do was get wood, so I borrowed a canoe, Michell and I paddled across the Red River to collect driftwood. We found some fair size logs and began sawing. We piled all this in the canoe, brought it back to the opposite side of the river and hauled it all the way up the hill to our house. It was hard work.

There was not much food in the house, so I had to get some food for us. I went to see the Hudson's Bay manager to ask if I could charge what we needed to Dadda's account. He said that I had to wait for Dadda's return. This manager knew who I was. My Dadda worked every summer doing maintenance for the Hudson's Bay Company. Dadda did all the chores, stacked shelves and cut wood. Anything needed, Dadda did. Yet, this manager said no.

That was my first negative experience with a white man. Race did not enter my mind. My teachings said that because white people were raised differently, they do things differently. In my mind, he was simply a mean man who had said "no" to us. We were just three little kids; I, the eldest, was eleven years old. The Hudson's Bay was the only store in this little town, and Dadda spent all of his money there. It was not as if Dadda did not have a job!

I began to think of ways to make money to buy the things we really needed such as sugar, rolled oats, milk and macaroni. I had an idea. If I had flour, I would make bread and pies and sell them to the people of the community. I asked Odella for her bread recipe, as I used to like the way her bread smelled and tasted. If my bread tasted like hers, everyone would buy it!

My first batch turned out terrible, but to my surprise, I sold it. My brothers said, ""No one will buy your bread because it's hard as a rock". However, probably because people felt sorry for me, they bought it anyway.

I was glad to have the money. It bought the groceries that we needed, including dried apples and raisins. Now I could also make pies to sell. In those days, there was no such thing as recipe books to follow. I made the pie crust using the same recipe for the bannock dough; I did just that, then rolled it out flat and placed it in the pie plate. It looked good when it came out of the oven. The crust was hard, but I sold my pies.

Along with the fresh fish we got every day from other people, we made out fine. We were able to take care of ourselves until Dadda arrived back from Aklavik.

We children came back from school so happy. Our summer vacation began with great joy because we were all back with family and friends. Little did we know the tragedy that awaited us?

A Family Tragedy   My cousin Agnes was a year older than I was. She was my Uncle Amos first born, followed by her brother Greg, Elsie and Louise and Joe. Joseph was just a baby when their mother died, and Amos raised the children with the help of his parents, Didii Paul and Didoo Camilla, and my Auntie Annie. The boys stayed with the grandparents but Amos looked after the girls during the summer holidays.

Earlier that year, my uncle had built a new house for Agnes, who was now old enough to take care of her sisters and run a house herself. The furniture and appliances were all new; he had ordered them from the Eaton's Company. He had them delivered by boat before we got home from school that summer.

Uncle Amos had also purchased rolls of fabric for Agnes to sew into clothing. When we arrived home from school, Agnes asked if I could come over to see what her father had done for her. I especially liked the cook stove that she had. It was chrome allover, white, and yellow. The big clock had beautiful chimes that rang every 15 minutes. I told her that someday I too would have a beautiful cook stove like hers and a beautiful clock that had the same chimes.

One beautiful sunny Sunday morning after church, my Uncle Amos dropped by the house and asked Dadda if we all could take a trip to Pierre's Creek. His friend Otto Natsie and his family were fishing there, and he wanted to take tobacco, tea and sugar to his friend. Since it was such a beautiful day, we could make a picnic of it. Dadda agreed, and since our canoe was a 22-footer, there was room for all of us. It did not take us long to get ready! Agnes and I walked down the road and told our friends that we would be gone for the day.

I remember that day so well. We stopped at Konnie Bay and visited with Edward Nazon and his family and Nicholas and his family who were fishing there. After we had tea with them, we continued on our adventure, arriving at Pierre's Creek sometime in the afternoon.

We had the midnight sun during this time of the season, so there was no worry; we had sunlight 24 hours. As soon as we arrived Bernadette, Otto's wife, began cooking for us. This was the traditional practice of our people, to make tea and feed the visitors. While the meal was being prepared and the adults were visiting, we children played on the shore, throwing stones and wading. After the meal, we began to play again while our parents sat around and told stories. The creek was about 100 yards from Otto's camp. We wandered up there and someone suggested that we go across. It was about 18 feet wide and deep so Burnaby, Otto's son, went to get a canoe.

In a short time, he was back, paddling a little canoe. Now he transported one child at a time to the opposite side of the creek. We began to wander along the shore throwing stones and looking for colorful ones. Burnaby asked if anyone wanted a canoe ride. I said that I did, so he came ashore and I got in. My cousin Agnes also wanted a ride and they let her get in too. Dadda always said that if a canoe was small, sit on the floor to be safe. A small canoe can tip very easily if not balanced or overloaded. I sat on the floor at the head of the canoe. Agnes got in and sat on the cross bar at the middle. I remember telling her to sit down on the floor. Then Barnaby pushed off and the next thing I knew I could not breathe. My lungs felt as if they were going to burst.

I could see the sun through the murky, muddy water and realized we had tipped! I had to do something or I would drown. I was wearing big, heavy gumboots and I did not know how to swim. Somewhere I had heard that if you find yourself in deep water the only way to go forward is to move your feet back and forth and paddle your arms. I did this, but once again went down. I fought hard to come to the surface. I prayed to my Holy Mother to save me.

As I paddled very hard, my toe gripped something. I thought that maybe it was a rock. "Oh please God, let it be the bottom I prayed, but my feet slipped off. I tried again to paddle with all the strength. This time I felt the bottom under my feet and hung on until I reached the shore. We had walked some distance away from the creek, so it was on the Mackenzie River that we had tipped.

Although I was weak from the ordeal, I saw some driftwood, found a long pole and rushed back into the water, the children were crying and screaming. With the long pole I reached, Barnaby. I could not reach my cousin as the current had swept far out. Although I waded out until the water was up to my chin, I barely could reach Barnaby. I pulled him out but I was not able to reach my cousin Agnes. Uncle Amos, Otto and Dadda tried too but they were unable to save her. She never came up again. None of us dreamed our day would end in such tragedy. We all cried and cried.

Dadda said that he and Otto would go back to town to get the police and report the accident. We were to wait there. He told me to take care of my uncle. I did not know how. I did not know what to say or do. After they left, I remember sitting on the shore crying and holding Agnes's youngest sister Martina in my arms. I was very angry because my cousin Agnes had drowned.

How could she die so young? She had so much to live for. She was like a sister to me; we were partners in everything we did. We shared our secrets; she was my friend at school and at home. I remember sitting with Martina on the shore looking out at my uncle. He was paddling back and forth to the creek and down the river then back again, all the while groaning and moaning as if it hurt so much. It was not a normal cry. In addition, the water was so calm, like glass. How could anything so pretty be so cruel?

About two hours later Dadda, Otto, the police and everyone who could help with the search arrived and began to drag the river. They worked in shifts all night, but by noon the next day, they gave up. The police said that the swift current from the creek could have taken her further downstream. We would just have to wait until her remains surfaced and hope that someone would find her. A few weeks later, Cliff Hagan and his family were fishing up the Mackenzie River, just around the bend from Arctic Red River. Cliff was looking out on the river and saw something floating. He went out to check; it was the remains of my cousin Agnes. Finally, the family was able to put her to rest.

Dadda had a twenty-two foot canoe with a nine-horsepower outboard motor, or kicker. One day I asked him to teach me, how to operate the kicker and he gave me the instructions that I needed to use it safely. When I felt that I had had enough lessons and could operate the outboard motor alone, I asked Dadda if I could go out on the river. He said, "Go ahead, as long as you're careful and don't have an accident". I was excited as I started to cross the mighty Mackenzie. Once across, I decided to surprise Dadda with a load of wood. I cruised along the shore, searching for logs that looked good and dry. Seeing a big log close to shore, I decided to land nearby so that it would be easier to load the wood. As I was landing, I tried to stop the kicker but misjudged my timing and rammed into the log. It made a dent at the front of the canoe. I was afraid to report this accident to Dadda, but knew I had to tell him. His expression told me that he was not too pleased, but he said nothing.

One thing I was sure of when I left residential school was that I was not going back. I had to have a plan in place for when the mission boat came. I worked on one throughout the summer months and learning to operate the outboard motor was part of it.

In late August, the mission boat came by on its way to Fort Good Hope to pick up students for the school year. It would pick up students from Arctic Red on its return trip.

When a boat was coming, everyone went around yelling, "Booaat" and there was much excitement. This time when I heard someone yell, I wasted no time. I took off down the hill, jumped in the canoe, started the motor and took off up the Red River. I traveled about eight miles, then shut the motor off and began drifting. The current was slow, and was about 10:00 pm. when the boat reached the bend. I could see the town and a faint light here and there but the shore was pitch black. This meant the mission boat had left! Although Dadda would not have liked what I had done, I was not going back to the mission school. I landed the canoe in our usual spot. As I climbed the hill to go home, I did not know what awaited me. Will Dadda be angry?" I wondered. "I went against his wishes."

I knew that he meant well but I wanted to stay home with him so he would have company. I would cook for him, and he would not have to travel out on the land by himself. I was afraid that maybe I had gone too far with my Dadda this time, but I might as well face the consequences because it was my own doing. I went into the house with a heavy heart.

Dadda looked at me for a very long time, and then said. "Sending you to school is not what I wanted, but at least at the convent the nuns would take care of you. The land is too hard for a young girl. When I am traveling out on the land, I am gone many days from camp. Our way of life is difficult. We have to work very hard in order to survive.

It is especially hard for a woman; this is one reason why I sent you to school every year. I hoped the nuns there would teach you other kinds of survival skills that will make your life much easier."

My answer was, "Dadda, I don't want another way of life. I love our life, I love the land, and I love all the work that you and Mamma have taught me. I want to live as you have because it is a peaceful life. In school, I cannot talk my language, and that life is much different from ours. I have to learn to survive on the land where I have my own diet and practice my own traditional skills."

He smiled and buried my head on his chest.

I thought, "I will learn everything out on the land and make him proud of me because he did not scold me for going against his wishes."

SPRING BREAKUP AND REMAINS OF MY FATHER'S HOUSE AT PIERRE'S CREEK

CHAPTER 3

Mackenzie Delta

It was that winter when I reconnected with the land and the beginning of my relationship with her from the adult point of view.

I wandered on the land alone as much as possible. I felt the peace from her. I also felt her energy. My heart soared with joy and contentment. She was a special friend and servant of the Righteous one. She fed, clothed, healed, quenched our thirst and gave life from the One who created her. Our Creator was everywhere through her. I took it all in and loved every minute of it. He had prepared me for this journey of life. I remember what Dadda and Mamma taught me so well that I was never afraid when I was alone out on the land. I felt peace, freedom, joy and contentment.

Many years have passed since that golden time. I remember how my people took care of the land and nature and how they had great respect for her.

Today I feel sad. I want to cry with the land, the universe. Mankind has been thoughtless and has destroyed so much of her natural beauty. Garbage and chemicals pollute the air and our rivers and lakes. The earth does not produce naturally, as she once did; pollution has destroyed her health. All nations should ban these chemicals, as the future belongs to our children and their legacy is not ours to destroy.

As long as I live, I will never understand mankind's greed, to destroy the very life that gives us life, the air, the food and the water. Although

Dadda had no money to bequeath to me when he departed this world, he had the land's legacy to leave me, which I will enjoy just as he did, and the generation before him.

When it is my turn to leave this world, I will repeat this pattern and I hope my children and their children will repeat it. If we continue to extract all of the land resources through greed there will be, nothing left for our children's future. Let us stop this madness and take a few steps back, realize the mistakes of the past and have a new vision.

My memory flashes back to Mamma's wise words:

- "Hear the earth speak silently when we appreciate and respect her.
- Hear nature sing softly, sometimes fiercely, but never with anger.
- Hear the birds as they sing their songs of joy, and animals wandering in freedom hunting for their food, storing food for the season they know how to prepare for. Do you hear their soft songs?
- Sometime they let you know their strength too; all this is beauty that we must take care of for our children.
- If you know the land as I teach you, you too will also do the same in the future."

Many times this teaching came to mind through the years, but today people degrade the Earth, mankind for greed, love for money, pleasure and power. I want to yell, "Stop for a minute! Let us ask ourselves the question, 'what have we done? What are we doing today? "What are we going to do for tomorrow?' "It will take a lot of courage to speak out against all things that will endanger and harm the future of our children and grandchildren.

In the fall of 1948, Dadda said he did not want to trap at our bush camp up Tsiigehtjiink (Red River). He wanted to spend the winter close to other people because if an emergency arose, I would be able to get help. He chose to winter at Big Rock, my birthplace and my grandfather Paul Niditchie's country.

When you leave Arctic Red River to go down the Mackenzie River, Louis Cardinal and his family bush camp is at six miles; then there is a white man named Larson at Point Separation, then at East Branch are Fred Cardinal and family and Pierre Tazzie and his family. There is a small river, which runs in the back into the East Channel; this is where Tom Throne and his wife Philomena stayed.

At East Branch you leave the Mackenzie River and take the East Channel at the river junction, this will take you to Big Rock and Inuvik.

At this junction, there also lived a white couple, Earl and Louise Mirander. They trapped this area for many years. Taking the west channel from the river junction leads you to Loche Creek, which was Pierre Coyen's camp. Pierre and his wife Marceline lived there with their two children and three grandchildren. The grand children's parents had died when they were very young; their father drowned and their mother had tuberculosis.

Pierre and Marcelline, who were my godparents, trapped, fished and hunted, and lived year round at their bush camp and only made an occasional trip to Arctic Red River or Aklavik to get supplies.

Next were Pascal Baptiste and his family bush camp. Then on to the Roz's camp. The west channel flows again into the Mackenzie River and at the mouth of the river lived Albert Ross and his wife Sarah.

From the river junction you can also go to Chii stiideniilaa (Big Rock) Norris Camp, then on to Reindeer Station. There were people just miles apart and on a cold winter day, you could hear the barking of dogs from other people's camps. Dadda said this would be good for me so when I got lonely we could go visit families who had children my age.

We would spend the winter at Chii stiideniilaa (Big Rock) and for the spring hunt; we would decide when the time came.

Big Rock was now Fabian (Lalu) and Cecilia Coyen's bush camp. They too went to town a few times a year to visit friends and get supplies. We lived with them in their big log house. It was nice to have a grandmotherly woman in the house.

Across the river lived a widow, Rose De Lima and her two grown children. I would visit them often. Cecilia taught me how to lace snowshoes, sew winter clothing, mukluks, duffel (to line the mukluks) and all winter wear. She was the granny that taught me to use my thimble on the right finger. She said, "You will never sew well if you never learn to use your thimble in the right finger".

I remember telling Dadda I wanted to go jiggling for Loche and he said we would go to a place about two miles up the river, south of Big Rock, "when the time was right." One cannot use any kind of bait for Loche, just the gut from a fish we called 'crooked backs.' The Loche will only take this bait.

I collected as much crooked back gut as I could when we fished and soon it was time to jiggle. The day before we were to leave, we prepared supplies we needed for at least two days. By the time, we arrived at our destination and set up camp it was evening. Now I had to wait until after 8:00 pm. to go jiggling. Jiggling may be similar to ice fishing in the south, but we did not do this for sport. Loche is a delicacy. As soon as you catch a fair size Loche, you fillet it, take the egg and the liver out, wash and fry them; it is delicious. Loche liver makes another dish. Then you fry the liver mashing it; adding cranberries and sugar to taste. Then you 'mix well and freeze.' People eat Loche with bannock, or enjoy it alone when they get hungry while traveling. The meat and other parts are cleaned and frozen. Later the dogs eat the leftovers and nothing is wasted.

Dadda told me to bundle up warmly and to be careful. I remember how happy the mothers were when they prepared to jiggle for Loche on a moonlit night with their older children.

Dadda knew this land and could read the messages it sent so I always trusted his judgment. I arrived at the creek, chiseled a small hole in the ice and checked the depth of the water. It was too deep so I did another. This time the depth was right. I set my things down, and baited the hook at the end of the two-foot string on my two-foot stick. Then I began to jiggle. I dropped the hook into the water hole and sat very still. "Two jiggles of the hook, stop for about five seconds, and then jiggle your hook again." I reminded myself.

I wanted to jiggle by moonlight because it was more fun, but that night there was no moonlight. It was cloudy which made it difficult to see but I was fine. I felt a little tug so I tried pulling at my hook. I caught something. I dragged out a big Loche!

Instantly I thanked my Creator. Very early in our life, we were taught to give thanks for our catch. I caught eight Loche in the two hours that I was jiggling. Putting all my catch in a little canvas wrapper that I had made, I proudly headed home. As soon as I arrived, I cleaned and filleted a fish to cook for Dadda and me and clean and froze the rest. I was too excited to sleep. If I did not go through this process, Dadda would not allow me to jiggle again was we had to treat food with respect, at all times. Everything was cleaned and prepared for later use. This was one of the skills taught to us early in life.

A few days later, we returned to Big Rock with some Loche goodies for the Elders!

At Christmas, we went to Aklavik and stopped at Albert Ross's home on the Mackenzie River to camp. That evening while the Elders were telling stories, their daughter Florence took out a sewing machine to finish a parka for her brother Georgie as they were leaving the next day for Aklavik. (She made parkas for all her brothers).

She had already sewn the parka together, now it was time to sew the delta braid, the geometric design that would decorate the bottom. I asked Florence if I could watch her trim

I watch carefully the way she designed it, it was a good way to learn. I never forgot her for this generosity because it helped when I learned how to delta braid later on.

As always when we went to Aklavik, we stayed with Didii Kenneth Stewart and Didoo Annie at Pokiak Channel. At Christmas, Dadda and I went to midnight mass at the Catholic Church, and at New Year's, Didii Kenneth and Didoo Annie who belonged to the Anglican faith were going to their midnight services. When Dadda said we were to join them I refused to go. He said nothing, and went along with them.

Sometime later, he asked why I had not gone. I told him that the nuns said it was a sin to go to any other church, but ours. I was told if I went to another church beside my own, I would commit a great sin. Dadda then asked if the Anglican people prayed to a different Creator. I gave it some thought then said, "I don't think so".

Dadda said someday I would understand what he was about to say." People have different practices but pray to the same Creator as we do. Our culture teaches us to respect others and someday in the future people will realize that although the practice of our faith is somewhat different, our Creator is the same Creator they pray to."

This made sense! Imagine an old man who never had an education had an explanation, which taught me a lot more than those who told me not to go to any church but mine.

We had a nice visit with our people in Aklavik then we were on our way back to Big Rock. Didoo Cecilia taught me how to make pemmican, prepare meat and waste nothing. She also taught me how to clean caribou skins, and then cut them into thin strips to make babiche, used to lace snowshoes, sew sleigh wrappers, and repair a dog harness.

In February, Dadda said we would move to a place named (Delta) Jack fish Creek at the river junction when muskrat hunting began in March. Therese (Rose Delma daughter) stayed there with us for a month. She then moved to my godparents' bush camp at Loche Creek because Marcelline needed help.

One cold clear spring day while we were setting traps for muskrat we heard a plane. Looking up we could see a small white speck so far up we barely could make out what it was. Dadda seemed to upset seeing the plane. He told me that the Creator has bestowed intelligence to the white man so they could find good things to help people, but they abused that gift by never being satisfied. In the future, he said they would want more, never asking themselves if it would be harmful to anyone or anything. He said "They will stop thinking because of greed and power, it will destroy the land," At the time, it did not make sense to me but now I understand what he meant.

Before spring, break-up another family came to stay with Fred, his wife Annie and their children. While the men went hunting for muskrat, Annie Rose, her children and I stayed behind. When the men came back to camp, we had a lot of work to do. Skinning hundreds of muskrat was no easy work. We washed, cleaned and then stretched the pelts. Once they were nicely dried, we put them in a gunnysack ready to sell to the Hudson's Bay Company when we got to town.

I recall that spring when I tried a cigarette and Dadda caught me. Fred and Annie's daughter Ruth smoked. Her parents did not care if she did. In fact, she rolled a cigarette whenever she pleased.

One day when everyone was home and Dadda was visiting next door, Ruth came over and insisted I try it. At first, I said no but she kept urging me to so I took one and inhaled. Just then, Dadda walked in. He looked at me and said nothing. Because I was almost choking to death, I did not care if I caught supreme hell!

Early the next morning Dadda left without saying where he was going. He returned in the evening, explaining that he had gone to the Norris's and bought some supplies. When he unpacked everything, he threw me a carton of cigarettes saying, "Now! Smoke all you want!" I was so happy Dadda gave me permission to smoke and lit up one Camel after another. The next morning I was so sick I could not get up to do my chores. Dadda chuckled as he asked me how I felt." Rotten!" I replied. I never smoked another cigarette until I was nineteen years old.

The people we lived amongst that year were delta Gwicha-Gwich'in from Arctic Red River. Prior to that year I seldom saw them, because the only trip they made to Arctic Red River was for August 15th, the celebration of the feast of The Blessed Virgin Mary. People came from the village Mouth of Peel. People with houses put up visitors for a week, and some stayed in tents down on the flats below the town. During this gathering, we all gave thanks to the Creator for a fruitful and safe summer. The year I lived in the Delta I got to know the people there very well. The August 15 celebration started out with a high mass at our big church with everyone attending including the children who all had new moccasins and new clothes. Later, there was a big feast with enough food for everyone. The leftovers the Elders took home. In the evening, there was a dance. The dance always began with the drum dance. We sung the songs with joy and gave thanks for all food received during the season for winter use. "

> **"Once a person asked me if I was ever lonely and I replied that I didn't know the word. I only discovered what it was like to be lonely after I lost my Mamma."**

CHAPTER 4

Arctic Red River

During the winter of 1949-50, Dadda said this year we would go up the Red River to trap. He was lonesome for his country and the land had, had plenty of rest. However, Dadda felt a bush camp was no place for a young girl like me. There were long distances of traveling by dog-team from place to place and many times, you had to set traps that took more than a day's travel, sometimes a week or more. Dadda said, he was going to the bush camp alone and planned to leave me with a couple of Elders in town. When I found this out I tried to convince him to take me along. I was young, (fourteen), but I wanted to use all I had learned and show Dadda I could be responsible. I could travel a whole day and never tire. I was capable of looking after camp, cooking, sewing, and cutting all the wood needed. I told him I was quite capable of being on my own for days but his decision was final. I was to stay with Joe and Annie Natsie.

These Elders were good to me and in return, I helped Didoo Annie with the household chores and with the fishing and woodcutting. I was company to Didoo (grandmother) while Didii (grandfather) went trapping. The Red River freezes by late September along the shore of the Mackenzie River; usually in a couple of days people can go on the ice and set nets for the white fish run. You can cross it if you are careful to avoid places where the ice is thin, as it would be even in October. While

63

staying with the Elders during that time, I did as told, but I still had a plan of my own.

I knew Dadda would come to town earlier than usual. By dog team traveling to our bush, camp at Bernard's Creek took four days. Our trap line was the farthest and miles away from the nearest camp. This was one reason why Dadda did not want me to go with him. What would he do if I got sick with him out on the land alone and far away from people? In town, there was the police and the priest to depend on.

Just as I expected, Dadda came to town during the last week of November with a few furs including one mink pelt for me. I was so pleased for this meant I could buy some parka material and make a new parka for myself for Easter. Whether or not we would go to town for Easter depended on how many furs, we caught during the winter trapping season. I was going to ask Dadda to try to trap a wolverine so I could have the fur to trim my parka and protect my face from the wind and cold. Wolverine is our traditional fur trim because it lasts a long time and does not freeze as other furs do. There were so few of these animals that to purchase a pelt would cost between four and five hundred dollars.

For the mink pelt, at the Hudson's Bay Company I purchased two yards of shroud, bias tape for the delta braiding and thread (which only came in black and white). Shroud is a very fine thick material that the Bay imported from England. It was available only in red, white or navy. . When we drew designs on them to make mukluks or vamps, the ink did not go through when we did our transfer.

I prepared my things the day before Dadda was to leave. I knew when he traveled he arose around 3:30 or 4:00 a.m. so that evening I offered to load the toboggan with his supplies and make sure the dog harness did not need repairing. I added my own items to the load, keeping out my pack sack and my bedroll. Early the next morning while everyone was still asleep, I left on foot. By the time, when Dadda caught up with me I would be so far out of town he would not dare send me back. I did not care that I did not get much sleep; I was on my way! It was so dark and cloudy that all I could make out were the shapes of the hills on both sides of the river. There were no stars or moon to give me light, but I was not afraid. Peace and joy fill my heart; this was real life! Town life was so boring with not many exciting things to do, just the same old chores. Out on the land I could discover lakes and creeks and get to know the land like my Dadda did. I felt I was not alone anymore. My energy soared and my spirit became alive. The spirit of my family, my ancestors were with me in those familiar surroundings of rivers, lakes, creeks and hills. Memories of my Mamma, my father, my mother, and all the people who used to travel with us flashed back to me. I felt a tinge of sadness. Now nature and the land thrilled me as I was re-discovering them.

I remember many places from that journey. I particularly think of the foothills. When you travel over one hill and the next hill is higher than the one before, this means you are close to the mountains. On the third hill, which is higher than the other two, you can see for miles. As I traveled west I turned around to see where I was coming from and on my left I could see part of Peel River at a distance, then to the East I could see the outline of a narrow dent in the landscape which told me the Red River flows somewhere along that line. To the South, were hills and lakes? All of this was mine and I was in charge. This was my land, and I would take care of her.

I knew then what my Elders meant when they said the land gave them much joy and refreshed them. It does replenish your energy and restores your outlook on life. You feel the warmth of the earth's protection. Mankind has to admit that it has tried to take this right from Mother Earth and she is not agreeing with the plan. I grew up knowing about her as my Elders and my ancestors did throughout our history. Our foremost thought is to please her through the Respect you have for her, so in turn she also can please us with all her strength, richness and beauty. Gwich'in' in people have a special relationship with the land. They feel her kinship and her protection. Gwich'in' in people are always thankful for what she gives, they used too; my ancestors never at any time extract more than what is needed from her. In addition, they make sure that other plants and nature are not disturbed or destroyed for other animals - you always leave the land as it was. The teachings of my grandparents and my Elders created that solid relationship with the land, and today I respect her and hold her dear to my heart.

The Earth has plenty of food to share with me; it sends energy through me and always gives me hope. The animals, the birds, plants and all that the land and nature gives to me I am forever grateful. I am their friend, I have respect for them; they will in turn treat me likewise. The narrow sled trail was along the river. It seems I had walked for miles before Dadda caught up to me. He asked if I was tired and when I said a little, he invited me to "sit in the sled and rest." I was overjoyed because this meant I am going to travel with Dadda all winter. I was on my way to a year full of excitement and adventure and I said no more towns for me! It took us three days to get to our camp. We stayed at Jack fish Creek and the next day we arrived at Marten House and camped overnight. My uncle Amos, his children (George, Alice and Martina) were staying the winter there. Ernest, Mary and their three children (John, Ilene and Thomas) were staying the winter at Marten House.

Dadda said these families were having a difficult time. They were experiencing bad luck in hunting and trapping. For some reason the animals were not good to them. They tried to trap, but the animals were going around their trap and not even eating the bait. If they hunted, the moose heard them for miles and ran so it was impossible to get close enough to get a shot. We had to keep an eye on them the rest of the winter. At intervals, we checked to see how they were doing and tried to help as much as we could.

During that time in our history, the Federal government set some laws for the trappers to follow in the Northwest Territories. A family could trap fifteen martens from November to February and ten beavers during the spring season. There was to be no shooting of beaver, only trapping, and only one moose per family per year. If a trapper crossed the Yukon border, the number of marten he trapped was unlimited. Dadda's country was near the Yukon border. We went over the border to trap after we caught the quota allowed in the Territories. Dadda hunted and trapped in this area all his life as his family did before him. He said he knew every fish, lake, moose, marten and everything there was to know about the land. He knew the whole of Gwich'in country.

We had a main camp at Tghaa Tiyaazhaii between Marten House and our cabin at Enjuu dehtla chic (Bernard's Creek). It was a job traveling constantly from camp to camp as well as to Snake River. We had four camps set up before we got to Snake River so we were constantly on the go.

Trappers do not like it when a wolverine finds their trap line. They follow your trail and eat everything. Whenever these animals find that the trail leads to food, they know they do not have to hunt. They will wait a few days, then travel your trail and eat all that you caught. If nothing else, they eat all the bait and snap the traps. They are almost human in their behavior. If a wolverine found your trail, you had to be cleverer than him and trickier. This is one animal very difficult to trap. He knows if the trapper had set a trap for him, so he would avoid it. He does not go near this trap but he sure likes to snap the marten traps.

In Gwich'in legend, when man was half-animal and half man, the wolverine was a con artist and a criminal. He conned, stole and lied to people to get his own way. Therefore Atatt-chi-u kaaing, ordered him to live his life in hardship. He would have to hunt diligently for his food. There would be few of his kind because he would cause a great deal of grief to humankind who worked so hard to survive. If we saw wolverine tracks in our trail, the first reaction was "Oh no!" then anger because we knew what to expect, nothing! If caught in the trap set for him, he usually gnawed the pole and walk away with the trap. This happened when Dadda set trap for wolverine. He set a trap similar to the way we set our mink trap. If the wolverine tried to take the bait, he would be caught in a No.4 trap. He would think it was a little old mink trap but when it snapped, he would find out how large the trap was! Yes, Dadda outsmarted him and now I was going to have a wolverine trim on my parka.

At our main camp, Tghaa tyaazhaii, we rested our dogs for a couple of days. My tasks were to make sure they had fresh spruce boughs for their bedding and to cook hot miracle dog food. When we did not have this type of food, we boiled a couple of fish and mixed it with oats, never meat unless there was nothing else to feed them. Meat was always hard to come by so we used it only when there was nothing else.

I had an old Marconi radio, which used a 15-volt battery. This battery was about 14" long, 8" in height and 8" in width. It was heavy but it went everywhere with me. Dadda said our dogs had enough weight to pull and did not need the extra load. I offered to walk or help push the sled with the dogs if necessary, but my radio had to go everywhere I went. I do not know why because the only stations I could get were Anchorage or Fairbanks, Alaska. They were never clear and the signal always faded away and came back again. I remember listening to "The Whistler" and "The Shadow", each hour-long mystery. I did not want my radio and battery to get cold so I wrapped them both in my feather eiderdown. When we arrived at our camp, the first thing I did was to take the harness off the dogs, fix their bedding, and feed them. Then I would unroll my eiderdown and put my radio and battery beside the stove to warm them. Then I would eat. Later I would go outside to pick long poles for my aerial, which was rabbit snare wire. This done, I would settle down and repair whatever needed repairing or make bannock for our traveling.

My teenage life was never boring, but fulfilling and busy. Anyone who has lived on the land and experienced nature will know what I am describing. Words cannot truly express the beauty, the life, and the energy that one can experience on the land.

We felt about the land before invasion of what one called civilization and the colonization of the Native people in the far North this way.

Today, my Elders say the land is not the same. Before, they felt her energy soaring into their own beings. Today, she moans almost constantly from the destructive materials dumped on her and from the polluting air, she breathes. Elders say we should change our direction before it is too late. I know what they mean as I feel it myself when I go out on the land. I knew Christmas was coming soon but I was not sure when as I never thought of asking Dadda either. When we are out on the land, Dadda crossed off the days on the calendar with a big X. Dadda said we were running low on dog food and wanted to go to Ghaii ghiian (Fish Lake) across Enjuu dehtla shik (Bernard's Creek) to fish. We were going to set hooks and hope to catch big northern pike.

We worked hard to cut a fresh trail from our camp to Tghaa tyaazhaii, (Sand Sliding into Water) to reach this lake. It took two days of traveling and finally we reached Ghyaa ghyiin (Fish Lake). Once our camp was set and we had tea and something to eat, we went out on the lake to where Gwich'in traditionally set hooks for pikes. We began chiseled the ice until we reached water, and then set the fishhook. Back at camp, I fed the dogs then went through the process of setting up my radio. A Christmas Carol came on. The announcer said it was 10 pm. This was only another two hours until Christmas. I felt a tinge of loneliness, not for town but because I wanted to be in church for the midnight mass and sing Christmas carols.

I remembered the few times we had gone to town for Christmas and I had the opportunity to see my people celebrate Christmas. The excitement of the preparation, women busy sewing new parka covers, making new mukluks, mitts, or slippers. People attended Church reverently and sung carols, celebrating the birth of Jesus. Afterwards, visiting one another, eating and then the dance would begin. Now I was settling for Christmas carols pouring forth from the radio stations in Anchorage. I felt sad only for a moment because I miss this part of Christmas celebration. However, I was out on the land with my Dadda but I was content, as I had chosen this life.

We had stayed two days at Ghaii ghyiin (Fish Lake) but had not caught any pikes so decided to head back to our main camp. When we arrived, Dadda said he had to make a trip to Arctic Red River for some supplies because we were running very low. There was one moose hindquarter left at camp but hardly any dog food so the next day we headed for Marten House.

New Year's, 1950, was just a few days away Dadda rested his dogs one day and left next day with Uncle Amos for town (Arctic Red River). I stayed with my cousins as we had an older couple staying in a house just next door so they knew we were going to be fine.

The animals were still treating my people badly. They had not killed a moose yet. A week later when Dadda and Uncle Amos returned, I could not wait to see what he had brought back for me. I was thrilled to discover a case of oranges! Early in the fall, he had asked the Hudson's Bay manager to freeze them so they would not spoil and arranged to pick them up sometime during the winter. Dadda told me to eat the oranges frozen, because once they thawed, they were not any good. Today, I still eat my oranges frozen and so do my children.

Dadda had a day of rest and then went hunting for the people at Marten House. As was his custom, he left early in the morning, so was gone when I awoke. My cousins and I made the morning meal, washed the dishes, and carried wood inside so it would be nice and dry when put in the stove, then made sure there was water for the day.

If there was not enough wood the older child would go out on the land and cut some, then return for a dog team to bring the load in. There was the dog harness to check, also the sled and wrapper. When these chores were completed, it was time to play, even if it was late afternoon. Sledding, hide and seek, going out in the bush and chasing squirrels were pastimes we frequently enjoyed. Sometimes we shoveled snow off a spot on the hillside to look for frozen cranberries to eat. Dadda had luck; he killed a moose. He brought back the gut and kidneys and we all had a delicious meal. The following day three-dog teams went to haul in the rest of the meat. The day after that when we left for our main camp at Tgha tyaazhaii, Dadda took very little moose meat, only a leg and one side of the rib. He said the Creator has blessed us with good luck so we must share.

It was steady traveling from then on, as we had not seen our traps since before Christmas; there would be no rest for some time. When our dogs were tired, we gave them one day of rest, and then left for Bernard's Creek (Enjuu dehtla chic). There was much snow on our trail and it was hard pulling for the dogs. Dadda walked ahead of the dogs to break trail, and I was behind the sled to help push when it was stuck. We managed to arrive at Bernard's Creek late in the evening. Dadda said that since we were both tired and so were the dogs, we would rest a day before we continued.

The trail in the bush would be more difficult to travel, because each day there would be more build up of snow. In the bush (tundra), the snow does not have a chance to blow away as it does in open spaces. By 5 a.m. the next morning, we were on our way. Sure enough, there was so much snow the dogs had great difficulty pulling the loaded toboggan.

We were about five miles away from first camp at about 9:00 pm. We were so tired Dadda said we should stop, make a fire and have some tea and bannock. When we had rested, we could continue on our journey. Traveling was slow so it took one hour to arrive at our first camp. Where our tent once stood there was just snow. A severe blizzard between Christmas and New Year's must have blown down our tent. I was so tired I wanted to cry, but I was not going to let Dadda know. I tied the dogs and made their bedding; then I helped him shovel the snow off the tent with my snowshoes. Out on the land, one does not have a shovel; we used snowshoes instead. It was later than 1:00 a.m. when we finally had something to eat and went to bed. It was hard traveling the rest of the way. When we traveled, Dadda never wasted time. He would wake me at 5 a.m. and say. "Therese, there is your porridge, or pancakes, but first go outside and wash your face with snow." I found this would wake me quickly and would not be dopey the rest of the day."""

We were in good health so nothing was impossible. When we moved from place to place, sickness had no place in our lives. We dug out our traps and reset them again. Sometimes mice became our enemy. If the mouse finds a dead mink or marten, he gnaws at it and mostly shaves the hair off the pelt. This is another reason why we had to check our trap as often as possible.

Returning to the main camp between Bernard's Creek and Marten House was better traveling as we had a good trail. Once we were back, Dadda said we should go and see the traps towards Fish Lake after we had a few days rest. We had a few mink traps along the Small Beaver Creek and marten traps at Fish Lake. Our line of traps ended at Fish Lake, which was a one day round trip on a good trail. If there was much snow on the trail and we arrived at the end of our trap line by late afternoon, we would camp by open fire.

On our way home the next day, two moose had crossed our trail. Dadda noted that their tracks were not too frozen, meaning they had gone through the night before and had not traveled too far. It was good weather for hunting, and he would go after them. I tied the dogs and told Dadda I was going with him. We did not make a fire just in case the moose may be close by and hear us or smell the smoke. As always,

71

I carried the Axe, teakettle, a little sack of sugar, hunting knife and ban-nock. Dadda carried the gun and the pouch that had shells. He carried nothing else because he may have to chase after the moose. In addition, that day he did! I was always about 30 yards behind him when we were hunting. Suddenly he stopped, aimed and fired. Then he began to run. I though this meant he had missed and now was on the chase.

I picked up the gun case he had dropped and had walked almost a hundred and fifty feet when I came to a small clearing. I thought I would just take my time and follow Dadda's trail. If the moose really ran away from him, he would eventually come back and look for me. By the time I reached the center of the clearing, I felt or heard a movement to the right of me. There about ten feet away was the biggest moose I had ever seen. He was so close, feeding on some young willows at the edge of the trees. All I had was a pack sack with a bunch of junk. I had no weapon; I was carrying only an Axe with a short handle. I stopped and began whistling hoping Dadda would hear me. I stood there for about fifteen minutes, but no Dadda. I thought there was nothing I could do but keep going. The moose did not pay attention to me as I began walking. I looked at him once more but he kept right on eating. At the end of the clearing, I turned to look at him once more. He was looking at me too. I showed him the Axe and said, "If I was a man and this was a gun, you wouldn't be standing there, you would be long gone." Then I went on following Dadda's trail. When I finally met him, he said the moose had run away so I told him about the other one. As we circled back to where we started, I knew the moose would be gone.

We got back to our Tgha tyaazhaii main camp that night. We would rest the next day after cutting wood of course. That night Dadda said, there was good moose country about six miles up the river and then about two miles inland. We would go there tomorrow; it was probably where 'our' moose had headed for food and shelter. I made bannock and prepared our supplies for the next morning. Dadda and I left at our usual 5:00 am. It began to snow with the kind of snow that made the sled hard to pull.

When we arrived at the place we wanted to go inland I made bed-dings for our dogs, tied them and fed them a piece of dry fish each.

Dadda had made a fire and we had tea before we left. As we walked over-land, we came to a ridge that seemed to stretch a mile or more. Dadda said, "We will walk along this side of it to the end and walk back on the other side. You walk some distance behind me and if you see anything that is moving, whistle. I will hear you." With this instruction, we be-gan to walk the route he said we would go. We walked to the end of the ridge but there was no sign of the moose, not even old tracks. We started back on the other side. After about a quarter of a mile, I saw something black moving amongst the willow some distance ahead of us. I whistled, Dadda looked back at me, and I pointed. He slipped off his gun case and shot twice. The black thing disappeared.

Looking in his pockets, Dadda realized we had forgotten our shells. He had wounded the moose, and it would not go far. "We will come back tomorrow for him, "Dadda said." By the time we made it back to the tent to pick up the shells it would be dark." I said, "Dadda we are going back to the river to our dogs. You could stay at the fireplace and eat and I could home to get the shells. If the dogs and I can travel light we can make good time." Dadda was not too keen on the idea but I fi-nally convinced him we could do it. I told him what he already knew; if a hunter left a moose wounded for a length of time, the meat would not taste good, and we needed the meat, as our food supplies were low. I would not change my mind. It was slow traveling.

The large snowflakes were falling making the sled difficult to pull. It took some time but I finally arrived at our camp. I went into the tent, picked up the shells, turned the dogs around and was on my way again. By the time I arrived back at the fireplace, it was dark. Dadda tried to convince me that returning to the wounded moose at this time was of no use. I told him the snow would give us enough light and I would not even stop for tea before we left for the hill.

We just reached the top of the ridge and began going downhill. Suddenly there was the noise of willow breaking. We could see the out-line of a huge black figure about six feet away from us. Dadda slipped off the gun case and shot twice. When Dadda said "Thank you" to our Creator, I knew he had killed the moose. When we heard another sound further away, Dadda found the moose he had wounded that afternoon

73

and shot that one too. I was so happy! Dadda had killed many moose in his life, but he always gave it to people; he always shared the gifts given to him from the Creator. Now we were alone up the Tsiigehtjiink (Red River) with no one else around for miles. I would take my time to work with the meat, as mama did. I would ask Dadda to set camp at the kill site. I would make dry meat, and bone grease and work on the two hides if Dadda would make bone tools for me. For the first time I would have the moose head all to myself! I was thinking out my plans in those first few seconds while walking around to find a clear place to make fire. I found a small clearing where I did not have to cut any brush, and made the fire. I was going to do just what I wanted with all this meat. The gut I would clean, and the meat I would cut up.

Then I would send Dadda down to Marten House to deliver some meat to the families who lived there, but the moose head I would keep. It is the best part and considered a delicacy. While I made tea, Dadda had cut the gut out, cleaned the inside, and buried it in the snow so the meat would not freeze. Tomorrow we would do the rest. By the time, we rounded the bend to our camp it was after midnight. Our tent was all lit up; someone was there. Instantly I knew I was not having the moose to myself; the planning I had done at the kill site was gone.

"Isn't this the way things always happen?" I asked myself. "I should be used to it by now." I had thought we would go back the next day and set up camp, live there for a month, eat and enjoy, and prepare the moose hide for tanning. Now I knew this would all change. It was not because I was stingy. It was because for once I would prepare the moose all by myself. There were no women in my life to teach me this but I remembered how Mamma had done it I was going to do the same. Anything I was not sure of, I could ask Dadda. Then I could tell the story of how I had cut dried and smoked meat and tanned the hide, from remembering Mamma at work.

The dogs at camp were barking as Uncle Amos came out of the tent. He shook hands with Dadda and they went inside while I unhitched the dogs and fed them. They made all the arrangements by the time I finished and joined them. Dadda and Uncle Amos would be going to the kill site the next morning. They would cut the meat and load as much as they could take. On their return, Uncle Amos would just stop for tea and continue on to Marten House. My Uncle Amos came to our camp because the families back at Marten House had hardly any food. They had begun to boil moose hide for their dogs, as they had nothing else to feed them. Uncle Amos had come to ask Dadda if he could hunt with him, but now he did not have to. He was going back with a load of meat. The people at Marten House would be happy but my dream of staying at the kill site and working with the meat and the hide had to wait for another time. We had very little food left. Dadda said, "We will soon get more. The families at Marten House need it." Uncle Amos asked Dadda if his children Alice and Martina could stay with us at our camp for at least a month, to trap and hunt. It was fine with Dadda.

The wolverine pelt Dadda had trapped for me was tanned and put away for the parka I was going to make when I had the opportunity. When we had brought the wolverine home, I skinned it, dried it and worked on the pelt every chance I got. Wolverine skins are thick and take many hours to tan. When the wolverine skin was finished, it was so soft. I was proud of the work I had done. I had wrapped it and put it away until the time when I would sew it on my parka. When my cousins came, the fur on their parkas was old and worn out. Dadda told me to take it off and replace it with my wolverine fur. "The weather is cold, their fur is so worn, they have nothing to protect their face from the cold wind," he said. I was angry. Goodness, we gave them all the moose meat; now he wanted me to give the wolverine skin too. I had put so much work into it to make it soft. It did not matter how disappointed I was, I had to do what Dadda said. Someday I would have my own way though. Dadda would get me another wolverine, and he did.

Now that everyone had meat, Dadda told Uncle Amos he could stay at our camp with his children. We had to go pick up our traps towards Gyuu dazhoo jiink (Snake River). With so much snow on the trail, it took a week to pick up all the traps and return to Hehnjuu deltyah tshik (Bernard's Creek). We camped there and the next day started back to our main camp. Because Dadda knew we would not have enough meat for the spring, he said we would set up camp about 12 miles below Hehnjuu deltyah tsiik and would hunt there.

Of course, he had to pick a place on a hill where there was plenty of dry wood. Big Beaver Creek was only a short distance and a good country for moose. As I busied myself, with making tea and cooking a meal, Dadda went to cut firewood and I laid out the spruce boughs for the flooring. I did not hear Dadda approaching the tent. Suddenly he was there, blood pouring from his mouth." My God, what happened, Dadda?" He pointed to his mouth, then to the tea. I remembered Mamma telling me all the things that were good to clot blood, including tealeaves. Quickly I emptied the tea into a different pot, put the tealeaves into a cup and handed it to Dadda. Then I boiled more tea. We continued to do this until the bleeding stopped. I asked him to open his mouth so I could see the damage. Whatever hit him in the mouth had cut his tongue. Now I was worried. There was no way Dadda's tongue would heal without medical help. I suggested we go to town but Dadda said that we would wait until morning before deciding what to do.

Later when he could speak he said, "I had my pipe in my mouth and when I had finished cutting the wood it went down, the tail end came up and hit my pipe which in turn almost cut my tongue off". I barely slept that night because I was so worried. Dadda will not be able to eat. I had to think of some way to get help. However, just like always, he was up when I awoke the next morning, drinking tea and smoking his pipe. When I asked how he was he replied, "Fine, a little weak from the loss of blood, but fine". I asked to look at his tongue, and it was almost together except for what seem like a small cut.

The next day, Dadda portaged to Big Beaver Creek where he knew there was good moose country. He left very early in the morning so I waited for an hour before following his trail. He did not mind me going hunting with him, but my snowshoes were small and they did not keep me above the snow. I went deep down which always made me fall. He said I should not put myself through this hardship, but since I enjoyed hunting with him, I did not mind. Following his tracks for what seemed like hours and still not catching up with him, I came to a top of a hill overlooking Big Beaver Creek. It was a breathtakingly beautiful sight. The creek was winding with trees, willows and birch on both sides. The view just captured my being and I thanked my Creator for all this beautiful land we lived on. I rested for a while then continued to follow Dadda's trail. For the hundredth time I fell in the deep snow and was so tired, I began to cry.

Did Dadda have any idea I was following him? Quickly I wiped my tears away as covered in snow I picked myself up. It was then I heard the most beautiful sound, almost like a whistle, except it had a soft, high melodious note. Could it be a bird? I had never heard a bird with such an intriguing sound. I looked around but could see nothing. I knew then, that the sound was sent to me so I would not feel sad. It gave me the energy I needed to continue my journey. I remember thinking I would never hear this sound again because songs of this nature do not belong to this world.

Finally, I saw smoke. Dadda had built a fire and was making tea. As I arrived, I heard his chuckle. I said if he had had the slightest inclination I was following him, he could have tried to break a better trail. (The tracks of his snowshoes were far apart because of his 3' ft. large, long snowshoes my steps were shorter and my snowshoes were smaller so I had to break my own trail again). I told him when we got back to camp; he had to go in search of the biggest, straightest birch to make me the biggest snowshoes for the next year. Then I would be the one who would be waking away. Little did I know I would hear a very familiar sound again?

In 1991 when I was living in Arctic Red River, a group of us went cranberry picking. It was September and the ground was very cold. Cold makes my feet cramp up and the only treatment is heat, as hot as I can take it. I had wandered a distance from the rest of the berry pickers and was looking for a spot to build a small fire, when my both feet took cramp. Massaging them with tears streaming down my face I did not want the others to know until I had time to make the fire to give heat to my feet. I would have to massage them until I was able to stand. It was then I heard the same melodious tune. Because I had heard this before I was all "ears" and was happy. I looked around me but saw nothing. Suddenly it seemed out of nowhere a bird landed beside me. Such beautiful earthly colors were his feathers and he sang again then asked how my feet were? I had forgotten about the pain, - it was gone! I said fine. I had the strongest desire to just touch him and hold him close to my heart.

I asked him why you come only when I cry because I hurt and I am so tired. You should come more often because at this time in my life I need someone like you to sing to me so I can continue the work I am doing for the length of life I have left.

He sang again this time a little longer then said, "This will carry you and I am always at a hearing distance, never far from you. I too am not so healthy! I am at the mercy of mankind's thoughtlessness and greed. This has great impact on all life on earth. I am part of nature, the air we all breathe, the soil of the land and the water, which at one time was so pure, the sky, and our food now making us ill. You have to write and tell your story. You will have a difficult time but all work that is for a good cause is always more difficult than others and remember I am never far away."

I asked how could I do that, I have very little education, I only have work experience, I will not know how to start. He answered, "We will help you". With this, he sang a short note and flew away. I quickly forgot the pain in my feet and lay back on the ground. I was so much at peace that I did not want to move ever from this spot. , Someone was calling me; they said that someone had already picked berries there. Nothing was left to pick, it was fine with me.

So much has happened to me since then, it is unbelievable. In my traditional culture when things of this nature happen to you, one does not question, you just accept it as part of your life. As a believer of the Creator and life after death, I believe in all happenings, as one of my teachings is that the spirit world makes contact with us through many forms, whether it would be people or whatever form they choose to be for that occasion.

Dadda hunted for a couple of days but did not get a moose. We left for Leth nejihtakii, our main camp. Uncle and his children were still there. They were making plans to return to their camp at Marten house. He had no luck in his hunting. The day before they left I got very ill. They left anyway as uncle had to picked up his traps. The trapping season would soon be over. Dadda told me later I had a very high fever; at times, I was delirious from the high temperature. All I remember was that Dadda prayed to the Creator asking him to spare my life. Our

Creator had called his wife and son home many seasons ago, now I was an only child left with him and he did not want anything to happen to me. He went out on the land to pick some medicinal plants, which he boiled and made me drink. I recall this but nothing else. I wanted to tell Dadda that the Creator was not about to take me. After all, he had to leave someone to take care of him; but I was too sick and weak to say anything. My faith and the faith of my Dadda had a lot to do with my recovery. It was two weeks before I was able to travel. Most of the time, the dogs pulled me because I was not strong enough to walk or run. Dadda said we have much to thank the Creator for, never forget to say, thank you, for all the blessings we receive during our lifetime.

We had to pick up our traps towards Fish Lake, towards the east of Tsiigehtjiink. As soon as I was able to make the trip, we left our main camp. Dadda said to prepare enough bannock just in case our trip took a few days. As we made our way, Dadda stop suddenly and came back to where I was standing. He pointed and said, "Wolverine has found our trail but I don't think he has bothered our trap line, he is more interested in something out there. Stay here while I go and take a look."

He was gone for almost half an hour and when he returned, told me that the wolverine has found a beaver dam and was killing all the beaver as he had dug a hole in the dam. He was killing them one by one then pulled them out of the dam dragging them somewhere else.

Dadda thought the wolverine may be sitting in the dam, "I'll go back there. Just make the dogs comfortable, and then follow my trail." In no time, I finished and went to follow Dadda's trail. I arrived at the lake, which was just a short distance away; Dadda was sitting by the beaver dam with a long pole. He said that the wolverine was inside and when he poked the pole through the hole, there was a growl. Now we had to close off the hole with large piece of wood then chop at the beaver dam to get him out. Beavers; build their dam like a fortress, wood, big and small, criss-cross, it was tough cutting.

It took us hours of chopping, but finally we were close because the growl was heard clearly. Dadda said I should go back to the dogs; make a fire for tea and a meal. "I will have my parka trim now!" I thought as I happily walked back to the fireplace. As I finished, drinking my hot tea

Dadda was coming back with wolverine. I was happy. While Dada ate, I said, I was going to go back to the beaver dam. There I began shoveling the soil and wood back into the hole. Why I did, I do this. In those days, there was a law in the territory against cutting beaver dams. Dadda and I were the only people who live and trap this area so if the game warden somehow came to this place and found a cut-up beaver dam, Dadda and I would really be in big trouble.

Easter was in a few weeks and Dadda said we were going to town (Arctic Red River) for the celebration. It would be nice to visit friends, and finally get some news. My Stroud parka was worked on feverishly while Dadda hunted and trapped beaver and a few muskrat. It took us three days to travel. Because there was no radio station, we did not know news from our region. If no one went to town, we would not know anything of what was happening during our absence, the whole winter season.

When we arrived in the village we were told Frankie Jerome, Andre Jerome's son, who was about my age had passed away. I felt sad, as did everyone else. Andre said Frankie got sick suddenly out on the trap line. By noon, he had got worse, he decided to bring his son to town, but he died on the way. They said it was appendicitis. Dadda said I was lucky to be alive. This was the reason why he did not want me far out on the land. I asked him since he had so much faith in the Creator, should not we leave the caring of us up to Him. He only smiled! Easter was a sad time because there was a death of young person that everyone knew.

When we left town, it took us a week to get back to our camp because we gave the dogs two days of rest at Marten House. They were pulling a big load of supplies.

At the beginning of May, Dadda said, "I am going to make one more trip to town; I will get someone to stay with you during the spring break-up. I do not want you to stay alone at camp, if I leave you, alone I will never be able to do my spring hunt. He brought Rosa from Town. She was my age and we had a lot of fun.

The spring season had twenty-four hours of daylight so the men hunted during the night and slept for few hours during the day while women worked on skinning of beaver and muskrat then stretching them to dry. During this time of the spring, the blue flies were out. We did not want them on the carcass to lay their maggots so everything was done as quickly as possible. There was no time to waste! Once the skinning was done they were put on stretcher to dry, the meat was clean split, bones and gut removed and dried to smoke. It was the season of light, the midnight sun, who wanted to sleep, for the women it was beaver or muskrat skinning during the day. Rosa and I tried to hunt but we never killed anything. We untied my five dogs and they came with us. Maybe we were too noisy and chased the animals away. It was fun trying.

The spring hunt ends on June 15. Once all the pelts were dried then everyone prepared to leave for the town. As young people, we felt the excitement- we were going to see our friends and all the dances and feasts we were going to attend. To the elders it was visiting one another and sharing stories of the past year, where they had traveled and their hunting. The "Banana Boat" should have been in and there would be fresh apples, oranges to eat, eggs, and potatoes. The "Banana Boat" was the first boat that came right after the Mackenzie ice break-up. This boat came from Fort Nelson, B.C. through the Liard River and down the Mackenzie River. After the long winter months of traveling on the land, just to see our friends and our people we had not seen during those months, and to be able to go to the store, and the feast and dances at these gatherings was looked forward with excitement.

UNCLE AMOS, JOSEPHINE, ALICE, TERRY ILENE
COURTESY OF WILLIAM CLARK

CHAPTER 5

Learning The Ways Of
The White Man

As a young adult, (fourteen) I was still chaperoned by older women when I went to dances. They picked me up at home then delivered me back after the dance. I had a couple of crushes on men but just from a distance. I could not imagine myself married to any of the boys my age, or the men for that matter. I grew up with them, played ball with them, fought with them; they were more like brothers to me or were part of my family. They used to tease me so much that sometimes I would beat them up. The boys used to say; they would feel sorry for whoever married me because he would be black and blue from the beating. In my culture, we teased those we like a lot. I could take jokes and give them back. I was a trooper. Some of the young girls' talk about whom they would like to marry. Being in love meant; the guy had to be good dancer, protector, and good provider. Money or looks never entered the picture.

At fifteen, Dadda felt I should go to Aklavik Roman Catholic hospital to learn to work for the nuns so he went to see the mission priest and discuss this idea. The priest agreed with Dadda that I should learn other skills, as the land was no place for a young woman to make a life. Arrangements were made for me and I left for Aklavik in January of 1951.

I did not want to go. I begged and cried but Dadda's mind was made up.

He said, "My baby I will not live with you forever, the Creator will call me home one day and you will be left by yourself. The life on the land demands a lot of our time so we can survive. At the mission, you will have a warm place, a bed to sleep and meals. You have to learn about the white man's work so you will survive much differently than I did. I am thinking of what is best for you and preparing you for the time that I too leave you."

I knew he was right but it was so difficult to leave him. The only plane that flew between communities in those days was a one-propeller six-seater mail plane and it came only about twice a month. One wintry day I left my Dadda, my home, and my community. Sadness filled my heart. I thought of Mamma. If she were alive, I would never be sent anywhere. The first month I cried a lot, but come hell or high water I was determined to adapt to a new way of life even if it killed me. I would make Dadda proud of me. Deep in my heart I knew he was right but it was hard to accept. Later I understood that Dadda wanted me to be independent and responsible. Who could do this for me better than the sisters whom I already knew and trusted? They were stricter than Dadda, and I began work the day after I arrived.

The mission and the residence were all in one building almost two blocks long and one block wide. The boys' residence was at one end and the girl's at the other end. In the center was a very large chapel. On the first floor was a classroom called the "High Classroom" and at the other end near the boy's residence was the "Baby Classroom; next to the girls' residence was the Grey Nun's residence.

In another wing was the hospital. There were four floors, the basement, main floor, and the upstairs then the attic. My first job was to work as a ward-aid. There was a private room, used only for an emergency case; the other rooms were used for TB patients. The attic was where we slept; some of the nuns also had their small bedrooms there. On the second floor were the women TB patients with an operating room and a private room. The male TB patients, a small lab, an X-ray room and a tiny room for medicine occupied the main floor. The basement was being renovated into rooms for the staff.

The big kitchen was where all the meals were prepared and then brought to the small kitchen to be served to patients. This was one of my tasks.

At 6 am, sister woke us up and we attended Mass. Later we went to give patients a basin so they could wash up. Next, we prepared the trays with food and then served it. We were given just enough time to eat. The ward-aid mealtime was always rushed. Then it was time to pick up the trays. As soon as all this was finished, we emptied and washed the basins and bedpans, changed beds, dusted and washed floors. This went on every day, except for a break between 3 pm and 4 pm. In that hour, we could rest or catch up on personal things that needed to be done. I thought of home many times those first months. At home we were taught to take our time to eat as we might choke on the food if we rushed. I was taught to do my work properly so that it will give me satisfaction and if not I would have to do it over again, even if it takes the whole day. Here was rush, rush, rush, and given a few minutes to do the work, time was allotted to do each chore, which caused so much stress. However, if this was the way to work in their world I will learn and that damn clock went so quickly that you were running to beat it all the time. Oh my goodness, I wanted to go home and work on my own time again. Some of the work on the land needed quick attention, for instance preparation of meat and pelts was enjoyed because one had a fire going with hot tea and fresh air.

This place was like a jail, so closed in; windows were all frozen with thick ice. We were never allowed to go anywhere unless we asked permission. If this permission was granted, it would be to the Hudson's Bay store which was located just on the other side of the priest's and the brother's mission house. We were old enough to work but still treated very much like schoolchildren. Today, when I think about this I have no regrets because it taught me about rules. I had to follow them whether I was a young or mature adult.

In my culture, we had a way of life. You had to get up early, eat, and do the task given to us. One learned all this since childhood. You can play when you have done all the work.

Here people had to follow the clock. There was time to do this, time to do that; there was pressure trying to keep up to that clock. I worked 12 hours a day for thirty dollars a month and my board and meals. In a way I was happy once I knew what I was doing and for what. My way of looking at this was for the patients who were bedridden. Many had families and never knew when they would get well enough to go home. My own problems were trivial compared to theirs. Although we all slept in a dormitory, we had our own bed and a table beside it. Tuesday was the day we were allowed to go to the Hudson's Bay store.

I met Annie and her sister Jane that spring. They too were brought to the hospital to work. The whole family was brought to Aklavik because Annie and Jane's parents had TB. The parents, Hyacinth and Frances had advanced case of contagious tuberculosis. They were put in the hospital immediately. The girls' two youngest brothers were put in the convent school. Jane, the younger of the two girls, was very shy; Annie was just the opposite. They did not speak a word of English, but we had some patients at the hospital that could speak Slavey and English and they translated for us. This made teaching them their work much easier.

I was always a fast worker. I liked to get things done and always tried to do my best. I never took short cuts. Because I wanted to do things properly and took pride in my work, I got myself into trouble. One day during lunch, preparation Annie and I got into a fight. Just as she grabbed a table knife, our head nurse walked in. She had to stop us. I have never forgotten this incident because later we became lifelong friends.

When the river ice broke and began to flow then the river began clearing and the mission launched its boat "the Immaculata". Even though there were ice floes on the river, it was time to haul wood from the bush. This had to be done before the mosquitoes were out and the children had to leave for home. Some children never went home, it was best they stayed at the convent. Some of the children were orphans; others were Inuit children whose parents lived far off in the Eastern Arctic.

By the time they made it home, it would be time for them to return to school. In Aklavik, canoe, whaleboat, or dog team was used for traveling, which took days or even months. Some of the girls got married from the convent and some finally went home when they were old enough. Some went to work as a ward-aide at the hospital or as a kitchen helper.

The mission boat had to travel 30 or 40 miles to collect the wood that the brothers had cut during the winter. It was hard work as the wood was 3 feet long. However, it had to be done so we could have heat for the next winter. In May of 1951, I began feeling sick, I thought it was due to the cold I had. In June, the flu-like illness continued so; the nun took my sputum for testing. I was not well, but one day, the sister said it was my turn to go. I went. I needed to go out on the land to rejuvenate my energy. My strength was slowly draining from my body and I had lost weight. It was an effort just to get up in the morning and go to work.

I never forgot a trip. One was because I was so sick and yet I had to go, another was something that happened which was difficult to believe without proof. At one time or another I had heard, this one brother used to expose himself to the children but I did not believe it because I have never witnessed this behavior. It was said that he should not to be trusted. I did not want to believe this because I was brought up to always respect the religious order and I had not witnessed or saw what was said. I must never make a judgment on what I hear. During the trip, one of the children approached me and asked to come and look in the engine room. What I saw was gross. This brother was exposing himself. Instantly I was mad - madder than hell. I asked him what he was doing. I swore and said some terrible things and then told him he was going to hell for what he was doing. I was only 15, but I was not afraid to protect others. He did not say a word but started zipping up his pants. I said, "If I ever so much as hear you do this again I am going to Father Superior and report you." Why didn't I just report him? I was afraid the priest wouldn't believe me. I thought to myself, this man was going to hell for sure, because he was sinful. The nuns and priest said that we should never say bad things about priest and nuns as they represent God on Earth, this made us afraid.

I Spent many years in the mission after this incident but never heard of him again. I was very young when I had lost my loved ones, because there was no one to protect me and dry my tears or heal the pain in my heart from rejection; I never wished pain on others. I felt protective of my brothers and sisters and other young children. This incident made me realize that there were some sick people who would go to any length to satisfy their own sexual desires. This made me mad especially when they did this in front of children. I still feel the same way today and hope the people who do this great wrong will be punished and wiped off the face of the earth.

CHAPTER 6

My First Bout with Tuberculosis

A few days later, I ended up in hospital. At that time, because X-rays and sputum's of patients were sent to a lab in Edmonton, Alberta, some length of time elapses before the results were received. The mail plane does not fly into communities during break-up, April to the middle of June and during freezing, September to November. There was no way for us to know if we had TB, unless they took our sputum and did their own testing in the small lab at the hospital.

At the time of the season x-rays were not of any use, the nurse thought it best to take my sputum. I had worked with TB patients, so it was possible I had contracted the disease. The sputum had TB germs. I was contagious so they did not waste time to admit me to the hospital. I was too sick to care what they did with me. I was very ill the first month.

One day in July, I felt better and it was a beautiful sunny day. I went out on the veranda with the rest of the patients to get some sun. I was still very weak, so I stayed only a short time. Later that evening, I felt something warm coming up. All at once, I began vomiting blood. The girls in my room rang for the nurse; they managed to stop the blood. I was very ill, but I never thought of death. I believe this was one more experience to learn and it will pass.

A week later, the same thing happened. Our head nurse, Sister Lemire said very sternly, "Therese listen to what I have to say is for your own good. You young people are not listening to what we are saying; we keep telling you bed rest is important. You have active TB, and the only way you can recover is through bed rest. We are serious. If you do not follow this rule, you are not going to get better. Maybe the next time this happens, you will die. Maybe next time we may not be able to stop the blood. When we say you are to have strict bed rest, we mean strict bed rest. It may save your life. You should think of your brothers and sisters who look to you as their older sister and the only family they have. You will let them down through no fault of theirs except, your own."

When she finished, she stomped out of my room. She made me so angry I took my two pillows and threw them after her. From then on, I laid back flat on my back and for the next seven months, I laid in the same position. I was very sick, so they moved me in the same room with Frances Cook, my friends Annie and Jane's mother. She passed away sometime in the fall. I felt very sad for them, especially for the youngest boy because he was so little. They all needed their mother. I knew what they were going through as I had gone through the same thing not so long ago.

For seven months, I laid in the same position, flat on my back. The nuns bathed me and rolled me over to make my bed. Although the food put in front of me did not appeal to me, I ate it. I drank lots and lots of milk made from powder milk because they said the calcium somehow helps in the recovery. In February, Dr. Orford came from the Charles Camsell hospital, Edmonton, Alberta. He complimented me on the improvement I had made since July. I ate everything, drank milk by the jug, and rested. Something should have improved; I did not intend to do this for nothing. Everyday the nun nurses came and gave me a needle. They said it was a medicine called strep. And three times a day, I received an ounce of something called P.A.S. The months of getting the shot made my butt as hard as leather.

They always had a difficult time looking for a soft spot where they could give me the shot. They were afraid they would break the needle. All patient x-rays and reports of their condition went to Charles Camsell

Hospital. Decisions were made, and the reports made on our recovery, which came back to Aklavik hospital.

From this information, the doctor of this hospital told us what stage we were at, in our recovery. Sometimes we would receive good news; we could get up once a day or twice a day to exercise. Many stayed strictly in bed year after year and eventually died.

When Dr. Orford came to see me he said, "Therese, you are an example to other patients. A few months ago, we had no hope for you. You sure surprised us all. Since you are progressing nicely, you may get up once a day, first by just going to the washroom" It was another year and few a short months before they discharged me. I left for home. The rules they gave me to follow were to rest at least three hours a day, eat three meals daily, no heavy work.

During my stay in the hospital, I learned to sew unique embroidery work on parkas, mukluks, and moccasins. I met a young woman who was also a patient, Rosie, who at the age of fourteen, was brought to the Aklavik hospital with her younger brother George. They were from Fort Norman Community that was further up the Mackenzie River. She was a beautiful person, and we became close friends. Her mother taught her how to sew, and she sewed beautifully. There was no flaw in her work in both the sewing and the designing of patterns.

When the nurse told me I was going to room with her, I was pleased. This would give me a chance to learn to sew better. Because I had no one to show me the art of sewing and drawing, I asked Rosie if she could teach me how she drew her leaves and made the flowers look so real. I would draw them and show her my design. If it did not satisfy her, I had to do it over again. It was the only way to acquire the skills. Rosie said it was the way her mother taught her to sew and design. I had my own ideas on flowers I would like to draw and how my sewing should look when finished. However, to get to this stage, I needed help.

I recall the day when I said I was ready to make a beaded vamp for a slipper. Because it was my first time to sew beads, I decided to use some leftover beads. I was going to make a full beaded vamp with multi-colored beads. When I finished my sample was nowhere close to the vamp she made. Mine was like a board.

Rosie said, "Undo it Terry, then start all over again." I agreed with her; it was terrible. She said the mistake I had made was that I had pulled too tightly on the thread and that made it stiff. She said to loosen them a little. She also said that if I wanted to be a good sewer I had to sew every bead down and I should never be too lazy to do this.

I have followed this pattern all my life. Everything that I have accomplished is because I had the determination to learn and to do it well. The encouragement Rosie gave me helped me to continue to master our unique Native people's art.

Rosie then told me a story of how her mother had taught her. Ever since the time she was very young, on several occasion she wanted to give up but her mother would not let her. She made her undo her sewing repeatedly until her sewing was satisfactory to her. Her mother was a craftsperson's and artist in Fort Norman. Rosie said in spite of all the frustration she went through she was glad she never gave up as her mother died just a few months before her hospitalization. She had learned all there was to know about the art of sewing, and all the skills she needed to survive, and to live on the land. Rosie's mother taught her the crafts, tanning, and the preparation of the meat of moose and caribou.

Some years later George recovered, but my dear friend Rosie did not. She spent the next few years in Aklavik hospital; later was transferred to Charles Camsell Hospital in Edmonton for further treatment. Sadly, she passed away in the early 60's. She was my good friend who never had a chance to try her wings. We both had dreams of marrying a cowboy someday and having a big ranch.

We would own a guitar and sing to our heart's content and there would not be any one to yell, "Be quiet" or "it's time to take a rest." Oh yes! We had dreams. Our life was going to be exciting; we would learn all there is to know of the other world - the world down South.

There were four of us - two Rosiest, Agnes, and myself. We were all the same age so our dreams were much the same.

Years later, I was in Fort Destiny when George came to tell me his sister Rosie had passed away at Charles Camsell Hospital, Edmonton. She had lost her battle with tuberculosis. I was devastated; I grieved for many months. She was a special person in my life. Today I have tears when I think or talk about her. She was such a good person, and I am sure all those who got to know her thought the same way I did. God rest her soul.

In June 1952, the hospital discharged me and I went home to my community, but I was there for only a month. Soon after I arrived home, I caught a cold, which did not go away. Dadda said that I should go back to the mission where the nuns could keep watch on my health. He was afraid I may get sick again.

That summer, the mission boat Immaculata was hauling gravel from above Arctic Red River, and I met Father Beanie. At the time, he was the Superior for the R.C. mission. Dadda asked our parish priest if I could return to the hospital and do some light work for the nuns. The priest said he was going to speak to Father Superior when they made the next trip. When asked, Father Beanie said it was fine with him.

Once again, I headed to Aklavik hospital. When I arrived, the Sister Superior said the light work I would be able to do was to take care of six little girls. I took rests in the afternoon for two hours. The staff and I all got along well. There was Jane, Annie, Lucy, Marjorie, Regina, another Jane, Winnie, and my cousins Alice and Martina. Rules were still the same as they were in '51, and we did not go anywhere except to the Hudson's Bay. Sometimes we wished we could go to Puffer's restaurant just to have coffee. We were treated like schoolchildren although we were eighteen. Maybe the Fathers and the Sisters considered themselves our guardians so they had to make sure we did not get ourselves into trouble.

Dear Father Beanie, we had heated arguments over this matter several times during those months. I tried to tell him they could not protect us forever, we were at an age when we needed to learn about life on the outside. We should be trusted to go out like other young people. We worked hard to earn our keep; the rest should be up to us. However, he would not budge.

Little did I know of the real world? Finally, he consented that on Tuesday nights after our work was finished we could go for a stroll, but would be chaperoned by two nuns. Golly! This meant we were not able to visit friends. They decided on the path that we would take us by   the river road to the point where the Post Office was, then towards the Anglican Church up the road and circle back to the R.C. Mission. Well!

This one night we decided to play some tricks on the nuns. When we got to the Post Office, we began to walk faster. We heard them calling to us, but we pretended we did not hear. As soon as they were out of sight, we ran to Peffer's Restaurant. People stared at us. Maybe they were surprised to see us, we were known as the RC girls. Did we look different? None of us ever had much money. When payday came around the end of the month, we had nothing coming to us because during the month we had advances. We walked in, looked around and walked out. Some friends lived not too far from the R.C. school building, so we went to visit them. We told them what we had done.

They suggested we should go back at once before we really put ourselves in trouble so we left. The higher grade school was a separate building from the main building. An American nun, Sister Gallant, taught grade 6 there. She seemed to understand and was a little more human than the rest of the nuns. We knew she worked late preparing for the next day class. There was a light in the building. We knocked on the door, and she let us in.

I told her what we had done and now we were afraid to return to the hospital because we had run away from the nuns. I said we did not mean any harm; we just did not think it was right for them to treat us like children. She chuckled; then said she was just leaving. She would escort us back to the mission. We hugged her and thanked her.

Before this incident, we had done something similar to this. We took our parkas, scarves and mitts and hid them; then we hid behind one of those huge old wood furnaces in the basement. At that time, we had everyone looking for us, the Brothers, nuns, the Father Superior.

I was the speaker for the girls, so I was looked upon as the instigator in all-sinful pranks that we pulled. The Sisters and Fathers blamed me. The girls wanted to say "we all shared the blame; it wasn't fair you just blame Terry". I told them it was okay. I knew the superiors would call me but I could handle it. Nobody talked to us for two days; then I was called to Sister Superior's office. She talked to me for an hour telling me

94

why it was sinful to disobey the rules. If we were to work for her, she expected us to follow the rules she put forth; I said nothing. Why try to explain? It was all said before. Next, I was called to Father Superior's office. He said they were responsible for us and as long as we were in the mission and under his care, he expected us to follow the rules. I could always talk to Father Benamie; he was the Superior then. He asked, "Now what are you going to say for yourself Terry?" "A lot" I said! Father Superior, I began with the rules, then the work, explaining how we tried to be responsible for all the tasks given to us, and that we never complained. Most of us were over eighteen years old; we just wanted them to start treating us as young adults rather than children. We had respected their rules, and the work given to us, how about showing us a little appreciation also. We did not want to run around town; we had some good friends in the community and sometimes we would like to visit them. Myself I just wanted to visit people whom I had become friends with, and I could eat rabbit and caribou meat.

I brought up another grievance about girls who were parent less. When someone asked to marry one of the R.C. girls, they would ask the Sister Superior. We did not think this was right; it should be up to us to say either yes or no. both the Superiors should respect our decisions. Many disagreements were done away with that afternoon, now it was up to them not to forget.

I always had great respect for Father Benamie. I could talk to him. He asked, "Why do you always take the blame? The others are just as much to blame as you are." I said, "It is better to deal with one person on all issues because our concerns are the same, so what I say won't be any different than what the others will say." He said he would meet with the Sister Superior, and see what he could do. I was pleased; I thought this was big progress. The incident made it possible for the staff to be free to do what they pleased during the hours off, during the day, but not in the evening, this made us happy. Dear Father Benamie, on one of his holidays back home to France he died of a heart attack. God rest his soul; he was special.

During the fall, I came down with a very bad cold. The nurse suggested taking my sputum for a test just to be on the safe side. Since I was an ex-TB patient, they were not going to take any chances. A severe cold may cause a relapse. I did not think I had to worry about anything.

I was sure wrong because after the sputum test, they did not waste time to admit me. The nurse said the sputum they took for test was full of TB germs. I cried; the girls who had become dear friends of mine cried. I stayed one more night in the staff dormitory, although they did not want me to. I may infect the girls but it was their pleading that made me stays one more night with them. I went upstairs and was admitted. Because the germs were active, it was contagious. They did not want the rest of the staff exposed to the disease.

I was eighteen years old. In June I was discharged just a few months ago. I was very angry the first few days. I did not want to eat, and cried a lot. The thought enter my mind, stay miserable and eventually die, or I could look at the bright side and tell myself that I could be out in two or three years if I did what I was told. It was during those convalescing years that I learned how much attitude plays a role in our life and how important it is to the way our life goes. It was then I decided to read and spend my time reading. I was going to learn everything by reading. I would read every book, magazine I could lay my hands on, and time would pass quickly.

One day I came across a Winnipeg Free Press and saw a page where young people were writing for pen pals. Golly, maybe I should try it. If my letter was printed, I could get some mail. We got mail twice a month. I was excited; I did not know if they were going to print my letter but I was going to try it. A few months later, the Nuns brought me a bag full of letters. Letters, tons of them! In addition, I received parcels with magazines and cookies. I shared this with my friends. People wrote to me from everywhere. This was my first contact with people from the South. It truly amazed me that these good people did not know me and yet took the time to write me. By this gesture of kindness, I knew there were wonderful people who lived outside of our country.

At the time a country to me was the where I traveled and lived most of my life. I did not think of Canada and how huge it was. There was not much contact between the North and the South then. Those who lived in the region and communities were a few white trappers, Hudson's Bay staff, RCMP, missionaries, and a few other non-native people. To be able to have direct contact with people in the South was a privilege. We lived and traveled in our region and did not know much else. This to me was a great adventure and experience to have contact with other people from other places. I shared my cookies and magazines with my friends. From then on, I lived for mail day. The reading, writing, and sewing took up all my time, so I had no time to be bored. During this time, I also learn to play the guitar, so that was another past time I enjoyed.

CHAPTER 7

First Encounter

Joanne, an elderly lady from my hometown writes me once in awhile and tells me the latest community news. I always did look forward to her letters. She was the only one who cared enough to write. Dadda could not write. Occasionally someone would write for him, I received a letter and a parcel. I was thankful for these two people. This time when Joanne wrote, she said I had an admirer. He was an RCMP. WOW! I guess she had mentioned me in one of their conversations and he wanted to know who I was. She showed him a photo, and he wanted to meet me. I could not believe this. Me? I was so scrawny, and kids always called me ugly names. I did not think I was pretty. I did not think I had any personality. I was shy, but I always spoke my mind. Kids always said I looked like a Chinese or an Eskimo because they said I had eyes like these people. I sure did not have any looks. I never thought of myself as being attractive.

This person's name was James. When he saw my photo, he told Joanne I looked cute and had a smile that stole his heart. Ouch! I considered it such a compliment. I was twenty years old and I dreamed of loving someone someday. If I was lucky, I might just get married, but that was someday. I did not think too much of romance. When I did get married, I wanted that person to love me very much and be a good dancer as I love to dance, I wanted to be number one in his life, and he would love me forever.

I was very naive. In the meantime, I was in no hurry or so I thought. However, when I heard this, my heart missed a beat. I know that a young woman from town was always sending him requests through our small radio station, but if he cared enough about her, he would not be interested in anyone else. She was probably chasing him.

Once again, Joanne wrote to let me know James was making a trip to Aklavik, and he would pay me a visit. He did not know how to go about it so she was sending a parcel, which he would deliver to me. It took James a few weeks because the RCMP at the time traveled by dog team between settlements in the North. Not very often did they have the luxury of traveling by RCMP plane. My girlfriends and I talked about guys in uniform and how good they looked. It added a little more masculinity and style to their image. I admired them from afar and only dared to daydream about them in a make -believe world.

No one was interested enough to want to meet me. WOW! I was filled with excitement. One day, the nun said I had a visitor. This man walked into my room wearing his uniform. I wanted to die right there. First, I was shy, and I was not prepared. I looked a mess, but all he said was "finally." He gave me the parcel from Joanne, and then he sat on my bed. My heart was beating so hard I was wondering if he noticed my pajama top thumping like crazy. He had to be blind not to notice. I was speechless. This surprised me because I was such a yapper. He was 6' 1" tall with blond hair and blue eyes. He introduced himself and he did most of the talking. I just sort of answered questions in a daze. My friends were curious, so they pretended to borrow something from me and I introduced him. My roommate was so taken in by James she hardly said a word the whole time he was there. When he tried to talk to her all she did was smile. Visiting time was only an hour, but probably because he was a policeman, the nun let him stay longer.

Up until then, I always thought if I was to marry someone someday, it had to be from outside my community. Although my friends and I said we were going to marry cowboys, it was only in a make believe world. James asked if he could visit me again before he left. I said yes.I heard from people that the RCMP officers were not supposed to get involved with Native girls. If the CO heard of any involvement, the person would be shipped out.

Anyway, I decided I should not let one visit bother me. He might never show up again. However, he did. He came back to see me before he left and said he wanted me to recover so I could come home. I was twenty years old, but something like this had never happened to me before. It was hard for me to believe.

I learned very early in life from my grandparents and parents, that police are very highly respected people because they uphold the laws of the Crown, in the name of the King or Queen of England. During that period of our history if the Natives had a red carpet, they would lay it out for the white man, RCMP, bishops, church people, and the non-natives. My people looked to them as people who knew much, who were educated, and would do no wrong because they knew the interpretation of the law. Our people respected and trusted them. Joanne wrote me twice again before I went home in July, and each time she delivered a message from James.

During my hospital stay, I learned to play the guitar and sang, mostly Kitty Wells songs. I have been a fan of hers over the years. Two boys downstairs played music frequently. I could strum on my guitar and sing, my playing the guitar was good enough but the boys downstairs played better so I asked if they could play the background music for Clara and me, as we sang duet. We sang for people when they came to visit us and we sang for our radio stations. I was discharged once again from the hospital. I was happy and excited to be going home but sad to leave good friends that I had made.

Somehow, I knew I would never come back. I wished them quick recovery, and with tears, we said our good-bye. I made many good friends amongst the Aklavik people, both the Indians and the Eskimos. Many I sang for and many I sewed for; many we drew designs on vamps, mukluks tops and fronts.

CHAPTER 8

Forbidden Fruit

In July, I the hospital released me, and once more headed for home. I was terribly excited and afraid at the same time because James was working at Arctic Red River. I did not know what awaited me, it was like going into somewhere where I knew there was warmth but there was a foreboding and the need to find this special place.

In a way, I was sorry to leave Aklavik. In those days, the Catholic Church did not allow me to marry outside my faith, unless they were Catholic or turned Catholic. I just had this thing about not marrying someone from my hometown, not because I thought I was better than them but because Dadda had many relatives amongst the people. I grew up with these people and I wanted to reach out as far as I could and absorb all that there is to know. I was not going to be satisfied living in one place. I had never had a relationship with anyone and I knew James' RCMP superiors forbade this type of contact.

The float plane landed in Arctic Red River. Many people came to meet the plane. Amongst them was James. This was a something I had once dreamed about, someone who is so handsome that my heart fluttered and did flips over when I looked at him.

I had very, very mixed feelings as I walked up to the house. Right now, I did not want to think, about what I may fall into as it may cause me much pain and tears. I did not want any regrets. I reminded myself

I was old enough to make decisions. I did not go into this relationship with my eyes closed. The outcome was obvious, it may be brief or it may be for the length of time he was here.

I had many arguments with myself that this was not really happening. I was an Indian; we had no freedom to live like white people. (I did not know what prejudice or discrimination meant yet). I just knew we were different in the way we speak, our lifestyle, and the way we think. I gave myself time to think things out. A month later, I told my friend Rose. Why not? James was nice, handsome, very thoughtful, and he did not seem to care who knew he was interested in me, so why not live a little? He may have used me because he was far way from home and he was lonely, but I used him too because I wanted to find out all about the white man's world, their lifestyle, their work and just their plain everyday life.

The first month was fun, with laughter, my first experience with love, or infatuation, whatever you call it, staying up late, and enjoying the midnight sun. I dared, but I was afraid. I knew it was going to end someday, but I did not want to think about it then. I hoped the end would not be too devastating. I hoped I would be strong enough to handle it well.

In late August, James asked if I could work for them at least twice a week, doing house cleaning and their laundry. I accepted. It was light housework. He knew I could not do heavy chores because of my health so he was careful not to give me tasks that could affect it. I was asked to do this for the Bay boys (Hudson Bay manager and clerk) too and I accepted.

Now I had some income, though it was not much. Fall came and I made all their winter clothing. I made new parka covers, mukluks, duffel liners, and mitts. In October, James was promoted to a Corporal and I sewed on all his badges on his uniform.

At the beginning of December, things began to change. Maybe a feeling of inferiority took over. I thought I would be satisfied with just a halfway relationship, but I found out I was not satisfied with just pretending. I did not want to have a relationship for fun anymore. I wanted something more real. I began to have doubts, not about James.

He was satisfied with whatever today holds; as long as he was stationed there this would continue.

He had a photo of a pretty girl on the living room table. One day I asked who the girl was. He said she was a girlfriend he had down South before he was sent up North; he wanted me to think of us not her, as she was far away in the south and we were in the Arctic. I knew we were living in the present and I had no problem with that. He was so gentle and thoughtful with me; he taught me that a love shared between two people no matter how short it is precious as long as it is shared with respect of one another's feeling.

I loved him for the person that he was, hoping he would marry someone who would appreciate the man that he was. I wished this were real. Things changed tremendously between us by Christmas. I had so many doubts I knew I was the cause. When one knows the relationship they have will never become a reality, something changes. The excitement disappears and one asks questions such as is it worth wasting my time? Then the realization that the relationship will go nowhere, it is not fun anymore. This was what changed my behavior and me. James asked why I was acting strange. I pretended I did not hear the question so I did not have to answer. For one thing, we could never be together for real. It was like a fantasy, or living in a dream world. Someday I would wake up and nothing would be there. When James had to finish his contract in the North, I wanted our friendship o remain with no regrets, and to ease slowly off. Now this would make it easier. The end had to come someday.

At this time, there was a young man in Arctic Red River who had spent most of his life living out on the land with his family. He had a good dog team, was a good hunter, a good provider for his family. He had taken care of them since his father's death. That Christmas he came to visit Dadda. He said he wanted to marry his grandchild (meaning me). In the old days, I would have been told all the good qualities that this young man had and the answer would have been made for me. However, my Dadda had told me previously that he would never force me into marriage. It would be my choice when the time came. Dadda took this calmly then said it would be Therese's decision.

John said to Dadda, "I will treat Therese well, she would never want for anything." Because he took care of his mother and he did what she asked, she made all the decisions. He would not tolerate a wife who disapproved of the decisions made by his mother. He felt strongly about this so he brought this to Dadda's attention. Dadda said if he felt this way, there was the door and never come back on the same matter, case closed. His grandchild was an orphan, and he did not want to see her treated like one, especially by the person who marries her because husband and wife should be first with each other. That was the end of that and I was happy Dadda did not say yes.

CHAPTER 9

Fort Destiny

In January of 1956 Father Levesque, our parish priest paid us a visit. He said St. Ann Hospital in Fort Destiny wanted three good workers from the community of Arctic Red River. He wanted to know if I was interested. At the time my cousins Louise was the only one working outside of our community. Elsie married a local boy. Interested as I was I took some time to think about it. I decided to take the job. I went to see the mission priest and told him I was interested in the job. He said he would make all the arrangements. It was a chance to get away, so I could think clearly again. At that time, parents still made decisions for their children as long as they were not married and lived at home. The young adults helped their parents with household chores, if it was a woman; if it was a boy, it was hunting, fishing and trapping. As their parents were getting older, it was the children's turn to take over the care of their parents as a way of saying thank you.

I was 21 years old and still living at home. Dadda let me make my own decisions. He was there to give advice and guide me, and sometimes gave stern advice. Dadda said I was an orphan and this meant when he was gone there would be no one there for me. I had to be well prepared to take over my life. He made sure I had the skills of the land and the skills of the white man to survive.

I wanted to get out of James' life and this was my chance. I discussed my decision with Dadda, and he agreed. Two other girls were going, so I would not be alone in this new country. We boarded the mail plane for Fort Destiny one cold day in January. Dadda said he would miss me but I had to begin to live my own life.

Who knew what a disastrous decision this was that continued to play a major role in my life. The effect of the decision led to a traumatic experience, which has affected my life to the present. At the time, I thought it was for my own good. When one takes a direction, which will help towards a better future for oneself, one tends to think it is a decision wisely made. I would return to the safe haven of the convent, and to the nuns who at the time were a big part of my life.

Fort Destiny was like any typical northern community. The native people spoke a different language, I did not understand them, but their lifestyle was similar to ours in the far North. As far as I was concerned, we had traveled half of the continent. The major disappointment was that there were no white fish. The people there had caribou and moose meat, but the hospital only served buffalo meat. I found that meat very tough and tasteless. Probably because of the way, it was prepared. However, I was not too keen on the diet. The rules for the staff at this institution were not as strict as at the Aklavik Hospital. The staff was allowed to go out to visit or attend any recreational activities in town, if they wished to do so.

The people of this community were friendly, the only disappointment I had was that they spoke their language whether there was someone in their midst who did not understand. Later I was glad because I understood their language quite well and even began to talk some. Dadda taught me many years ago that out of respect for those who do not understand your language speak in a language everyone understands, if not, translate what is said. It is rude to exclude anyone in a conversations Therefore, I found this very disturbing. It would help me to better understand their needs. The friends I made were the staff and patients at the hospital. Through these acquaintances, I met the Métis people in the community. Once settled into the routine, I was busy and did not have time. I loved my work and loved my patients I took take care of.

They became very special to me. I did extra for them such as going to the Hudson's Bay for the things they needed. I wanted their stay at the hospital to be less stressful than it already was, and to assist them in my own little way was a blessing, just to help my fellowman. I was a hospital patient at one time and was concerned about the patients. The other girls, Iline (Porky) and Bella (BN) were busy finding out the town recreational activities that was nil, except for the hockey game that was played twice a week in town at an open skating rink. The first month all I did was work and did sewing. I knew I was not going to see the color of money for some time. We were to be paid by the month. Our salary was $45.00, but it had to go towards paying for our plane fare to Fort Destiny

I can't remember who but someone introduce me to a sweet old lady named Celine. She was very religious, and she loves to play cribbage. I went to visit Celine and her husband Joe frequently, and we played crib. Celine had four children of her own, three girls and a son. Her children were all grown up, but the oldest of her girls was deceased and now she was raising her three grandchildren. She was a sweet old lady who dedicated her life to the well being of her family. Her youngest daughter was about my age, so spending time at her house was enjoyable. The invitation from the daughter to come over for visit was hard to resist. In addition, the English language was spoken in the home, so it was not hard to feel part of the environment. The Lafferty's, Eddie and Margaret, were the musical family of Fort Destiny. Eddie, his brothers, Maurice and Peter all played musical instruments and sang. They often got together just to relax and sang songs. I was still very shy, so I did not get into the singsong party very much.

When it was hockey night, the girls used to rush around getting ready to go to the game so they could cheer for their favorite team. I had never heard of hockey before so I could not understand why there was so much excitement about this game. One night, Iline (Porky) asked if I would like to go to the game with them. I was curious as to what their excitement was about, so I went along. To my surprise, it was fun. The star of the game was a handsome young man by the name of Brent. As time went on, the hockey game made some sense and with some explanation of the game from friends, I began to enjoy it. I looked forward to these games and went whenever I could. Brent was the star of the town team and always seemed to score. The other team was "the wireless boys" as they were called in those days. They worked for the Department of Transport (D.O.T.). The girls went to the game just to cheer for Brent and his team.

I heard everyone talking about the spring carnival. They said it was the event of the year. Again, I did not know what a carnival was about. Someone said it was an event the town sponsored every spring; it had recreational activity, which could be enjoyed by all ages. Just preparing for it was fun. There were girls who would be nominated to run for the Carnival Queen. Two girls were chosen, one representing D.O.T. and one for the town.

I guess someone nominated me for the hospital, because the Carnival Coordinator came to ask if I would accept. I excused myself; I did not have any talent and sure did not have any looks, who would buy my tickets. I made some feeble excuse and declined but they would not take no for an answer. How stubborn can they get, they picked me and I would sure be a loser plus I didn't know the town people so I would not be able to sell too many tickets. They were persistent, so finally I accepted.

I was sure I did not have a chance against the other two girls who were born and raised in this community. They were both pretty. Laura represented D.O.T. and Florence was for the town. I was so busy working, I did not campaign nor did I try to sell tickets. I did what I was told to do and no more. The eve of the Carnival came, along with a dance and the crowning of the Queen. This event was to be held at Andy's Hall. Our work finished at 7:00 pm, and Change from our uniform, dressed in our best clothes we were on our way to the hall. I was crazy for dances and this is what I am going for, nothing else. Someone met us and said to hurry, as they were waiting for me. The coordinators of the event were waiting, as they wanted to announce the winner. The hall was filled with excitement. We found some seats and sat down, and then the candidates' names were called to make sure that we were all present, the people who were responsible for counting the tickets were identified.

When they called my name as the winner, I could not believe it. I was shocked, speechless, and numb. The coordinators asked me to make a short speech. All I managed to say was "thank you," and "it is nice to be here." The community presented me with gifts, and I had an escort for the evening. He was Archie Hardisty; he was good looking, fun and a good dancer. Sometime through the course of the evening, Brent our hockey star asked me to dance, "Oh my goodness, he was sooooo handsome." He smiles as he looked at me, and I wanted to melt. However, I was not going to let him know how much he had affected me. I heard through the grapevine that he had a steady girlfriend, but that evening we danced every chance we got.

Before the Carnival, Ilene (Porky) talked constantly of Lee, a guy she met. She pointed him out that evening. Then she introduced me to him - not bad I thought. He was a lot older than we were. Lee danced and flirted with me but I did not pay too much attention, because I was interested only in Brent and how handsome he was. Sometime during the following weeks, Brent asked me out.

I was not surprised as his eyes told me he was interested in me as much as I was. He introduced me to his grandparents who had raised him. I also met his uncles and aunts, nieces and nephews. They were all nice people.

I had arrived in Fort Destiny in the early part of January and by April; I still had not received any wages. We worked 10 hours a day and yet BN, Porky and I were never paid. Finally, I got brave enough, approached the Sister Superior, and asked about our wages. She said we had no money as what we made went towards paying my plane fare. I never did find out what the fare cost.

To cover my few personal needs, I had to sew crafts and sell the product to the townspeople. This gave me the extra dollars I needed. I did not question the nun again. In April, I ordered a Swiss watch from Eaton's catalog. The parcel came by the end of May. The cost was $21.00. Every day I wanted to ask the sister Superior for money to take my parcel out of the Post Office, but I was afraid she'd say, no money; you are still paying for your plane fare.

It was almost the end of June; in a few weeks, the mission boat "Saint Anna" would make its yearly trip from Fort Smith down the Mackenzie River and we would board it to go home. I got brave enough one-day and I asked the Superior about my salary. She said very sternly that the month of June would just cover the cost of my plane fare.

Ten hours of work, every day and no money, this made me very upset. I was not going to work another hour. I took off my uniform and went to the staff house. Before anyone came after me, I left. I did not know, where I was going, I just left. I walked all afternoon. Sometimes I just sat for a while looking out on the Mackenzie River. Thinking of home, I cried. Much later, I went to May's house. I knew her parents and her sisters were supposed to come in from Rainbow River and bring some wild meat. I could have something to eat then, cooked beaver or ducks, at least I would have something nourishing. This was a disastrous decision.

When I arrived at May's, she said her parents were not in but her brother Lee was. I told her what had happened at the hospital. She asked if I was going back later, I said, NO! She said if I was afraid to return to the hospital and confront the nuns, she would come with me. I thanked her but I did not want to see them, not then, maybe sometime much later. Later on, Lee came over and he sat around. They spoke in their language, so I could not understand what their conversation was all about. I guessed she told him what was happening with me because he asked if I wanted to walk to the Hudson's Bay with him. It would take my mind off things so I accepted. On the way, he asked if it was true, the nuns would not give me any money for my parcel. I said it was true. He wanted to take the parcel out for me (no strings attached). How naive I was.

For many years of my life, I felt guilty for every little thing I did wrong. What I have learned from the nuns that every bad thought, action, words; every human mistake was a sin. Only a prayer was not a sin. It was a good thing my Mamma taught me to love, but during the school days, it sort of got confused with the teachings of the nuns. Later, I had to go back to Mamma's teachings. She told me I should always remember the Creator loves us very much and forgives us all.

Lee walked me back to his sister's place. May said I could stay with them until I could clearly think and decide what I wanted to do. We sat around and talked. I told her about my Dadda, Mamma, my parents, my sisters, and brothers. She also told me about her family. They were a big family, and she said I would love her family once I met them. Sometime in the evening, Lee came over. His house was not too far from May's house. He asked if I wanted to come over because Ruby, a girl I worked with at the hospital was at his house with her boyfriend. I knew both quite well so I said yes. Ruby had befriended me from the time I had arrived at the mission hospital and helped me to know the routine. We got along well at the hospital so I did not see any harm in going over. During my misery and confusion, I forgot Brent. Somebody should give me a good kick. "My God, how could I?" When we arrived at Lee's house, Arnie and Ruby were there. I was glad to see them so I did not know they were drinking until later. It did not take too much coaxing for me to join them. After a few drinks, I forgot all my sadness. In fact, I was normal and happy. I was still there the morning after, not remembering too much of the night before. I said Oh God! What did I do? Now I am worse off then I was yesterday.

Mamma said if we believe in Our Creator's forgiveness, in his love, this means we love him with our whole being. However, for several years I forgot those teachings and confused them with the teachings of the convent. If I had bad thoughts, I was going to Hell; if I said bad things, I was going to Hell; if I did bad things, I was going to Hell. The nuns teachings did not teach me about love, just hell fire, condemnation and punishment. It was not until much later that I remembered my Mamma's words. Our Creator loves all of us and forgives us and I should forgive myself when I do not do things right.

Only much, much later, did I remember the words of Mamma, and began dealing with the guilt feelings, punishment, and hell. Yes, these teachings have affected my life. No matter how hard I tried to be good, someway, somehow I seemed to make drastic mistakes. I was always feeling guilty. I am human; I am no saint, I will do my best today, and it is all I can do.

Things happen in life and from this I gain more experience. Dadda said to look at them as one more experience learned. My thinking seemed normal, but sometime later I looked back and I thought I was sure confused then. When I make mistakes, I try to make a better decision, which may make it as right as possible. Because of the way, people treated me in my life, many times rather than trying to explain, I just buried all my hurts and pretended to others that I was not hurt at all. I cared a lot, how someone treated me or what someone said to me, but because some people hurt me so much and when I tried to tell them, they would not listen, I just said, "I don't give a damn. What is the difference? I am going to hell anyway".

All this was wrong thinking if I believe truly, in the existence of my Creator. However, I thank my Creator for reminding me of my Dadda and my Mamma's teachings, which did change my life before it was too late. During my childhood and adolescent years, I was much influenced by my Dadda's and Mamma's teachings and then later by the nuns of the convent. I remember Mamma taught me to pray since I was a child. I recall my first prayer. Creator, I thank you for Dadda and Mamma, the land and the food. As I grew older and began to understand, more she made me add more thank you to my prayer. Now with the teachings of the convent, I was so afraid, for just living, their teachings taught me guilt and fear.

Lee had the skills I wanted in a husband someday or so I thought, I did not know much of the world outside Dadda's home and the convent. I tried my childhood prayer,

Creator, thank you for all that you have given us. First off all My Dadda, for his health so he could hunt for us, Mamma so she can sew our clothing and cook for Dadda and me. Thank you for the land and all your creations you have given us to give us life, clothe and feed us, thank you for this land that you gave to take care of us. Creator send your mother to help me now as I have no where to turn to, my spirit is gone and as long as I don't feel whole by what I have done and where I am I will ask your mother to intercede for me.

I woke up Ruby so she could go to work. Then I had a wash and began cleaning, washing the dirty dishes and cups. Although Lee said to leave the cleaning and go back to bed, I said I needed this time to think. The guilt and humiliation of where I was and what I had done weighed heavily on my soul. I wished I could die. I wanted to die. However, I survived and I hated it! Lee said I could stay at his place if I wanted too, it was fine with me, now I didn't have to go anywhere, see anyone, or talk to anyone. I knew nothing about this man but he seemed to be very nice. He was confident in himself; he seemed to be a good provider. What more should I ask for?

He would help me and I, in turn, would do the same for him. A couple of days later Brent came to the Lee's house and asked if I could return to the hospital, he was willing to bring me back because he still cared. I looked at him tears streaming down my face. Oh, how I loved him! How I wanted to turn back the time to last week when everything was okay. I wanted to leave with him. Many times, I asked myself, "Why didn't I leave with him?" "Could it have made a difference in my life?" I wanted him to hold me and tell me everything was going to be okay. I wanted to tell him I was not worthy of him. However, he had loved the other Terry. This Terry put herself in hell and did not know how to get out. I felt so unworthy of him so I said, "NO". Lee asked him to leave. With what I know today, many things would have changed. Today I would have left with him and returned to the hospital, as he wanted me to. The nuns also came to Lee's house to ask if I could come back to the hospital to work. With the guilt feeling weighing heavily on my soul, I could never be a part of that innocent life again. I said 'no'.

I assume my life with Lee began like any other relationship. He had a big family. He had been married before and his first wife had died leaving him with three young girls. His first wife's mother had taken the granddaughters and was raising them. Lee got married again some years later but the marriage did not last. He was divorced at the time I met him but the deed was done. I had to live with my shame and my sin. Today one can walk away from this sort of conduct; not feeling defiled and label it as a bad experience. At the time immoral behavior was frowned upon, it was shameful and disgraceful.

Dadda always said, "Therese you are an orphan. I cannot tell you things that a woman can and cannot do. Being an orphan means you have to accomplish more than others. Your behavior is always watched and your work has to be almost perfect before it is acceptable or recognized. As an orphan there will be no halfway for you will have to perform your best all the way. Some girls have children with no fathers.

They have their parents who may be angry at the time their daughter has the baby, but because it was their child, they have to stand by their daughter, and the woman's name becomes dishonored. She may never have a chance to marry. You have no parents to stand behind you. If you bring a child into the world, you alone have to be responsible, and it is hard to bring up a child alone."

All these teachings made me feel guilty and I felt ashamed for my behavior. The humiliation I felt made me decide to stay. There was no way out. As a woman, I had my rights violated. Nevertheless, I was as much to blame as Lee. I should have never accepted the invitation to go to his house. All of the heartache I could have avoided. If Lee would accept me, I would try my best to make a home for him. I would do this using the ways that I had been taught.

In July, Lee and Mark got a contract to cut logs for East 3 (Inuvik), a new town under construction in the North. We all moved to Green Island to cut logs. In addition, I was hired to be their cook. On weekends all the hired help went to town, Lee and I stayed at the camp. We worked on Saturdays and Sundays. He drove a caterpillar and I was the swamper, (a person who chains the logs) to be moved from one location to another by tractor. I kept busy and tried not to think. The logs were to be delivered to East 3 by the end of July or early August, time was valuable.

One weekend everyone was going to town and we decided to go. We needed at least one more week of grocery supplies. When we had arrived in town and did all our shopping, we then visited with his family.

It was good at the beginning with Lee because he did not drink much and if he did, it was a social drink. May asked if Bunny her little girl could go with us for the remainder of the week at Green Island. Bunny was about 7 or 8 years old at the time. May said Bunny never gets to go anywhere and it would be good for her to go on a little adventure. She would enjoy the trip. Lee said it was fine with him if it was okay with me, as I would be the one looking after her. I said "Sure, no problem." Bunny was a shy, quiet little girl. She would be no problem so we took her back to Green Island with us. Mark and Judy had a little girl Bunny's age. Her name was Lena Bunny and they now, would have someone to play with.

I cooked for the crew on the boat. Some ate out on the barge on a nice sunny day, and Lee and I ate in the boat. When I was busy cooking or cleaning up, I always asked the little girls to play along the shore and not on the boat because it was too dangerous, they might fall in. It was not safe and I was afraid for them. The water around Green Island was strong and swift all year around. There were small rapids in some places. If they fell in, they would be carried down the river so fast that it would be almost impossible to save them. With two little girls around, I did not feel safe. There was Judy, Lena's mother and me, but her tent was set a distance away from the boat. The men were cutting logs far back in the bush. If something happened, they could not help. At the time of our arrival at Green Island, I had made a loop with the rope that was used to tie the boat. It was free as the barge was the one tied securely to the shore. I made sure the rope behind the loop was several feet long. One day, after everyone had eaten their noon meal and gone back to work, I began to clear the dishes and started to wash them. The girls went to the boat to pick up something of Bunny's. I asked them to go back and play on the shore, and when I finished my chores, I would join them. I turned to put the silverware away, and then turned to watch them get off the boat. They were gone. If they had walked off, they would still be in view. I ran out. They were nowhere in sight. They must have fallen in the water. I grabbed the loop and jumped in. As I was going down, I could see a red sweater, which Bunny had been wearing at the time. I had never learned how to swim. Ever since my near drowning in 1948, I did not care to get into deep water. Now I did not have time to think. I just started to move my feet and put my arms forward and pushed back. It is a wonder what one can do in an emergency. One does not stop to think, one just reacts. I must have been doing the right thing, because the next thing I knew I had them both. I held on as tight as I could. By this time, we came to the end of the rope. It really gave us a jolt as the current was carrying us swiftly. Lena panicked which made it difficult holding on to both of them.

When we managed to get above water, I screamed as loud as I could. Judy heard the screams and came out of her tent. She saw us and began to run. She waded out as far as she could and handed me something to grab. She pulled us out. All this happened so fast that I never once thought of me. I just had to save those little girls. God was with me! I did not panic. Bunny is now a grown woman, but when she sees me today, she always says, "Auntie if it wasn't for you, I wouldn't be here today. I will always remember you and be grateful to you for saving my life." She was just a little girl when I did this, but she never forgets. It gives me much joy to see she is living a full life, which gives me happiness.

All the logs we needed had been cut. Now we had to build a raft. Lee had a boat, so we were going to float the raft down to East 3. His brother Allen and sister, Amy, were to come with us.

After we built the raft, it took us more than two weeks of traveling to get to East 3. On our way, we stopped at every community along the Mackenzie River. It was nice to meet people. Then we landed in Arctic Red River, my hometown. My Dadda was not there. He was at Big Rock fishing with my Uncle Amos. Therefore, we left almost immediately. When we left the Mackenzie River and began our travel in the east channel, I piloted the rest of the way.

We stopped at Big Rock to visit with Dadda. I was happy to see him, but I did not say much. When I was, alone I cried for the many things that had gone wrong. I wanted to say I was sorry and I wanted to come home. However, it was too late. I wanted to be a child again; then he could fix it all for me, but I could not. I just cried. Lee was with me, so I could not say much. It was okay for him to talk his own language in front of me, but I could not. By then, I was aware of how angry he got if I did not do what he wanted me to do. I introduced Lee. Dadda, who was always friendly with everyone he met, did not say much. I saw the disappointment in his eyes, but it was a decision I had made, and he did not want to interfere. Not until much later did he tell me that he knew at the time how this relationship would turn out. If he had told me at the time, I would not have believed him. He said sometimes we just have to learn from the mistakes we make and realizing it and changing our direction is what is important.

I wanted so much to go back to the security of Dadda's home. The logs were supposed to be delivered to East 3 by the end of July, and we were going to make that deadline. Once we arrived in Inuvik, Lee and

Allen sold the logs; then they both went to work for a construction company. During the month of July, I suspected I was pregnant. This was one reason why I did not go back to Dadda's home.

East 3 (Inuvik) was booming and the weekends were filled with parties and dances. On the weekends Lee seldom came home and when he did, he always found something to complain about which flared his temper. Then he would begin slapping me, kicking and punching me. I tried to make things normal. If I ever questioned where he had been I would be punched, so I never dare asked. At times, I prayed he would never come home. This one night he came home and began beating me. Someone called the police, and he was locked up. I knew the next time he drank he would say it was my fault and he would beat me again. Much later, I realized he was trying to make me fear him right from the beginning, so I would be afraid of him and would never leave. I did not want to anger him, so out of fear I did whatever he wanted me to do. I never saw violence neither in my Dadda's home nor in my parent's home.

One night in late September, he began beating me up in one of his drunken rage. I guess someone called the police; he was taken to jail overnight.

I met Robert. He was the one who came to arrest Lee. Later he came back to ask some questions. He asked, "What are you doing with a man who physically abuses you?" I told him a little about myself. I did not want to say much because if Lee knew I talked to someone especially an RCMP officer, the beating would be repeated and much more severely. I made him promise never to repeat what I had said. I told him I was pregnant. I have no choice. I did not realize I was not dead, I was alive and I could make changes. Robert said if I ever wanted to leave, he would help me return to Arctic Red River and my Dadda. It was up to me to make this decision. A few days later Lee began beating me in front of the dance hall. He was again taken to jail. Robert took me away and made me stay with some people he knew. By this time in the fall, the lakes were on the verge of freezing, as were the rivers. The day after Robert put me on the plane to Arctic Red River. I arrived home.

Dadda was so happy I had come home. Why didn't I stay? A few days later, the RCMP plane came and Robert was on it. He was being transferred to the Arctic Red River detachment. I was glad. Being afraid made me paranoid; I was always expecting Lee to come to Arctic Red River, beat me and drag me back to East 3 (Inuvik). At least there was some one here who knew of my situation. I was glad that Robert knew so I felt protected. I did not tell Dadda why I had come home, and he did not question me either. He was just glad I was there with him.

Dear Dadda, if I only knew then what I know today.

CHAPTER 11

The Beginning of a Nightmare

Almost immediately, I went to work for the RCMP preparing their clothing for winter and doing their house cleaning. Dadda did odd jobs for the Hudson's Bay store as always. Then the Bay manager asked if I could do their house cleaning as well. I said "yes." This kept me busy with no time to think and the fall passed quickly. When I was going to have my baby and what I was going to do never entered my mind. I would worry about that when the time came, for now I would enjoy my freedom.

Robert became a special friend. He would come to our house and visit. He asked if I thought about what I wanted to do after I had the baby. One day Robert in one of his visits asked if I wanted to go south, stay with friends of his, and go back to school. The plan he had for me was appealing, but I was afraid to leave the safe haven of Dadda's home again. I was only 23 years old but yet I felt I was too old to be going to school, and the fear of leaving the North Country to go to some unknown place was too scary. Robert taught me the meaning of friends. Good friends care what happens to one another. They are there for each other. He said, "Sharing our thoughts and talking about what we fear in life with one another always helps." When you talk about the concerns you have and share it with a friend, it does not seem as bad as it looks. God bless and take care of him always wherever he is today. There are not many friends like him.

On January 9th 1956 I left for Aklavik hospital. Because I had been ill with TB for a number of years, the doctor wanted me to spend some time in the hospital before I had the baby. They were afraid of a relapse. I was very sick after the baby was born because of a long labor. There was something wrong with the baby's spine. If she did not get proper care, she would die. They had to send her to the Charles Camsell Hospital. She died a few weeks later. Deep down in my heart I blame Lee for my baby's death. When he used to kick me or threw me around maybe, he did hurt her. Now I know why it is difficult for me to say I forgive him. I remembered all the things he had done to me and so much hatred seems to surface again.

After so many years, someone please tell me how to forget. I pray to my Creator to forgive me for not forgiving, but there was too much harm done to me both physically and emotionally. The scars are so deep. I have no hope of healing, but maybe telling my story may help me and the prayers for my spirit to heal. Because I have buried it so deep, I have not dealt with it. When some incident happens, that relates to physical abuse, the anger and hatred surface. Now I try to keep going the best I know how.

When I was told that my little baby had died, I did not cry. I just felt sad and empty. I knew she had become one of God's angels and she was safe. I heard Lee had gone back to Fort Destiny for Christmas, and had returned to East 3 at the beginning of March. When he heard I was in the hospital, he flew over to visit me. He said he was sorry and asked me to forgive him for hurting me. He asked for another chance and he would make it up to me. I said I would have to think about it. After several, more visits, I began to believe him. He treated me as if a man was supposed to treat his woman. As I said before, I was naive.

One weekend he flew over to visit, I went back with him. I had begun to work at the hospital after I had my baby. I left this job to go back to East 3. When we arrived at East 3, I applied for a job at the Department of Public Works (DPW) kitchen and was hired almost immediately. Lee was different. He was more attentive, and did not drink much. Now, when he went out, he took me along with him. Sometime in April, my friend Robert made a trip from Arctic Red River to Inuvik by dog team. He came to the dining room where I worked and he saw me. He came over and asked, "Is this what you want? Do you want to live in fear the rest of your life? I had no answer. He said I was smart and I could do a lot better with my life. I did not know what he meant at the time. Gradually I felt things began to change. I did not know much about other people and behaviors, especially outside my home or the convent. I thought, if a woman does her best in her home like the one I was taught to do she will be well taken care of.

I thought if certain behavior hurt another person they will stop as this was against the law of respect. At the time I could not see what I had done wrong to be treated so horribly. I could not even see why promises made were not kept.

At the beginning of June, everyone came down with the measles. The kitchen staff all became sick. There was just the cook and I working. I thought, maybe I was going to pass this one but when everyone began to return to work, it was my turn. I was very ill with the measles, and then pneumonia set in. I was sent to Aklavik Hospital. I was in the hospital for almost six weeks. The doctor was afraid I might have a relapse because of my history with tuberculosis. However, six weeks later I was discharged and on my way home.

I knew Lee was playing around, and this hurt me but I dare not say anything out of fear. By this time, he had gone back to his usual self and had become more abusive.When one gets to this stage, depression sets in, there are many guilt feelings, and I was totally without hope. I wanted someone to love me and take care of me. I wanted to be happy and to feel secure, but I felt there was none of that in this relationship. I felt alone and trapped. However, I wanted to make it work. I thought, maybe I will try to talk with Lee and how much my heart and my spirit are hurting by how he treats me.

My cousin worked as a clerk at the Hudson's Bay Company store, which was located down at the waterfront. At the time, she was staying with us. I did not have a key to our place, so I stopped at her work and ask her to give me her key. I had plans. Lee should be at work so I was going to surprise him with a nice supper then I would talk to him about my feelings. My cousin looked at me funny; then said, she may be wrong but she was almost certain Lee did not go to work. She gave me the house key and I left. As I unlocked the door, I had a dreadful feeling, I was afraid to walk in. As I walked in, I saw our bedroom from where I stood. I saw a girl leaving the bedroom quickly and in the middle of the day all the curtains were drawn. As I entered the front room, Lee came out of the bedroom. I wanted to ask what was going on, but I was afraid to. I would get a severe beating for asking such a question.

Why did not I leave then? As I saw myself then, someone with no future, hopeless and bleak, the happiness one feels when they began to have; their own home was taken from me in its place now I just felt worthless.

Rather than leave I went to see a friend of ours and got a bottle of over proof rum, brought it home, and drank the whole bottle that night. I intended to die; I wanted to die! I was calm, and I did not say a word. That night some of our friends came over and brought more drinks. I knew I was going to die; I was drinking to do just that!

About 4:00 am, I began to get very sick. I thought the drink would knock me unconscious and I would not feel anything, but it did not happen that way. I began vomiting, and I was so sick I could not describe it. I was sweating. I was using towel after towel and they would soak up in seconds. Drinking a 26-ounce of over proof rum is lethal. I heard this somewhere, but it was not doing the job! It just got me deathly ill. Lee thought I was sick because I had just got out of the hospital, and I should not have drunk. Maybe God saved me for a reason, but at the time, I could not understand why I was not dead. It was a week before I returned to work.

Maybe, the feelings of guilt Lee experienced made him behave better for the next few weeks. In September, I found out I was pregnant again. Having a child while not married I wondered who would want to marry such a woman. Once again, the guilt made the decision for me. Here was not too much I could do about the destiny that fate had set for me in life. I would have to resign myself to the situation and make the best of it. My child needed a father and if this was to be, let it be. I would suffer for my sins. While making this decision, I asked the Holy Mother, the mother of God and my mother to intercede on my behalf to her Son. Maybe there would be a way out of this whole nightmare some day. However, save me because I see no way out; I was caught in a world of evil from which I could not escape. For me to survive this there had to be a miracle from the Creator I was doomed to hell before I had even begun to live.

I thought about the turmoil I allowed myself to go through. I had nowhere to turn. If I went to the Nuns at the convent, they would look at me with accusing eyes. If I went to see a priest, he would condemn me. There was no one in the world for me as everyone sat on the judgment seat. How I wished my Mamma or my mother was alive. I am sure that they would have been there for me. They would understand. However, they were not there. The only friend I had was the Blessed Virgin Mary and I hoped she would not desert me; she must take care of me as her Son had called my entire love ones home. She would have to take their place. Somehow, I had to keep on; I had a baby coming I had to think of.

I buried my fear and started a life of just existing from day to day. I knew if I held on to my spiritual beliefs and faith, my Holy Mother would come to my aid and I would find my life again.

When the camps began closing for the winter months in November we left for Fort Destiny. The camps would reopen again in the spring. Things were better, so I thought. Desperately I grasped every little hope I could, it kept me going; it was like food for my emotional strength.

Winter passed quickly. I was making fancy embroidery clothing for Lee and buying a few clothes for my baby. At the beginning of February, Lee borrowed a dog team and we went to Rainbow River to visit his family. His father, Jonas, had passed away that year with cancer. His mother and her two daughters, Amy and Laurie were home with their mother. Katherine and her husband and all their children were also living at Rainbow River. Lee's mother cared for me very much. She was glad I had returned. I enjoyed the trip. When we returned to Fort Destiny, Lee left for Calgary. He was to take a welding course. Lee never cared about all the hard work I had put into sewing the clothing I made for him. When he had a few drinks, he gave them all away, sweaters, gloves, parka, slippers, and mukluks. Everything went to who ever he was drinking with. I was also fully aware of his unfaithfulness. He bragged about it when he was drunk.

My son Fredrick was born on April 8, 1958. The joy and love I felt when I held him in my arms was overwhelming. He was a special baby. I promised myself I would take care and live for my baby. I had assumed that now Lee had a son, he might change. He might even quit drinking, but fatherhood did not stop his behavior. I stayed at home with my son for a couple of months but I wanted to go back to work. The Hudson's Bay Company had advertised for a clerk trainee so I applied. I got the job and began training. I learned quickly, in no time I got into the routine. I was fast and good with people so Mr. Craig said I was going to be the number one cashier. I liked my job.

How I presented myself working with the public did not matter to Lee. Now he was jealous of my work and of the other staff. He accused me of cheating with them. My God, this guy did not know when to stop. I was beaten up almost every weekend and dear Mr. Craig had to put me in the back room taking stock until my swollen face got better. I remember July 1 when Lee hit me with a two by four lumber right across my face. I had some cuts and I could not see through both eyes the next day. In those days, there was no place for a woman like me to go to. I ran away many times, but it was a little town and one cannot hide out very long. Lee found me, and out of fear, when he said to go home, I did.

The police could not do much either. If I had laid a charge, he might get ten days, he would be home again, and then I would get more beatings so I could not even win if I tried. Lee would beat up anyone who stood up for me, even his mother. I ran away from him one day when he began beating me. I ran to his mother's tent. She said, "Sit here beside me Terry and I will talk to my son. He has no right to hit you like this." He walked in and my mother-in-law did not have much chance. She began to say something and he ploughed her one then he threw her around too, because she was trying to protect me, she got hit too. He must have punched her good because the next day she had a black eye and she told me she was sore all over. I wanted to kill him, but that would create more problems for me. There was no support for women in those days.

Rather than put this on anyone else, I did what I was told. I did not dare say a wrong word nor do a wrong thing. I felt I was slowly being caged. I was trapped with no money to leave. Today, I am not that woman who was afraid of her own shadow.

I would make plans, steal a car, and steal a boat to make my get-away. I will consider doing whatever it takes to get away. The emotional, verbal and physical abuse has not been forgotten. When I hear of abuse being committed, I feel a surge of anger because it brings back memories. The people who experience this form of abuse, verbally, physically, emotionally know what I am speaking about.Even the word abuse does not describe it correctly; it was more like a torture because whatever you did was never satisfactory, what you said was always wrong, so you existed with fear. You felt tormented and scorned for every move you made.

Lee asked me to answer him when he spoke to me. If I did I was punched, if I did not I still was punched. If I was punched and I fell, I was kicked until I got up. Whatever I did was wrong. My Dadda and Mamma said that a woman is to be respected, as she is the woman behind the man. She takes great care of his hunting and everyday clothing. She is the one that rears his children. Because of her hard work, her home and children are tidy at all times. The abuse against women was very unacceptable in our traditional culture. If an abuse of this kind was committed, instantly our Elders dealt with it.

Gene was born December 9, 1959. Lee said he was overjoyed now that he had two sons. I asked him to quit drinking and he did for three months. When there was no drinking our life was good. We went out on the land, fishing and hunting for moose or spruce hen. This was too good to last; he began hitting the bottle again and as he continued the beating seems to be more often and there were no more apologies afterwards. At first, at least he said he was sorry but now he seemed to enjoy it, the more afraid he made me it seemed he was like a person who had achieved his goal and now he was celebrating.

One summer, when he did not come home for a few days, every minute of my life was filled with fear, wondering what he will do to me when he comes home. The night I was making kindling to start the fire in the morning in the cook stove. The door was locked and he knows I locked the door when I am going to bed. The big noise at the door made me jump; I look at the door there was a big Axe blade showing through the door. I began trembling with fear, what is he going to do to me. I open the door. The face I saw is the face so many times throughout my life, hate, leering, ugly. I went back to continue making kindling. He mumbled something, he grabbed the Axe from my hand and it came down on my head. I got so weak I was falling to the floor, I was waiting for another blow, but he drop the Axe and went to the bedroom. Slowly I stood up, blood streaming down my face and already my hair was soak in blood, I took a clean towel, wrapped it around my head, took a pillow and went to the couch, did not phone anyone, I prayed he would find me dead in the morning when he woke up. I wanted him to be charge with murder, put in jail, and then hung. Then my spirit would come to him and say, "Lee now others are in control of your fate, you cannot abuse me no more, now you will pay the price." In those years I wanted and prayed for death so often, I was in total despair. Sometime during the morning, I woke to hear Lee calling my name. He said, "Honey, what happened to you? You are full of blood." The pillow I on was soaked in blood and my hair was matted with dried blood. This was the reason I wanted to die, just so he would feel the helplessness the hopelessness, the pain in my heart and the tears he had made me suffer. He asked what happened to me. I said, "You hit me with an Axe last night after you got home". He took me to the hospital and I got twelve stitches. The nun then said to me, "Therese you live in such a dangerous situation. Do not forget to say your prayers. If you continue to stay in this abusive relationship one day you may not make it. Think of your children

I said who knows better than I do and I am praying for a miracle to happen. This incident made Lee stop drinking for few months. I recall the night he began drinking again, it was on Halloween night. The same abusive pattern was repeated; I cried many tears those years. When the mainliner left the airport to go north, it usually passed over town; I wished I were on that plane.

CHAPTER 12

Wife and Mother

I hoped things would get better so I worked extra hard, snaring rabbits, preparing all the meat that Lee killed, making dry meat. However, nothing seemed to please him in fact he probably felt manly being in command, the controller of a little Gwich'in woman.

Donna was born May 14, 1961. Lee was disappointed because she was a girl. He wanted all boys. This man thought he could order fate to what he wanted, everything and everyone had to be or had to do things his way, especially me.

I was still working for the Bay and I loved it. It was different from the jobs I had at the hospital. There, I always worked with the sick. Here I worked with healthy people. At times, I did not want to go to work because my face was swollen and I had black eyes.

Many things that Lee did to me I tried to hide from others; I was ashamed. However, Mr. Craig the Hudson's Bay manager was a kind man. I tried to be honest with him about what was going on in my home but asked him never to repeat what I had told him or indicate he knew what was occurring. He understood and at those times, he did not let me be at the cash out to face a questioning customer.

One day I was fed up going to work looking battered. I told Mr. Craig I would not be returning to work. I wanted them to hire someone who would be presentable and one they would not worry about. After a few weeks at home, I went to work for the Nuns at the hospital.

My daughter Marlene was born November 14, 1962. Again, Lee was disappointed because it was another girl, he said, "Are you going to produce bitches?"

By then, Lee had a mistress, Bea, and he drank and he would say, that she knew how to please a man. They did not hide their affair. In fact, they were open with it and people in the community felt sorry for me.

I was past caring what he did. I prayed he would leave and move in with Bea, but he did not. On many occasions when he was with Bea, I prayed he would not come home. Several times when the door was locked, he would break it down. I knew where he had been so I did not want him to touch me but he would tear off my clothes and rape me. He accused me of not doing my duties because I was f------ someone else.

My prayers became my strength in those days. I began to play two roles, one as a woman who was resigned to her fate and another planning her getaway. For Lee it had become almost a sick thrill to beat me, to see me squirm and begging for mercy. He threatened to kill me if I left and I believe now that it was my spiritual faith that saved me.

Somehow, I had to keep my sanity. I told myself that he might think he had me under his control. My physical being might be in his control but I had control of my mind and my spirit, I was not going to let him have that. I could still plan and he may even suspect, but my mind was my own and only my Creator has that control, and me.

This thought made me stronger. Only a woman who goes through these types of abuse can understand the desperation one feels. You are being punched and kicked, and you are looking into the eyes of someone who is full of rage. You are a woman and your strength does not match his. The despair, the helplessness, and the hopelessness you feel drains all your energy.

Many times, I wished there was something I could grab. I would not care in that moment if I killed him or not. Many times memories flash back. The eyes that are filled with rage during and after the beatings are one of the things that I do not forget to this day. You always feel so afraid; even if the man who abused you is 1000 miles away, you constantly feel fear as if someone is constantly watching you. You never feel safe.

After he got another woman, he was even more difficult to please. He said, "Jump" and I did, because I would get a beating if I did not.

In early October, after I was beaten up bad, I ended up in the hospital. Mind you, my mind kept very active. Now I was not only planning my get away but I was planning to kill him so he would never hurt anyone again. Probably because I was still sane, enough I did not do it.

I was not feeling too well so I made an appointment with the doctor. I was pregnant again. What was I going to do? At the time, Donna was in the Charles Camsell hospital going through one of her treatments. There were the boys and Marlene at home.

Though I was afraid to tell Lee I had to, he was not too happy with the news. The way he looked at me while I was telling him told me I felt that I was in deep trouble by the way he was looking at me. He swore, and then left and when he finally got home, he had been drinking. As soon as he walked in the door, he asked me who the father of my child was.

I thought this man is insane. He said he would beat me until I miscarried. I felt like I was a bitch who was there only to breed boys. How I hated this man. I told my Blessed Mother I had the right to hate him; he had no respect for me. He took and took and he was not going to stop. I had to leave fast.

Lee then gave me a terrible beating. He said, "you will probably have a bitch again, I won't let you have this one," and he began throwing me and kicking me.

Early the next morning he and another friend went hunting up the Liard River. I had to go to work but I could not get up. Even to roll my eyeballs hurt.

A friend of ours dropped by to see if he had left found me in this condition and took me to the hospital. They were afraid I would miscarry. Although Lee wanted this to happen, I wanted all my babies. I said to the doctor and the nuns, "Please let me go home, if Lee comes back while I am here he will beat me worse the next time and I cannot take that chance".

They let me go home. Late afternoon of the next day, they were back and had killed two moose. That evening when supper was over, Lee said he was going to his friend's place as they were going to haul all the meat to his warehouse. We would cut and package all the meat there except for what I would take to make dry meat.

He got home about 2:00 am and he was drunk, though not drunk enough to beat me. He finally fell asleep. I had a gun, a 25-20 rifle that he had given me when we first met. It was one of those old rifles; I had a hard time getting shells for it. I had ordered the last box of shells from the south and only had a couple left. I was going to kill him.

We had a trailer-shaped house that had one entrance. As you came into the house, there was the kitchen; then you went into the living room. There was Marlene's crib. Then there was the bedroom. On one side was a double bed, which belonged to Frederick and Gene Opposite their bed was another double bed, which was ours.

Sprawled out across the foot of the bed fast asleep was Lee. I got up very quietly and went to the living room closet to get my rifle. I took it out and put the two shells into the chambers, and then I crept back to the bedroom and pointed the gun to his head.

Suddenly my son Frederick made a sound in his sleep. This startled me and made me realize what I was about to do. My mind flashed on how the scene would look if my boys had awakened. This stopped me or maybe it was the hand of my Creator.

My sons would have waked up screaming, they were always afraid; they saw too much violence at their tender age. If I went through with this, I would be put in jail and my babies would grow up without me.

I put away the gun and asked God to help me to be strong enough to endure what lay ahead of me. I would let Him be the judge and ask him to help me. No matter what I never thought of harming someone again.

That night has come back to me often in my life, especially when I hear similar stories to mine. I am glad Frederick did move and I thank God many times that I did not go through with my intent, not for Lee, but for my peace of mind.

Because I had some sanity left, I went to see my doctor and told him how I felt. People like Lee are not human; they do not deserve to live. How could they? They hurt so much and cause so much misery. The doctor said he would try to help me because one day I might end up dead, and I would not be there for my children. What would happen to them then? I knew Lee would be good to the boys but not to the girls. In one of his drunken rages, he threw Marlene across the room because she was crying. She cried because she was afraid of Lee's loud, angry voice. Luckily, she was not hurt.

In October of 1963, another beating occurred. I do not remember leaving home and arriving at the hospital, but the nurse said I was crying when I got there. I remember the day so well though. It was Sunday morning and I left at 6:45 am to go to work. At 9:30 I went home to pick up the children for Sunday Mass. After church, I brought them home and went to the hospital to prepare lunch. It was a little after 1:30 p.m. when I left for home. Approaching my house, I heard music and people laughing. I suspected what might be going on.

At the time, Amy was staying with us; she was sitting outside on an old mattress and the children were playing around her. My dear Amy, she was like a sister to me and today she still is. She did not drink and was always there for me; she did not have to say anything, she just listened. I asked her what was going on. She looked at me sadly and shrugged. I knew then that this would be one of those frightening times.

As usual, Lee was not in a good mood. After I made the children's bed and he had been cooking, he brought a plate with food, salt and a knife but I wanted to finish the work that I was doing.

He gave me this murderous look and he said eat or I will stick that knife in you. I ate a little then I made an excuse, saying I forgot to put out the Father and nun's lunch. I had to go back to the hospital.

He let me go but he told me to hurry back. I know that I left the house. I kissed my children and I left. I did not remember anything else until I came to. I was on the couch in the staff lounge. The nurse said my mind was sending a message and telling me, I had enough. I wanted the children and me to leave as soon as there was enough money for the plane fare.

Earlier I had told the Sister Superior to pay me in cash and put some of the money aside for our plane fare. If I got a check, Lee would know how much I made; with cash, he would not know. I asked the Sister Superior how much money I had saved and she replied there was enough money for my ticket.

I was admitted to the hospital and the police told Lee he was not allowed to see me. I asked to go to the court so I could take the children. The police and the doctor said that Social Services might be able to help. I wanted to leave as soon as possible.

In the meantime, Lee phoned and asked me to go home to the children but my mind was made up; I was going to leave even if he kills me, I have had enough. There was no Social Services department in Fort Destiny but a regional office in Fort Smith, a two-hour flight away. I asked if someone could come from this office. Maybe they would give me some assistance with the children's plane fare. Dear God! If they had maybe, my sons would be alive today.

I wanted to take my children and I would tell them the reason why. Two workers were asked to come to Fort Destiny. There were many that would testify on my behalf, the doctor, police and nurses from the hospital. When they arrived, we met with them to tell my story. I asked if they could help with my children's plane fare, so we could all return to my home community, Arctic Red River.

The answer they gave that day I have never forgotten." We are here to help in any way we can, but we cannot help to break up a family." My God! Were they not listening when we told them this family had been going through sheer hell? What about the children? When the beatings began, they cried and screamed; they were so afraid.

I had to be strong for my children's sake. The boys would be fine with their dad for the time being; he had always paid more attention to them than he did to the girls. I could only take Marlene because Donna was in the Charles Camsell hospital at the time. I would let them know where I was so they could send her to me. The day I was to leave Lee was working just outside of town. I went home, snatched Marlene out of her crib, took a bottle with some milk and left for the airport. My boys were crying, my heart was hurting and I hated the man who had let this happen. He was an adult and he should be responsible, but he was not. I could not understand him. I felt safe because the police were at the airport to make sure that Lee would not cause trouble.

I promised my sons I would send for them. I told them to go to Auntie Amy; she would take good care of them. I boarded the plane to Fort Smith where I was to connect with a flight to Inuvik, NWT in three days time. I was to stay at the hospital in Fort Smith, but three days seemed like a hundred. I wanted to get as far away from this monster as soon as possible.

The nurses who were training at the Fort Smith hospital had given me some clothes, as I had nothing. In addition, the hospital gave me clothes for Marlene. I boarded the plan for Inuvik; I thanked My Blessed Mother for taking me out of that situation.

She would have to look after us because I had nothing except for a $20 bill that a nurse put into my hand as I was leaving the hospital in Fort Destiny. God bless her.

That $20 is a symbol that reminds me of the determination I had to leave my abusive environment for the sake of my children's survival and mine. The twenty dollars someone put into my hand gave me hope and renewed my strength and my determination to survive.

I was filled with fear but now it was up to me to make a home for my child and the baby I was expecting. Lee had repeatedly threatened me if I left. He said, "This world is not big enough for you to hide in. I will come after you and kill you. If I can't have you, no one else will." This I found stupid. He was the one running around. I thought he should be glad I removed myself and I was no longer in his way to do anything he wanted. It did not make sense but I knew he meant it.

The abuse I had suffered at his hands affected my life tremendously. I was suspicious and afraid to trust. Physically and emotional verbal abuse leaves scars that never go away. I got out of this brutal relationship but I built a wall around me and vowed no one would enter my space again. I was afraid that if I did I would lose control of my life. The hurt that I caused because I was afraid, I bitterly regret.

CHAPTER 13

A New Start

Finally, I was boarding the plane leaving for Inuvik. Half the battle was won; I was on my way. Our next stop was Norman Wells, NWT. Marlene was cranky during the flight so I kept checking her. She was running a slight temperature, and I was worried. When we were told we could get off the plane for a few minutes, I took Marlene to the washroom and bathed her with cold cloths to lower her temperature,

In the meantime, someone said we would be delayed and had been lucky to land without an accident because a part from the plane had dislodged along the way. I looked out the window and saw men searching the landing field. Finally, they announced they had to order the missing piece from Yellowknife, NWT. Once these parcels arrived and repair the problem we will continue on to Inuvik.

We had arrived in Norman Wells about 4:00 pm. and it was 9:00 pm. before we left for, Inuvik. Our Creator must have been with us because there was no accident. Arriving at Inuvik I was so afraid. I had no money, a sick baby and did know where the people I knew lived. Father Taiyuan, a priest I knew from my school days, was at the airport. We were glad to see one another. He told me he was the director of the R.C. Hostel, a residence for Catholic students whose parents were out on the land. The children kept him busy, he remarked as he asked what I was doing back in Inuvik. I told him I had left Fort Destiny, that my baby got sick on the way and I had no money to take her to the hospital. Dear Father Rayuant offered to take me to the hospital, then he offered to let me live at the Hostel until I found myself a place to stay. God bless Father Rayuant. He had a compassionate heart and always gave a helping hand to those in need.

I use "God Bless" a lot in my story because true kindness that my Dadda and Mamma taught me was not shown towards me much in my life so rather than feeling so alone I always turn to the Creator and to the Angels, to the spiritual world. The people who have shown they really cared what happened to me were few, and I want my Creator to take care of them and their families during their lifetime. Today they are remembered in my prayers and I will always recall them with fondest memories.

Father drove us to the hospital and they admitted my baby, as her temperature was very high. Her tonsils were the problem, but there was only so much they could do for her because she was too young to have them out.

The day after my arrival in Inuvik I went to apply for work. The following day the hospital phoned Father Rayuant to tell me I could start at 10:00 o'clock the next morning. I said a prayer of thanks as someone was really looking out for me up there.

I was hired as a dietary aide. Now I had to find a place and someone to look after my baby. She would stay at the hospital a few days but I had to be ready for her when she was discharged.

A friend from my hometown said I could stay with her until I found a more suitable home for Marlene and me. She had been widowed the year before and she had four small children of her own. Her place was small but I could stay until I could get something more permanent.

It was a difficult year as I began a new life, but I was not hungry and I had a good job and best of all there was no violence in my life. Lee coming to Inuvik to make good his threat was a possibility and I lived in fear for those first months.

Throughout the year, I lived at several places - at Beth then Alma and later Barb. Finally, we got a 5/12. A 5/12 is a trailer type of a house. As you come in the door the washroom is to your right then you enter a large room, which is a combination of both living and kitchen, then there are two bedrooms.

I worked right up to the time of my baby girl's birth. I was overjoyed. I thanked the Holy Mother that my child was healthy and was not harmed by all the beatings.

I named her Arlene after her aunt. My cousin Louise worked at the hospital as a ward aide and stayed at the nurses' residence. I spent a great deal of time with her and at her fiancé's place. Dr. Stephens had been the Doctor for the Inuvik General hospital for some years. He was a special person who had a compassionate heart for the people he worked amongst.

Stephens and Louise helped me through those first difficult times when I thought of the children I had left behind and shedding so many tears. In those days, there was no help for an abused family. There was the Social Services Agency but they believed very strongly in keeping a family together. Many people believed that no matter how bad things were in your home you had to keep the family together. If you left you were made to feel you were the one who was in the wrong.

Louise and her fiancé Dr. Stephens always tried to find ways to cheer me up. They were always there for me because I needed someone to constantly tell me everything would be all right. I had to believe this in order to survive.

Time passed quickly. I kept busy at my job and making a new home for us. Gradually the fear began to disappear but in its place, anger began to surface. A destructive, suspicious person emerged; I no longer believed in people. They would be nice to you only if they wanted something, especially men. They lied to your face; they wanted to control and they wanted to dominate. They always saw women as a housewife, a mother, the bearer of children and someone to be there at their beck and call. Well, I knew different! I was never going to be caught in this type of situation again.

I quit my job the summer of '65. I rested and stayed at home with my babies for a few weeks. Then a friend of mine Diane who had worked with me at the hospital asked if I wanted a job as a cook's helper at a construction camp. I said sure; it would be something different. The job was seasonal. Diane was a great person and she was fun too. We were busy, as we had to cook for about 40 men who were all from Edmonton. We were constantly cleaning, baking and cooking. Garnette was a man at camp who seemed interested in me, but I did not want to get involved in any serious relationship. We did become friends.

Diane and her husband Jim, Garnette and I all hung around together. I went to parties a lot. When I finished work and went home there was always a case of beer waiting for me. Garnette had brought it over or had it delivered to my place. It was nice of him because by then beer was something I looked forward to at the end of the day. Garnette was good to me but he wanted more than friendship. I could not make a commitment to anyone, as I was still hurting inside and believed I would not be good for anyone. I liked him and wanted us to stay good friends.

Bernie was another one of the men at camp and from the first time I met him I disliked him. At the time, I was angry and trusted no one. Anyone who reminded me in any way of Lee made me assume his or her character was like his. If they had a good sense of humor, were fun to be with, and would not get serious it was fine with me.

To me Bernie acted conceited. He was the type of guy every girl hoped her boyfriend would look like - tall, dark and handsome. Even the way he walked told you he was sure of himself. He always teased me even though he knew I did not like him.

Words used to pass back and forth and from my lips, not good ones. Bernie reminded me too much of Lee - a macho-man type. Those type never stay faithful to you I warned myself. (Remember I was very confused in my thinking at this time of my life) Bernie had girls chasing him and I was determined not to be one of them. He was fully aware of my dislike for him, but he never gave up.

Parties filled the weekends. Garnette was always bringing me the things I loved. I felt I ought to repay him because I did not want to feel I owed him; we were not even dating. But he said my friendship was enough, he hope someday it would change. My salary did not allow us much as I was making just $136 a week. Garnette said I should not feel this way, as he just wanted to see me happy. He was a good person, and I always treated him with respect and valued his friendship. A serious relationship with anyone was out of the question. He respected my wishes and said we could remain friends. Maybe when I felt I could handle a relationship, I would change my mind. We worked hard, we partied a lot and we had fun.

One evening in November, a group of us decided to head for the Zoo (the Mackenzie hotel bar) after work. I did not feel too much like drinking and decided to leave early. I noticed Bernie did not seem to join in the laughter and jokes. He was the type who never drank much, but he always tagged along, probably just to be nosy I thought, and to watch everyone make a fool of themselves.

Once I told him, he should join the girls who were chasing him. He just might find himself useful. We were just old fogies who drank too much, but we liked what we were doing. Later he asked me to dance. I thought if I did not dislike the person so much, this is the way I would like to feel when I meet that special someone someday.

As I left, the hotel Bernie caught up with me and asked if he could walk me home. I said sure, if he did not mind wasting his time walking with the old lady. I got to know Bernie that night. We sat around drinking coffee and talked. He told me of his mother, his brothers, his step-brother and his sister. His stepfather had died recently and his mother was widowed again.

I found myself attracted to this very interesting person. He was not conceited but thoughtful, considerate and down- to-earth. I told him about myself but did not go into much detail. I told him about my marriage and because I got hurt badly I was a very angry person and very suspicious. I just did not trust anyone at this time.

Bernie said he admired me, as I was spunky and a hard-working woman. He had suspected I was hurting, and was hiding my true feelings by pretending I always had fun when I wasn't. He said I looked sad at times; I told him it must be when I thought of the children I had left behind. Sometimes the hurt was unbearable. I missed them and worried about them.

Bernie and I became good friends and our relationship slowly developed into something more. I had this thing about never going out with anyone younger than me. He was 26 and I was 30 and I felt old.

We enjoyed each other's company, and we liked the same things. We began seeing each other as much as we could before he was to leave. It was a month to Christmas and the camp was shutting down until spring. Everyone was leaving for Edmonton and wherever else they came from.

Although Bernie said he would return with the crew in the spring, it was hard to believe him. What man would get involved with a woman who had two small children and three more that she left behind?

I would miss him terribly. He was all a woman could want in a man. I had always dreamed a husband would be kind and gentle and would give me a feeling of security. How could a handsome person like Bernie be interested in someone like me when he could have anyone he wanted?

My heart ached but of course, as always I hid that feeling from him. I did not want to let him know I was so smitten because I did not believe he would be back.

Little did I know Bernie was a man of his word? In the few weeks, that we had begun to know each other I slowed down on my drinking and took life a little more seriously. He was good for me, he made me feel I was worth something, like a person with a spirit and this gave me belief in myself.

I would miss him. He was all I wanted but I dared not say anything. Maybe it was just a fling for him. A few weeks after Bernie left I went back to work at the hospital. The holidays came and went and there was no word from him. My friend Garnette wrote, asking me to write back and let him know how I was doing. He included small gifts with his letters. In the spring, Garnette sent a photo of a house he had built and said it could be mine if I changed my mind. I can still remember the house; the walls were paneled with wood. My mind said, Terry, there is no love, but there is friendship, based on this maybe it could work.

It was tempting, but the values that my grandparents taught me, treating people, as I wanted to be treated, would not let me use Garnette, for material gain. My friend deserved more than that. Someday, someone would give him the love he deserved. God bless him; I hope his life has been good.

When I was in school the kids would call me, names and this continued when I returned to my community and Lee had flung verbal abuse in my face daily. All of this contributed to my low self-esteem. I never saw myself as pretty, always ugly, and throughout my life, I believed this. The only thing I was ever good for was work. I was my worst enemy. My work had to be perfect. If there was a flaw, I was not satisfied with it. To this day, I feel the same way. I have never used make-up, not because I am against it, but I did not think it would do me much good.

Summer came and still no word from Bernie; obviously, he was not coming back. Although I felt I was not ready to have a relationship, I missed Bernie terribly. When you are single or divorced, it is better to have someone with you amongst your married friends, otherwise, you are left out.

Late in the Spring Peter came into my life. He was from Germany but had lived and worked in Canada a number of years. Like Bernie, he was a painter. He was handsome in a rugged sort of way with piercing gray eyes. His eyes and smile was the first thing I noticed when I met him. They always looked mischievous. Peter was bachelor who did not give a damn about anything so it was sort of a challenge to make him fall for me.

We went out together and partied often. Peter had a great sense of humor and being with him was never dull. I told him about Bernie, how I had fallen for him but had not heard from him, and was afraid of experiencing heartbreak. It would be some time before I would get over Bernie but in the meantime, we could live a little.

Peter agreed but then one day he phoned to tell me Bernie was coming back. He was expected in a few days and Peter said he would understand if he could not be part of my life. I was glad I had told Peter the truth at the beginning but I did not find out until much later how much he thought of me.

I did not know what Bernie's intentions were but he had promised he would be back and now that he was returning, I felt guilty for not believing him.

My friends said Bernie was back in town, but he did not call or come to see me. A few days later on my way home from work I passed the building that Bernie was painting and stopped to say hello. He said since he had heard I had a boyfriend he felt it was better to keep his distance. What did he expect? I did not hear from him. I thought I would never see him again.

When he asked if I was, free that evening I said of course. It was the beginning of a relationship that I never dreamed I would have in my lifetime though I knew in my heart I was not ready for one. I was still angry and did not trust.

Ours was the only relationship I regret letting go. I loved him very much and thought from the way he treated me I was special to him. He showed great love to my children. He was security and a man dedicated to the well being of the family that he had adopted. I blame myself for the break up, the tears and the heartbreak. Because of my distrust and suspicions, the relationship lasted only two years. Bernie was six years younger and women chased him and flirted with him constantly. When they began to phone him at home, it was too much for me to handle so I ran. I should have trusted him. Although he swore he loved only me, I did not believe him. He wanted us to get married as soon as possible and even went to the parish priest to get some information. He asked me if I could file for my divorce so we could get married but I was afraid to make a commitment to anyone.

Fall came and Bernie moved in with us. The decision was made for me. I came down with a kidney disease and became very ill. I had to stay in the hospital for sometime. When I was discharged even though I did not fully regain my strength I went back to work. I did not know my feet and my legs had to be kept warm at all times. Not aware of this I ended up in the hospital a number of times that year.

During this illness, I really began to know Bernie's because of how much he cared for my family. He worked during the day and got a babysitter for the children, then visited me at the hospital evenings One of the times I was hospitalized my temperature was dangerously high, and the nurses said would try to bring it down with ice. They covered me with just a sheet and began pouring buckets of ice over me. As soon as it melted, they changed the sheet and poured ice over me again. This they did several times but they were just able to bring down my temperature to 102. When Bernie came, he offered to continue the treatment because he would feel better if my temperature was brought down to 99 or 100. His father died because it was too late when they tried to bring his temperature down and he did not want the same thing to happen to me. He worked very hard to bring my temperature down to 99. I owe him my life; God bless him wherever he is.

I remember the nurses with fondest memories, they were very caring people. The ones that I met through my stay at the hospital were a lot of fun. Everyone I got to know most of them and they had a sense of humor, which turned out to be my recovery therapy. Sometimes I wonder about these ladies, God bless them. I hope that life was good to them. When their contract was up some renewed and others left for the South. I was sad to see them go.

Winter went quickly and in the spring, I discovered I was pregnant. We were glad, as we wanted children of our own. Bernie left for two weeks to do some painting in Fort McPherson. After he returned he received a phone call from a woman named Lucy. He said she was just a woman he met and talked to in Fort McPherson. I wanted to believe him but the suspicions overpowered my good sense. I was afraid of being caught in the same situation that I went through with Lee and Lena surfaced once more. Rather than be hurt again I planned to leave during the summer.

It was August when I got a place of my own. One day I moved my few belongings while Bernie was at work. God forgive me. I will regret that day for the rest of my life. A person who has gone through emotional torment cannot believe that something good is happening in their life, so subconsciously they begin to destroy whatever positive thing is taking place.

How well I know the saying "if I knew then what I know now" and how bitter is the regret. Then, would I have grown in my faith and beliefs that I have today, if I had not left Bernie?

I always felt inferior since residential school days. This was compounded during my marriage to Lee who always did his best to reinforce those feelings of low self-esteem.

I keep telling myself, I am Terry and what is wrong with Terry? I am Dadda and Mamma's child. I am God's child. Some way I have to learn to believe in myself and even now I often think how?

During those turbulent years, I was full of fear. I did not even consider staying and trying to make thinks work with Bernie; I just ran. I thought if Bernie walked out on me, I would never survive. This made me deathly afraid so rather than do the right things and say the right words I did them all wrong. I would leave him before he left me.

I thought that a relationship should be like the relationship my Mamma and Dadda had. As a child I had never experienced loud voices, only a stern voice when what is taught to us is not obeyed.

I remember one summer when my parents were at Pierre's creek, fishing, I was spending a few days with them. My brothers and I were playing outside when my father came out of our tent with his bag and said "Therese get in the canoe; we are leaving for town to go see Dadda." This made me happy and when we got to Arctic Red River, my father stayed with us until the boat from up the river came and he went to work on it for the rest of the summer.

I did not know if there was an argument, I just know we left in a hurry, and my mother did not see us off. In my Dadda and Mamma's home, there was never an argument. Therefore, as a child I dreamed that my own marriage would be the same and as a teen, my views did not change much. Even though my first relationship was a disaster, I did not want my relationship with Bernie to end. However, I did not know how to save it. As a child, I had lost my Mamma, then my parents. There was no one I could go to for womanly advice. I wanted to cry but I felt dead inside.

I survived the next few weeks only because of my children. I kept telling myself that they needed me and I could not let them down. Bernie came over often for a visit and when he did, I wanted to cry my heart out. I wanted to tell him all the fears within me. I did not know how to say it; it was such a long story. He wanted to be a part of our baby's life but I would not let him. How could I have been so cruel and selfish? I tried to justify my actions by telling myself I did the right thing. I wanted so much to tell him I was sorry for doubting and that we could start over but I gave in to my fears and stayed stubborn.

Bernie left in November. He had a dream that he would travel to Edmonton, Alberta by dog team. He barely made it to Fort Good Hope and flew the rest of the way. I believe if I had gone with him we would have made it because of the experience I have with the land.

Marie born January 20, 1967 was the picture of her Dad. Because of registration requirements they asked me at the hospital who her father was. I said I did not know... I told my friends she was my baby and my responsibility. I was going to look after her the best way I know how. Everyone fell in love with her, she was healthy and she had so much hair for a newborn. My children may have missed a father but I did not want them torn between two parents. There may be arguments so one parent was better no parent. In addition, I had a lot of love to give them.

In May, my children caught whooping cough and the doctor quarantined us for a week. Once a day they came to check on us. I was alone, my two oldest were very sick and I was afraid for my baby who was only a few months old. Again, I turned to my Blessed Mother for help. I asked her to be with me, to make me strong and not let me panic. I also asked her to please not let my children get too sick.

I stayed up for three nights, packing one child on my back and carrying the other. It was unbelievable how I did not succumb to fatigue. On the contrary, I was constantly awake and alert. My baby Carol got a touch of it but thank God, it was not as severe as the other girls were. She would have not survived, as she was so tiny. Again my Blessed Mother helped She was and is real to me as she always helped me out throughout my lifetime.

CHAPTER 14

Centennial Year

In June I decided to move back to Arctic Red River and spend some time with my Dadda, I wanted to make a cup of tea for him for the next couple of years. He was getting to the age where I did not know how long he had, but while he was alive, I wanted to spend some precious moments with him. When he goes, I told myself, I do not want to regret not taking time to be with him. I knew it was the right decision. He was someone I loved dearly and I wanted him to know it and know how grateful I was to him for being a part of my life.

At 87, Dadda got around well; he was staying active doing small jobs. Somehow, he heard I quit my job and that I was planning on coming to Arctic Red River to he hired Edward Nazon and William Norman to come to Inuvik to pick us up.

At that time, there was no Dempster Highway. We depended on the rivers to travel back and forth to communities or used float planes during the summer season and skis during the winter.

Edward and William gave me one day to get ready. The next evening we were on our way. There was 24 hours of daylight so we could travel anytime we wanted. The only thing we worried about was weather. When traveling on these rivers, if a bad wind comes up the water gets very choppy in some places. We would then have to stay to a fire camp until the wind lessened.

1967 was centennial year for Canada; everywhere people talked of celebration. A boat with a mini-carnival was coming from up the river and expected to stop at every community. This was the topic of conversation when I arrived back in Arctic Red River. I was so happy to be home with Dadda and when the boat arrived the carnival was set up it was good to have fun with Dadda and my children.

The summer passed quickly. I did everything I always wanted to do, cook fresh whitefish on an open fire, pick blueberries and set snares for rabbits so we would have meat. The pressure of rushing around and punching a clock belonged to another world. I knew my children would have food every day and making money for survival did not enter my mind. There was no shortage. We had wood for our fire and fuel for our lamps when nighttime came. My Dadda always made sure that these necessities were looked after. There was always many whitefish in the river. All this was luxury. I did not need money here. I was just happy to rest and enjoy the life I once knew.

Fall arrived and Dadda wanted to set net on the ice as soon as it was safe. My people of Arctic Red River did this every year. They stocked up fish for the long winter months. Being home for a few weeks now I noticed some things were difficult for my Dadda to do. When he visited the net, his hands could not stand the cold and they turned numb; taking the fish from the net was difficult for him. I was glad I was there so I could do this for him. He went to see the net with me, just to supervise.

After the first snowfall, I went out on the land to set some rabbit snares. I left early each morning and returned in early afternoon. Marlene and baby Marie stayed home with Dadda while Arlene came with me to visit the rabbit snares. She was only three years old at the time and we had to climb a steep hill. She insisted on pulling her rabbit all on her own and even though the rabbit was fat and heavy and it was difficult for her, she made it. I was proud of her. I was surprised at how my children coped because they were not brought up on the land, but there were no complaints. They just went along with whatever I did and accepted whatever situations we were in at that moment without a fuss.

To stay with Dadda in a one-room house was no big deal and it was fun. They loved their great-grandfather and Marie stole his heart.

The Northern Affairs had a sawmill project about two miles up the Red River on the opposite side of the river from town. Shortly after my arrival, the boss of the camp asked if I was interested in a cooking job. I said not at the moment, I came home to spend some time with Dadda.

Some time later the camp changed hands and when Larry, The new leaser offered me a job I accepted it. The 16-hour days were difficult as I still had to care for my children, as I could not find a sitter in this little town.

There were from seven to 14 men working, depending on how much work there was. I was up at 5:00 in the morning and began preparing everything for the children when they woke up. Then I went down to the cook house to make breakfast. Again, I turned to my blessed Mother for help, as I was always afraid of a fire breaking out. We had a wood-burning heater and although I set the damper to low, I was always afraid the stove would overheat while I was away

At 6:45 am it was time to wake up the workers, put out the breakfast then go back to wake up the children. I dressed the baby and told Marlene to dress her sister and take her down to the cook house. She was instructed to touch nothing. The caboose we lived in was one room. It had a small table at one end, a stove in the middle, and a double bed at the other end. I worked Monday to Saturday and looked forward to Sunday, my day off.

At the beginning, I never partied on the weekend. I pulled my children in a little toboggan across the river to our small community church. By going to church during that time I felt closer to my Creator. I was surrounded with familiar places, faces, and all that I had known during childhood. During the years I had been away the life I knew as a child and later a young woman, I had shelve. Now that I was back in that environment, I began discovering that life all over again. It was like unwrapping treasures, because time controlled me in the other world, but not here.

The men I worked with swore a lot. When you hear this type of language constantly, you realize one day that you are speaking the same language as them. I felt bad about this but when you work with men; you learn to talk as rough and tough as they do in order to survive. Yet, it was fun; I enjoyed the kidding around and the jokes they told.

There was not much to do in a town the size of Arctic Red River. There was the R.C. Mission, the Hudson's Bay Company and a Community Hall, which was hardly ever used except for a feast and dance during the holidays. Recreation for the Elders was visiting one another and telling stories. For the younger generation, there was sliding down the big hill, driving a dog team and just plain playing outdoors.

My baby Marie was only a year old. I packed her on my back while I worked. If someone asked me now how I managed to work that many hours while looking after my three children, I could not tell them. However, if I had to do it all over again, I would. I did this for almost two years. The love I had for my children gave me the strength to bear the good and the bad.

Many times, I wished that my mother or my Mamma were alive. When you are worried because of just simple everyday problems, it is always good to talk to someone, to get another perspective.

I know what it is like to grow up without parents, to have no one to turn to and to felt nobody cares. Sure there were a person who cared but that was not the same as parents and siblings. Throughout my life, I have been suppressed and dismissed like a child by the priest and nuns, Governments (Indian Agents) and people. The interference in and of whatever I had to say was not important. I was wanted, only when my help was needed but appreciation was rarely given.

My heart goes out to all children without parents to love them. I have felt all of this so my children were the ones I lived for; to the present day, they are still my priority. In all my prayers, I pleaded to my Blessed Mother to ask her Son Jesus to give me the chance to see my children grow to adulthood. I always told her how it was to be alone in this world, how I was able to survive because of my Dadda's and Mamma's teachings and the strength I drew from the faith and hope that I had in the divine power. I had had close brushes with death but I was still here with my children.

Derek was one of the boys at camp, a nice-enough person but we never saw eye -to -eye. We always had disagreements over the least little thing. He did not like the way I did things and I found faults in him to. I went to parties with him because there was no else to go with.

Christmas came and was soon over. The saw mill started operating again. The new owner, Larry seemed to be nice; I admired the way he got along with his employees and treated everyone equally. He was married and occasionally his wife and children came and stayed at the saw mill. Everyone in town therefore knew them well.

I used to envy these people because they traveled when they wanted, they had any type of food they wanted and they wore the type of clothing I hoped to wear someday. I felt this family had many blessings, which they took for, granted. People should appreciate the gifts from the Creator.

The saw mill was operated by the department of Northern Affairs. I always received my pay with the rest of the crew. Nevertheless, this stopped when the new owners took over. Maybe they thought providing me with the shack and food for my children was enough. I was afraid to ask why they did not pay me. What explanation did they give to the income tax people; maybe I was not on the list of employees.

Every now and then, they would give me a $20.00 bill when I asked for some money but there was no receipt or cheque for all the work that I did. I knew that if my children got sick, they would provide the transportation and if there were something, wrong with my family they would be concerned. So I thought I might just as well say nothing. Later it did bother me a lot but I never tried to do anything about it. Larry always treated me with kindness; he showed concern about my children, that they were well fed and asked if our little house was okay for us and how my day went but the rest treated me as if I didn't exist. They did not have to say anything; behaviors and attitudes do not lie. Larry's concern for my family made everything else bearable. He made sure we were okay. In addition, there was admiration for each other. We both worked hard and long hours, Larry, so that the company would be successful, and I to clean and cook for the hard- workingmen.

Over the months, my admiration for Larry grew to attraction. I felt it and I saw in his eyes that he shared a same feeling. However, we made sure that it stayed as a working relationship. It was difficult though as we worked so closely together.

We were on a dangerous path and we tried to avoid one another as much as possible. Larry hired an additional cook as I was beginning to feel constantly tired and felt I was burning out. I cooked for the men and baked my own pastries and bread, looked after my children, cooked, fed them, washed their clothes and kept the cook house clean. Day after day, I did the same chores repeatedly! No wonder I felt tired all the time. I had to slow down.

Tania the new cook was a wonderful person to work with. At least she treated me humanly. There is nothing worse than these so called holier- than -thou people who sit in the judgment seat and talk and laugh about you, sometimes even in front of you like you were not even there. My feelings got very hurt so I would speak up. My teachings taught me it was wrong but they said not to take things so seriously. Well in my book, I did not make fun of people. I helped them to understand and as far as I was concerned, I had done nothing wrong. I tried to do things right but if they played the almighty so could I. Tanya was not stuffy. She had a sense of humor so I got along fine with her. Now that she was at camp, I had some spare time to spend with Dadda. I stayed on as a helper so I did not work the long hours as I had before Tanya's arrival. Now that I could live like a normal person, again I tried to fill my time with other interests.

In March, the crew was going to move 45 miles up the Red River to cut logs and Tanya was going. The children and I were to stay at main camp but because there was not much to do, I decided to move back to Dadda's house across the river. It gave me a chance to be involved in my community and I had time to visit friends whom I had neglected.

About the middle of April, I went to visit the gang at the camp. It was a mistake. I always thought I was safe as long as I was in a group of people but it turned out to be turning point for Larry and me. We did not say anything about love because it was not right. There were many lives to consider. At that time, the few stolen moments we had to ourselves make us become more attracted to one another. I left the next day. It was too painful to stay, to be reminded of what had happened and of what could not be. I was back home in Arctic Red River and I said to myself this was where I was going to stay from then on.

CHAPTER 15

A Doomed Affair

Few weeks later I suspected I was pregnant, I cried not knowing what I was going to do. I promised myself I will not tell Larry. I wasn't going to tell anyone. I did not want to move up to camp with the crew. I wanted to stay in Arctic Red with Dadda, but one day Larry came, he said " pack up Terry, you are moving up the river with us for the spring" Why didn't I say NO! But I did as I was told. Once my children and I settle at camp, I did nothing. I was just there. Tania did all the cooking for the crew. The boys worked all day and at night went hunting and whatever they killed I clean and cooked to open fire. I sure ate good food and had a rest. End of June we moved back to main camp. I was alone with my secret but I knew it won't be for long. I wanted so much to share this with Larry, but until I figure out what I was going to do I said nothing. I wore loose clothing so I was able to hide my condition until September.

One day I just told Tania I quit. She ask me if I could wait till Larry came back to camp, I said "no I made up my mind," Few days after I moved back to Dadda he ask me if I was going to have a baby, I said "yes". He did not say another word. I was glad for this as I didn't know what I was going to do either. Once Larry came back to Camp and Tania told him I quit he came across to see me. He wanted to know why I quit. I wasn't expecting him so with the clothing I was using, my condition was in plain sight. He said whose was it, my answer was, and it was for me to know and for him to find out. Not another word to me but spoke only to Dadda and left. The next day Larry was back, with groceries, he said for the children, He said whatever the children and I needed to let him know he will make sure, to get it for us. Oh! How I wish things were different, I love him so much for being concern. He must have done his own guessing because he was true to his word. Fall went by and we were never in need of anything and Larry visited often.

Millie was born Dec. 21 1969. I had to leave her at the hospital as the social services came to see me and said, they talk to someone in Arctic Red River and the information they receive was I did not have a proper housing for a baby so I have to leave the baby at the hospital and when I have the proper housing I could take my baby home. I wanted to take Millie home, she would get good loving care, and my children was in never in want of anything. But they kept her and I went home alone. Who are they to play God in our lives? My people did fine raising their children before they came. It brought memories back to what Dan who worked for the social services few months after I left Lee. He wanted me to go back to Fort Destiny because my husband wanted me to come home. "Therese, if anyone has to change it is you. You have a husband who loves you very much. He is giving you a chance to come back. Is this your decision? You should consider yourself lucky. Your husband still loves you. Lee always could manipulate people. He was the good person; I was the bitch. Fine with me! Only my Creator knows the truth and some of the people who saw him in action. When Dan said this I thought of all the times I heard the word SORRY but a word was never kept, so why should I believe anything this person said.

In January I got sick and the priest from the community had me flown to Inuvik. I had some test which was sent to a laboratory in Edmonton, Alberta. A phone call came and I had Appendicitis, I was wheel into the operation room STAT! I stayed in the hospital three weeks. The day I got out of the hospital I rented an old shack from an old Trader and began collecting my children. I came out of hospital the next day I was working for the H.B.C. They needed a janitor so I took the job. Now I have a job and a home, relocated to Inuvik. Because my house was an old shack, they will not let me take my baby. The next

153

encounter with Social Services was when I was going to sign the paper for Millie's adoption. How I hated these people. Lee had his fist and strength. He controlled in this way. Social Services with their policies had power over poor working people like me. An agency formed by the so-called government who set the policies for them and gave them that right to have control over people.

They did not even know the people they dealt with. I say this because I saw many of my friends who went through hardship because of no jobs at one time or another or they did not make enough money and were escorted right out the door. While able-bodied persons were helped, women still had to work whether we were sick or not. I was able to survive this difficult period in my life without too much damage. I wanted to go and raise hell with them, but I did not. They had much to say about what was best for Millie and why she had to be adopted. I was a single parent; I was the sole supporter of my family. If I gave her up for adoption, she would grow up in a normal home with a normal set of parents. Yes, I was in a vulnerable position but I feel that they could they have offered their help to get me better accommodations so that I can take care of all my children? No, they suggested adoption. Whom did they think they were to play God when all I needed was a little bit of help to get over one difficult hump? A little bit of caring would have helped.

These people did not try to understand, they just did their work by the book, which made them seem very inhuman to me. There was no compassion and there was lack of communication. I can understand if there was neglect of children but not because you cannot afford a decent house.

The values that I was taught like, caring and sharing were all gone from our everyday lives. In its place something else was formed, a cold, unfeeling, uncaring group which came to our community to say they had all the answers but taught nothing and hurt the children by taking them away from the parent they deemed unsuitable.

All the dollars spent should be used wisely, to help the mothers cope with what is going on in their lives. In addition, they need help to become independent. This would have been a positive achievement for the worker and the parent. For this I see most of our society today as selfish, uncaring and just existing. It may take everyone's involvement to regain the harmony we once had. For instance if we say to ourselves, today I am going to be kind and thoughtful and polite it doesn't cost anything and no one has to use physical force to practice it.

The decision to give up my daughter at that period in my life has hurt me for years. I asked my Blessed Mother to protect her for me because I could not do it myself. Eighteen years later, she walked back into my life; it was as if she never left.

I had wanted so much to approach her father for help then, but there was his family to consider. Rather than hurting many people, my family suffered. I was not going to put him through this scandal because I cared very much for him; therefore, I went on as always, to do the best I could under the circumstances.

I began to drink a lot during that year. Since leaving Arctic Red River, I tried not to see Larry. What I had done to Millie ate at my heart; I wish I could have told him. I made sure that when I saw Larry we were never alone together. I fought against loving him as the outcome would be too heartbreaking and who needed that?

Sometime in August, I moved into a new place. It was big enough for the girls and me; at least we had more room. Dadda lived in Arctic Red River but he came often to see us. Larry was traveling back and forth to the saw mill so it was not hard to bring Dadda with him.

Larry and I had not seen each other since I moved back to Inuvik, but now he came by once in awhile to visit and we just began where we left off.

Larry was a person who did not look at me as being inferior to him. He treated me as an equal. This made me admire him more and love him more. Because I listened to some of the conversation that went on around me, I became suspicious of the non native people. Sometimes they said things that hurt you and made you wonder what did you ever do to them to deserve this type of treatment. (This was my first encounter with racism.) Their actions and attitudes they considered normal behavior. It was not all of them but a majority of them.

I did not believe in in-equality of people as I recalled Dadda's words. We are all equal in the eyes of our Creator. It hurt very much when a remark was made about the Natives in front of me. I know this, because I worked amongst non-Native people all my life. Nations will never survive if we do not confront this type of behavior both in our actions and verbally. There will never be peace if this continues. There will only be abuse of power, greed, and bigotry. All these cause conflict, war and untold grief.

We cannot keep sweeping it under the carpet, we must address it strongly, deal with it like the adults that we say we are, and so our children can have peace.

Let us act responsibly and address what discrimination does to nations. We begin by communicating and learning from one other, and about the other nations so we can try to understand. Feeling superior and trying to control, not accepting others because of their color are very unacceptable.

Of course, I do not agree with some of my people's behavior, but they are humans and they are people with feelings and they have been hurt badly through racial slurs. I thought, someday I am going to address an issue that plagues nations. I will not stand by and see other people put down, no matter what nationality they are; I would speak up if my people were putting others down, too. What about love and forgiveness? What about trying to live a Christian life

I did not know then I was already going towards a mission that I will be doing someday, speaking to people on what equality really means and how important it is for us and our children to not see colors when we communicate with other people. As long as we see colors, there will be conflict and no peace. We all have something to give to each other - Love!

Whenever he was in town Larry and I spent the time with one another. He said I did not have to prove to people that I did not give a shit what they said. He said it in such a nice way I wanted to quit the drinking and just be happy for who I was.

Larry's contracts kept him busy and my work and my children kept me busy. I tried to do things right but no one else seemed to notice or care so why should I. I began to live just for him and my children. I knew people were talking but I was past caring. No one offered me help and I knew I was not going to get it any from anyone.

From now on, I decided to be like everyone else, just take, whatever the cost. We did not go into this relationship with our eyes closed. I was well aware of the consequences. Some have everything and never have to worry about where their next meal is coming from; they just do not know how to be grateful for the blessing the Creator has provided for them.

Food and lodgings was my priority. Clothes were not a worry as long as they were not torn and they were clean. With the little we had, I always tried my best to make them presentable in whatever we did. I wanted a husband like Larry who was thoughtful, romantic, and had a sense of humor and of course a good dancer. I was not going into this relationship blind, I was going to live for today and let tomorrow take care of itself. Larry and I were friends and lovers. I never tried to hide this. We never talked of his family no matter how angry they were with us. We wished we could change many things, like people being more spiritual about Nature, to be able to enjoy it, and not let greed take over to destroy it. We wanted everyone to appreciate and to have respect for nature, and see how beautiful mother earth and all creations are.

People may have condemned us but we found the understanding we were searching for in each other. Because there was so much anger, gossip, and conflict, we tried to create our own world where there was none of this bickering. The more we saw disapproval in the eyes of others, the more we drew closer and drew strength from one another. Outside in the world we did what was expected of us; we did not forsake our commitments.

During 1970 and 1971, I worked as second cook for Grolier Hall; a residential hostel was for children from outlying communities whose parents were out on the land. There were at least 200 students and 20 staff. Father Rayuant had been the director for the hostel since it had opened in 1960. I loved my work cooking for the students. During the week, the head cook planned all the meals. His shift was in the morning and my shift was always the late one. On Saturday, the main kitchen staff

157

had a day off. There were only the girls from the hostel and myself. They helped me plan their weekend meals. We had fun just trying out new recipes. The day was finished with a treat for all of them with vanilla ice cream topped off with blueberries. My second year, the Akaitcho Hall in Yellowknife NT was filled, so they sent some students to the Inuvik Hostel. We had students from South Mackenzie, Snowdrift, Yellowknife, Fort Franklin and Fort Norman. I got to know them all. They were great kids. My goal was to feed these students as best as I could so they would not be too lonesome for home. I got along very well with the students and I loved them all. They were like my own children.

Children are very important to me. I live for the youth and the children. They are my priority' I know they all need an abundance of love and caring. At a very young age they have to be corrected for the wrongs they do and learn why some behavior is a "no-no." The crucial ages are from the time they begin to talk and walk until they are 7 or 8 years old. After this age, you need to guide them. My Dadda and Mamma repeated this to me repeatedly, and I have not forgotten this through the years with my own children.

CHAPTER 16

The Last of his Generation

In June, everyone was preparing to leave for his or her summer holidays, and the students were busy with their final exams. Father Rayuant asked if I would like to work during the month of July and take my holidays in August. I said it was fine with me. The Grolier Hall hostel was used in the summer for tourists when the hotels were full. After the muskrat hunting was over in the middle of June, people from the surrounding communities came to Inuvik. First, we held 1st July celebration, and then the Northern games, so the hostel was busy during the summer months. My daily shift was from 9:00 am. To 2:00 pm., off for a couple of hours, and then back to work from 4:00 pm. to 7:00p.m.

One day I went home during my break and I returned to work at about 3:50 p m. I came over the Utilidor, (A Utilidor is an insulated pipe, 3 or more feet above the ground, which takes care of water, sewage and heat. Because of the perma-frost, the pipes cannot be laid underground.) I could see the hostel main door clearly. Father Rayuant was standing outside the door waving frantically. I rushed to him and he said, "Therese get in the car quick. The hospital just phoned to say they brought your father in from Arctic Red River. He had a bad accident. It is serious."

We got to the hospital and they hurried me to the X-ray room where my Dadda was lying on the table. Dadda said, "My baby I have a bad headache, please ask the nurse for an aspirin." I kissed him and told Dadda that I would bring his request to the attention of the doctor. They had just given me a few minutes to see him, and then I was led to another room where I had to sign papers. They wanted to take Dadda to the operating room as soon as possible.

Father Colaas, the mission priest of Arctic Red River, had brought my Dadda down by helicopter to Inuvik Hospital; the person who flew this helicopter just left what he was doing to bring dada to hospital.

Many times Dadda had said to me when it is our time to go we unintentionally do foolish things, we do not think and we become careless. In many cases, this is what causes many accidents to happen. I remembered this as I thanked the pilot for caring enough to bring Dadda to the hospital.

I really do not know how the following few hours passed. The next I knew, the doctor was standing in front of me. She said, "due to the injury your father received, we did all we can, but his injury is so severe, we have to medi-vac him to the University Hospital in Edmonton. There, they have surgeons who can do the job we cannot. Your father had a very serious injury to the back of his head. His skull is all smashed in. This has put pressure on his head and is causing severe headaches." I felt like screaming. This cannot be happening to Dadda.

I wanted ask the Lord, why? I needed him here. I said to my Creator, "you have all the people and all the angels in your kingdom. On this earth, I only have my Dadda. I wanted to ask my Creator to spare him; somewhere in the back of my mind I was told that my Dadda lived 89 years with me and he was tired. I had to be reasonable and let him go.

He was still active at his age. He was taking care of the Peter Bawden camp across the Arctic Red River. Twice a day he paddled across the river to check the camp. He also did a few odd jobs for the Hudson's Bay Company. To me, Dadda was always an independent person; he would never grow old. The doctor then told me that another doctor and a nurse would accompany my Dadda to Edmonton. I should go if I could get someone to take care of my children. Father Rayuant was still there, so I asked him. He said I could go and he could keep an eye on the children. He would make sure that they were well looked after. God Bless Father Rayuant.

I went home to pack a few things and told the children their grandpa had been in a very bad accident and they were sending him to Edmonton, where the doctors could fix him. I asked my baby sitter if she would be willing to take care of my children by herself during my absence. She said not to worry; they would be fine. I told her that Father Rayuant would be by every day to see if she needed anything. Her name was Agnes, and she was from Old Crow. I have never forgotten her. God Bless her.

We left Inuvik about 8:00 and landed at Edmonton Municipal Airport a little before midnight. I had phoned my cousin Louise in Edmonton before I left to tell her about Dadda's accident. When we landed, she was waiting at the airport. The ambulance was there too. They said we were all going in the ambulance. Louise said they would follow by car. It was my first time in the city, and I did not want to lose her. Before we landed the nurse told me to look out the plane window and look at the city lights, my goodness, so many lights, I could not believe how huge a city could be. This place had no end. I was afraid to land because if I got lost no one would find me.

I was glad Louise was there as I was beginning to be deathly afraid. Everywhere you looked there were people, lights, and houses. This was too much for me. How could these people know where they were going? What were they doing? To me they seemed like programmed robots, expressionless. They did what they were supposed to do, without blinking an eye. At least some of them at the hospital showed signs of real life. "Hi, how was the flight?" Remember, this was my first time in the city. Although business people commuted daily between Edmonton and Inuvik, the people I met, who came in from the south were friendlier and acted normal.

I did not relate a smaller community to a city then. In small towns, everyone knew one another, so of course it would be friendlier. In the city, they seemed only to exist. Maybe there was a programmed school here, where these people could be taught to do only what they were told. I would not want to live this way. Then there would be no joy in living.

In a few minutes of observation from the airport to the hospital, I concluded, that maybe I would get along fine with these people if I behaved just like them. Then I would make it back to the safety of my home in Inuvik.

As soon as we arrived at the hospital, they prepared Dadda for surgery. At the same time, they asked for his medical history. I told them all I knew which was not much. Then they wheeled him to the operating room for surgery at 12:30 am.

Louise tried to get a word to my brothers Pierre and Michell but with no success. Pierre did not have a phone, but Michell did. Michell worked as an orderly at the Camsell hospital. We phoned the hospital but were told it was his day off. We tried his home, no luck.

I asked the nurse if I could go home with Louise so I could shower and change. She said to leave a number in case they wanted to reach me.

Louise ordered Chinese food. When it came to her apartment I was not sure if I should eat it or not. The only thing that looked familiar on the plate was rice. The rest looked like leftovers from a clean the fridge activity. Louise told me what was on the plate. She said "taste it Terry, it is delicious." Surprisingly I found I really enjoyed it.

As soon as we ate, we headed back to the hospital and settled down in the waiting room with black coffee. At 7:00 Am., Dadda was still in the operating room. Louise suggested we go and find a restaurant and have breakfast; the nurse said even if the operation was done, it would be sometime before Dadda could leave the recovery room.

We left in search of a restaurant. The place we found I recall very well because we had to go downstairs. This restaurant was nice but gloomy. Maybe I describe it this way because I knew it was in the basement. In the North, we had no basements. The walls were painted with murals. As a craft person, I always observe; art catches my eye instantly. I learn many different ideas by just looking at the ideas of other people. I related this restaurant to a Hippie's place. All this was an experience for me.

When we arrived back at the hospital, Dadda was still in the O.R. A doctor came and said my father would be moved to intensive care but was still in the recovery." We did all we could," he explained. The impact from the helicopter propeller had crushed the lower part of my father's head severely. They had taken most of the bone fragments to relieve the pressure that was causing him severe headaches but his injury was beyond repair.

"A few weeks are all we give him. You will have to expect he will eventually go into a coma, and then it will not be long to the end. Your family will have to prepare themselves. I am sorry Ms Remi I wish we could have done more." I was devastated. Not until then did the full force of what really happened hit me. I knew the accident was bad, but the doctors were taking care of that. I had faith in their skills. I did not want to think of death.

Louise held me as tears trickled down my cheeks. My heart was breaking; I could not say a word. Louise said that Dadda had a very long life with us; not many people are lucky to see their children grow up to be an adult, and not many see their great grandchildren. We should be thankful and cherish the time that Dadda had with us. We have to pray for strength.

She had to phone some people she knew to go over to Pierre's place and tell him to come over to University Hospital as soon as possible. My sister Florence lived in Lethbridge and my other sister Lizzy lived in Saddle Lake. Neither person had a phone.

When we went in to see Dadda, he was conscious. He wanted to know why he was not feeling too good. I told him that he had had an accident. They flew him to Edmonton, they had operated on him, and he went through so much in such a short time he was bound to feel sick. It was normal to feel uncomfortable after an operation.

By then my brother Pierre joined us, he said Michell was on his way. Ever since I was a child, my grandpa was father and my Dadda. It was the only name I had for him. My brothers and sisters called him grand-dad. He held my brothers' hands and we could see from his look that he was happy to see that they were there. Now he asked for Lizzy and Florence. I told him we were trying our best to locate them but since they lived in cities some distance away, it would take sometime before they get our message.

All these years his only wish was to see his grandchildren before he died. This wish he was going to get. Maybe it was not in a way we expected, but he had this wish. I spent the next four days with him. Then he began to worry about his great-grandchildren back home, especially Marie; she was Dadda's special baby. Whatever her grandpa told her to do, she did. What she told him to do, he did. They adored one another. There was a bond and communication between these two.

Each listened to the other and had a respect for each other, which in today's society is missing between the elderly and the younger generation.

I, as a mother have always had to strive for stability and balance in my home. Having many children, I have had to know each of their needs. However, my love for all of them is unlimited. My Dadda taught me this early in life, but I had almost forgotten. It took an old man and a little girl to remind me. It takes one's effort and teachings to make it become a reality.

Because Dadda worried about his grandchildren, he told me to go home, as he had Louise and both my brothers. He said he would be safe. He also worried about his job because he was the security for Peter Bawden's camp. He wanted to make sure that there was someone there to take over during his absence. He also worried about the maintenance job at the Hudson's Bay Company. He wanted to know if there would be someone to fill the shelves and do the odd work around the Bay. I said I would make sure someone got these messages in Arctic Red River once I returned.

Two days later, I went home. The last words he gave me were. If I wanted to live with my children and see them mature, I was to do three things. (I cannot reveal this at this time in my life). I promised Dadda I would do as he asked.

I was exhausted when I finally arrived home. The children went out to play in my next-door neighbor yard. Jody will keep an eye on them while I had some sleep. I woke to the phone ringing. It was my brother Pierre calling from Edmonton wanting to know if I had got home safely and if the children were okay. He said Dadda was the same and if any changes occurred, the hospital would notify me.

I went back to work and prayed my Dadda would recover but I know in my heart this was the end. I prayed to my Blessed Mother to give me the strength to accept whatever the Lord had in store for me. The thought of having no one scared me. If Dadda died, there would really be anyone for us, and the children would just have me. My God, how alone can you get in this world? I would have to have the strength to keep going for the children's sake. I had to hang on. I would not let my children go through what I had experienced, God willing, I would see them mature and become adults, I wanted to be with them during the period of their life when they needed me most. I had to appeal to my Blessed Mother. She was the link between the Lord and me. She understood what I was going through so she had to help.

I went to Arctic Red River in July for my holidays. It was sad to see Dadda's house deserted. The last time I talked to my brothers, they said his life was slowly fading and the end could be anytime.

All of a sudden a message came from the RCMP in Inuvik. I was to contact my brother Pierre in Edmonton; it was urgent. Deep in my heart, I knew the news I dreaded to hear. The mail plane was expected that day, so I went to get our ticket. I got my children ready and prepared to leave for Inuvik.

I did not call my brother before leaving Arctic Red River. Once I was back in my own house in Inuvik, I phoned him. He said Dadda had gone into a coma and the doctor said it might just be a matter of days or hours.

My brother said if you want to come, do so as soon as possible. I phoned Dr. Habgood, head of the Inuvik General hospital. I was to leave for Edmonton on the next flight. I wanted her to phone the Charles Camsell Hospital asking them to prepare my Dadda for the trip back to Inuvik. I wanted him back in Inuvik where I could take care of him. If he was going to die, I wanted him to die in my arms. Dr. Habgood said she would phone Camsell, find out the latest information, and get back to me.

When she did phone back, she said, "As your doctor, Terry, I advise you against what you have planned." She spoke with the doctors in Edmonton and was told Dadda could not survive the trip and that I should remember my Dadda as he was.

Dr. Habgood said that after spending some time in the hospital, Dadda had lost a lot of weight. So to see him in this deteriorated condition would add more grief, because there is nothing worse than seeing someone you love like that and feeling helpless.

In no time, the news flashed around town. My friends phoned me and all advised me against going to Edmonton to get my Dadda. They said the same words that Dr. Habgood had said to me, remember your father as he was. I phoned my brother Pierre and told him I was not going. However, if by a miracle Dadda woke up, I asked him to phone me right away. I would be on the next flight.

A few days later, my brother again phoned me to tell me the dreaded news. Dadda had passed away peacefully without regaining consciousness. I was warned beforehand but to hear the news that it had really happened was devastating. Grief overtook my whole being. All that my Dadda had said to me, during his lifetime flashed before me. He was my father, my guidance, my counselor and my protector. I could only ask why he died.

My friend Blair and his wife Linda took me into their home for a couple of days, days I cannot recall clearly. Nothing seemed to matter. I cried for Dadda and the home I had lost. It did not matter where I was in this world; I had a home in Arctic Red River. Now this home was gone. The time that I had spent in Arctic Red River was only for a short time; mostly on holiday visits to my community. My Dadda always rejuvenated my energy so I could keep going. He knew just what to say to motivate me and keep that self-determination alive. When I talked about what a raw deal life had handed me, Dadda used to say, "Therese, life is as rotten as we make it. As long as there is life in us, we can change our situation. Any crises in our life should be looked upon as experiences, which will help us, deal better with future situations."

Those words constantly accompanied me during those days of sorrow. I was always trying to find what options I had just in case the plan I had at the time went wrong. The teachings Dadda instilled in me when he said "fire, water and food are important for survival; do not wait until the last minute; be prepared at all times". During my loss, I almost forgot all of these words. I am sure some time in our life that we are in total despair; we forget who we are, where we are, and what we are supposed to be doing. In the time of my great loss that almost happened to me, but the friends that I was with knew how deeply I was hurting, cared for me, constantly reminding of my children.

It took some time to get over this tragedy with their help and patience. There were times I thought of suicide but the love for my children kept me going and Dadda and mama's words that only Our Creator has the right to judge and he has the right to call us. Those words were with me often throughout my lifetime, that and a strong determination I would never let my children grow up orphans as I did.

I felt so much grief that everything seemed worthless, I tried desperately to reach out and get a hold of something, but there was nothing. When my Dadda's remains were brought back to Inuvik, Blair went to the morgue with me. Dadda seemed to be sleeping. He had not changed. I tried to wake him up; I thought that being there in the same room he would feel my presence and this would wake him. They took me away and the doctor gave me something to calm me. Blair and his wife Linda constantly reminded me of my main responsibilities, my children. For once in my life, I did not want to wake up. I did not want to know who I was or even think of living. I wanted to forget the identity of Therese Remi. I know today if it was for my friend Blair and his wife Linda I would never have survived that crisis. For Blair's unlimited dedication to help the people of the North, and the caring they gave me who brought me back to the living, I am grateful to them always. They have never made me feel like a third party; they made me feel always welcome.

Even today, I know Blair is there for me. When I feel down, when I am angry, I get on the phone and talk to him and I always feel better after our talks. He never tells me, "I told you so," but suggests alternatives. In his own way, he gives me that self-determination that I so strongly need from someone who truly believes in me. Dadda used to give me all this. It did not matter how much I screwed up, he made me get up and try again. To Blair and Linda I say "thank you." I look at them as part of my family; I am fortunate to have them.

We brought Dadda's remains back to Arctic Red River for burial. There were just the children, Dadda's coffin, and myself. We arrived about 11:00 Am.; but they buried him at 3:00. The elders and the younger generation both missed him.   I had the coffin open so each could say their goodbyes. Everyone came to the church service to do this. Some gave him messages, while others just kissed him.

I was like a zombie just going through the motions. The final moment was when I heard the noise of the dirt hit the coffin. I had heard that sound before. It was when my mama and my father were buried, and I never saw them again. I knew then that this was for real. I would never see my Dadda again. I guess I went crazy. They said I did not want them to cover Dadda coffin. As long as they did not put him six feet under the ground, I would be okay. The next thing I knew I was in Barney and Mary's house and she was trying to tell me to drink some tea. The people, each in turn, came and gave me kind words. I was so numb. I was so cold. Later when I felt better Mary walked me over to my Aunt Annie's house.

The children and I stayed overnight, and then we took a plane back to Inuvik the day after. I had to go back to work but my heart was not in it, not like before. It was just something that had to be done. However, my children and my friends' love slowly took effect. I realized what I was doing to my children. I was neglecting them. If Dadda was here, he would surely have looked at me with disapproving eyes. This woke me up a little. I had to ask myself who would care for my children if I gave up. I did not want them to grow up fending for themselves as I did. At least I had Dadda; they would have no one. If anything happened to me, they to would feel the loss worse than I did. They will grow up with no sense of direction. I cannot do this to them.

I began to think again of my surroundings. Dadda would have said," Therese you should look after your children". I was in charge of their life. They were given to me to guide and take care of. I would lose my spirit if I chucked my responsibilities. Grief belongs to this world and as long as I am alive, I will grieve at different times throughout my life. Each time I was sad it would be for a different reason. The confusion that I felt because I had lost Dadda had to come someday. Now I had to live my life without him and put to use what he had taught me. I began to see things differently. Something was still missing from my life. I could not put my finger on it.

Larry and I were still very much involved but I was far from feeling content. I prayed now and then but I was so full of guilt and I thought I was so bad I was afraid to really pray. However, I kept asking my Blessed Mother to help. I did not even know how. I said the "Hail Mary" whenever I thought of her, and asked God for his mercy. I was begging them for help. I began to drink more but at the same time, I became interested in the effects of alcohol. I began to see how much alcohol has affected our lives. The major cause of all problems is alcohol. It creates crimes, abuse in the family and amongst friends, as well as the neglect of children.

I wanted to learn to live without it. How? I wanted to learn to have a good time, but without the alcohol.

Memories flashed back which told me at one time I was quite a shy person, but I could sing and dance a darn good square dance, and did not need alcohol to do this. In addition, I sure as hell do not need it now. I wanted my children to grow up in a home without alcohol present. I wanted to learn the cause of why it was addictive, how it was the cause of family abuse and break-up, and I felt some type of prevention should be established which could be successful. What damage does it do the mind and body, and what type of cure is needed for alcoholism.

It was sort of taboo. I tried going to Alcoholics Anonymous, but they were so careful in hiding their identity, I thought they were not for me. Alcohol was beginning to be a major problem in the family life and in our community, and it should be intervention now before it took control of my people's lives and our children suffered the consequences. Somewhere I heard it gets worse. Dr. Schaeffer mentioned this in one of his lectures. He was my doctor in the early fifties in Aklavik when I had tuberculosis. At the time, I believe he was doing some sort of research at Charles Camsell Hospital in Edmonton. He made a yearly trip to the North to deliver lectures concerning health issues. I was always interested in the talks he gave. I would not have missed his lectures, so I tried to attend every one of them. I could not understand why there was so much hush-hush on this issue. Everyone should be concerned. I knew very little, but from what I heard at Doctor Schaeffer's lectures and what I had learned from Blair, I knew I did not want it in my life or in my children's. I did not know exactly what I was going to do about it, but it was up to me to find the answer.

At times Larry never drank and other times he did. The end to this relationship had to come sometime. I would be heartbroken, but I could not continue. I had to change my situation, but I did not know how to start I loved Larry regardless and to leave him just tore me apart. He taught me there were good people in the world. His vision of humanity saw equality as the answer to success; many things that were important to me were also important to him. He was concerned for things like caring, courtesy, gratefulness for the smallest to the biggest good things that happen to you. Nevertheless, I had to let him go.

Some years ago, my sister Lizzy had married someone in Alberta. She was in a very abusive situation almost from the beginning. I understood what she was going through but she was the one who had to realize she did not have to stay in this relationship. Over the years that we lived so far apart, she kept me well informed of her whereabouts through the letters she wrote. In one postmarked St. Paul, Alberta, she said she needed my help; she wanted to get away from her husband who beat her almost continuously. Drinking was always involved.

I talked to Father Rayuant who said there might be a job opening at the hostel and if she was interested, the job could be hers. I wrote her immediately and sent the plane ticket. In no time, she arrived in Inuvik. She had a job waiting, a place to live and could begin a new life. It was the fall of 1971. I had a 5/12, and it had a faulty oil stove heater that put out a lot of soot and smell. One day when we got home from work, the inside of our house just stunk. The snow outside was black, and our clothes all smelled. She became fed up and moved out. There was just my sister Lizzy, my baby Marie and I home during that year. I had put Marlene and Arlene at the hostel. Father Rayuant suggested it as the year before I had so much trouble with baby sitters. I brought Marie to the

170

baby sitters place. I would take my girls to the hostel early in the morning and make them sit in the staff parlor until they left to go to school. I was difficult on me and on the little girls. Now with both girls in the hostel, I would only have to worry about Marie.

I quit working for the hostel early in the spring. I stayed home for a few days and went to work for the hotel as a chambermaid. My working for hotels was always short. It was an income, not much but enough to feed us. I would rather do this work, in between jobs than applying for UIC. My children and I would starve while waiting for the first cheque to arrive. If something better came up I went for it, and I usually ended up with the job.

A construction company had begun building row houses the previous fall, now it was spring, and they were finished. I had filled an application to rent a unit when the project was finished. I had forgotten all about it when one day there was a phone call from Public Housing Management. They said public housing No. 1 was ready to move into. If I could pick the key up, I could move in anytime I wanted.

No more oil stove! I could wash off that oil smell. I was overjoyed to have a new place. I went to see my sister Lizzy and asked her to help me pack and move. My unit was No. 1 and I was the first person to move to this new place. It had three bedrooms, a bathroom upstairs, and a large living room downstairs with a kitchen combined. There were two extra rooms in the back and two entrances. This was luxury. I was still working at the hotel but I had to get serious and get a better paying job. I never worried about what type of job I had in those days. I always thought the more work experience I had, the better; I knew I would never be stuck for a job wherever I went. All I was interested in was being paid for my work and knowing I was providing for my children.

From the time, we began our relationship Larry and I had talked about money. The money I made ran my household. His money belonged to his household and his family. Larry worked hard and drank, but he did not neglect his work. I was accused of being after the money he made. This made me angry because I had no intention of this. I worked for these people for quite some time and I never got a cheque from them. The lodgings were a one-room shack, the children ate at the

171

crew's cook house and I know that if my children took sick, they would immediately fly them to the hospital in Inuvik. Now how did they account for their cook's salary? Then when they had brought Tanya in, what was the cost to bring her all the way from the South to Arctic Red River? I never knew much about what UIC meant in those days nor income tax. People who depended on their UIC almost starved before they began to receive anything; I always had a job to make ends meet. I was not fussy about the job I did. Income tax was another thing. I did not know what it was about so I did not bother with it.

On their part, how did they account for this? When I speak on unfairness and injustice, it is because there may be some cases of this still being done today. One should be able to trust their employers and be treated fairly, and employers should be able to trust their employees. This is one of my concerns because I would not like to see it happen to someone else. We should be able to trust the people we work for and be treated humanely.

We should do our best work because in a more harmonious environment people who are treated with respect they would produce more. I was too afraid to ask; at that time, I needed food for my children and their caboose for a roof over our heads. I did not question.

Dadda always said "treat other people like you want to be treated; smile. It will bring joy to other people's hearts, and by this you will bring joy to your own heart. Be happy with one another. If we carry our problems everywhere, we go it is not going to do us any good. If we created a problem, we can fix it at one time or another. But be happy with people; we have such a short time on this earth   Dadda was well liked by all generations, by his people and by the white people that he met throughout his lifetime. Dadda never worried about his broken English as long as he could converse in his own way and the other person understood him. He had a sense of humor, which captivated those around him. There were no color, age or language barriers for Dadda.

If Larry had any part in the unfairness, it would really upset me, as I trusted him. Looking back now, the only people that paid you honestly were the government and DPW (Department Of Public Work). They paid their employees for a hard day's work.

The Arctic Red River mill shut down and the crew moved to Inuvik. Larry was around more often. By then, his family' hatred of me was showing; threatening, name calling, the words I heard constantly out of their mouths was, slut, bitch, and Squaw. I had heard the term squaw before, "Squaws along the Yukon are good enough for me". I cannot re-call who sings this song. I had heard the word Indian used many times before.

Larry was so easy to get along with. When he came to my home and I was not there, he came looking for me. I would be sitting with friends in the bar and drinking coke; not once did he ask what I was drinking. He just had a coffee or a drink and said he would see me later. Sometimes I would leave with him; at times, I did not. Noline his wife hated me. So did her daughters Kassy and Charlene. However, Jimmy the second oldest and his sister Sherry never once said hateful things to me like the others. These two loved their father regardless. I had to find a way to slowly ease off this relationship and give Larry back to those two children. They had the attitude of their father, which made people love them.

I met my friend Danny that spring. He worked for Transportation Company. A jewel of a guy he was a lot younger than I was so it was not hard to become friends. It was his first time in the North. I had fun teaching him about the people in this part of Canada's North. He in-troduced me to Diane and her husband Frank who worked for the same company. I met the rest of the crew; they were all great and fun loving people, and I felt close to them. Diane became a friend; she was fun to be with and her husband was a happy-go-lucky person. They had one son who my children played with. This family reminded me of my par-ents. They were responsible for and committed to one another. When I looked at them I used to think, so there is a marriage like my parents after all. Sometimes when I was down, I thought of them. I had always hoped that there would be someone out there for me. It did not matter how old I got, he would enter my life someday.

A Friend and Protector

It was during this time, someone told me that a person who works at the Transportation Company had a crush on me. Really! They told me who it was; all I said was he was just not my type. I liked fun people, who loved to dance and liked music. These were People who accepted my traditional lifestyle and who were romantic.

I was always a person who spoke my mind because I was raised amongst people whose culture taught this; when I had my freedom back, I returned to the old way of mine. I love people I can communicate easily with and laugh.

This person just was not the type. His name was Darryl. Once he asked if I was married, and had a family or a boyfriend. I never said much more than a hello to him. I was not interested. I quit my job at the hotel and went to work as a cook for the Yukon Construction Company.

By then my sister, Lizzy was lonesome for her family so she decided to leave for the South to try once again to mend her marriage. Maybe it could work now that she had been away for a few months. I was afraid for her, but she was determined to try it. I felt sad for her; I wanted to tell her that once men begin to beat and abuse you, there is not much hope. It is like playing Russian roulette. You may come out of it alive if you are lucky or you may be dead. I wanted to say more but I just wished her luck and told her to keep in touch.

Before this time in my life, I would wait for Larry's call, but now I had made up my mind to leave the love of my life. It was not going to work as we had responsibilities to other people. I knew it would be difficult to walk away and I would miss him terribly. I wanted to cry when I thought of him but nothing would deter me from what had to be done. I hung around my newfound friends as much as possible and did not stay home too much. Some weekends I stayed over with Diane and Frank. Everything came to a head when Don's wife Ingrid who worked for many years at the Eskimo Inn Lounge asked to see me. When I went to the Inn the next night she told me that Noline and her daughter Kassy were in the lounge with some of their friends the night before having drinks. She overhead their conversation; they were going to do away with me. The law would justify their actions. Under no circumstances would Noline lose her man to a squaw. She would kill me first.

Ingrid said, "Terry, I always thought of you as a very nice person and I know you think of your children very much. The person you are involved with is not worth all the trouble. These people are serious. Whatever they plan, the law will be on their side." She said she cared about the children and me and did not want to see anything bad happen to me. This was when I phoned my friend Blair and told him that I wanted to break off this relationship with Larry but I did not know how.

Everything was getting to be so complicated, and my heart was breaking. He came over and suggested I stay over with them for a couple of days. That gave me the time I needed to formulate a plan. Just walking away would not work; I had to think of something else. I wanted to show everyone that there was nothing between Larry and me anymore. My children came first and I did not want them hurt because of my actions.

I came up with an idea. I phoned Darryl at the Transportation Company and asked if he could meet me that night at the Eskimo Inn lounge. He did not ask any questions but must have wondered why the change of heart. I have never said much to this person; I just saw him as part of the crew what would he say to the proposition I was about to make to him?

I had a couple of fast drinks to give me some courage; after some small talk I told him about Larry and me and the reason I had come to a decision, and that the plan I had included him. I told Darryl I wanted him to move in with the children and me. This would prove to Larry's family that I was involved with someone else. I told him I could not love anyone else, but I would be honest with him always as I was at that moment and as long as we were together. I would never hurt him intentionally. I wanted a friend and a protector. I was tired of fighting my own battles and taking all the responsibilities for myself. Up to then, I did not do very well in that department; I was always screwing up. My pay cheque did not go very far, but he would have a nice place to live, all his meals prepared, and his laundry done. I expected him to contribute to the household.

Wow! He said no one had ever made an offer like this to him in his life. This was too good to be true. It certainly did not take much to convince him. I thought to myself that was easy. What was I so afraid of? Darryl did not waste time moving into our place, which was fine with me. The faster things got moving the better. I wanted Larry to believe I was involved with someone else. This would make Noline happy. Let them think they had won; then they would leave me alone. Throughout my life, I always tried to hide my hurt feelings and I was good at it. I put myself in a position to be hurt rather than the other person. Darryl and I made sure that other people saw us together. Now Larry's children were angry. They called Darryl a cripple because he walked with a slight limp from an old injury. I did not know what would please these people. Darryl told me not to pay any attention to them. "You yourself have to live with your decision. I admire you for it."

He made me feel good. At least I knew I had a friend. We seldom went out, thinking it best to keep to ourselves. I did not want to rock the boat more than it was already rocking. The job at Yukon Construction would be finished soon, so I applied for a position as a kitchen helper at the R.C.A.F. base. A few days later, they phoned to tell me to report for work.

In February of 1972, Darryl said he was going on a trip. The Transportation Company he worked for gave their employees a trip once a year, compliments of Canadian Pacific Airlines (CP Air). I was delighted when he asked if we wanted to go too. I never asked about his money situation; it was his business. I thought he had saved for this trip so we boarded the plane for the south on March 31, 1972. We had a lot of snow that year and it was still winter and cold when we left Inuvik. The children were dressed in snowsuits, winter boots, scarves and toques. Arriving in Edmonton to see people wearing just light jackets and shirts was embarrassing. My cousin Louise of course, had a good laugh. I had not found it funny at first but by the time we got to her apartment, I was laughing also.

I remembered the last time I was in Edmonton and my Dadda. It was such a sad time then. This time I wanted to have a good visit with my brothers and cousin. I would be able to see a lot more of the city. We stayed with Louise for three days. I began to have an uneasy feeling about money, wondering why we were not shopping because things in Inuvik were so costly. I asked Darryl to offer a few dollars to Louise for letting us stay with her. She did not ask for anything, but I thought it would be nice to make the offer.

A couple of days passed and he still did not make the effort, so I asked him how much money he had. He said not much; we could not afford to go anywhere. I got very angry with him but I did not want to say anything that would cause some embarrassment to him. I wanted to take the next flight home, but he said he had already made plans to go to Calgary and visit his sister. His mother and father would also be there. He was going to ask his mother to lend him some money. He would return it after we got back to Inuvik. I wanted to believe him. After all, who would see a family stranded and does nothing?

We left on an airbus to Calgary. Someone picked us up at the airport, and we were on our way to a little town just outside of the city. A couple of days later, Darryl's mom took us on a sightseeing tour. We visited the Calgary Tower, and then we went to the Calgary Zoo. It was at this zoo that I saw my first real live polar bear. Imagine! I lived about 40 miles inland from the Beaufort Sea and I had never seen a polar bear in my life. I had to travel 2000 miles to see one! I have never gone to see the ocean. At one time, I left to go to Tuk on the winter ice road.

However, when the hills became bare of trees, I did not want to go any further.

I found it humorous. I had to come to Calgary to see a polar bear. Then it hit me. I had always worked and worried about the family needs. Life was passing me by, and I did not get to see anything or did anything much except the same old thing. Work and worry. Back in Inuvik, I went to the bar for laughs and fun. One gets to see friends and people from other communities, and sometimes go to an odd bingo at the family hall. I was going to grow old knowing only the place where I was born and the ways of my people. There was more to life than what I knew up to this present time someday; somehow, I was going to gain more knowledge of the outside world. The realization of all that I was missing came and hit me, just because I saw a polar bear.

We could not afford to go shopping or go any place, as there was no money. I was angry with Darryl for putting me in this position. If there was just him and me, it would not matter, but there were the children. I felt like a bum! The day we were to leave, I was happy; I would be home soon and this nightmare would be over. Because we were traveling on a pass, we always were the last ones to board the plane. We were bumped that day. Darryl called someone he knew in Calgary and the person came to pick us up. We got a bus ticket to Edmonton. Our luggage had already left by the airbus.

I learned another thing on this trip. Darryl's family must have suspected he had no money. I do not know if he had talked to his mother but they did not offer him any help. I learned that in the non-native world, helping or lending a hand was not one of their traits. They will defend their material possessions with their very lives. I was not brought up this way, because money and materialistic gain was not part of our traditional culture. Life came first and money was not as important. Dadda always said to take care of my family. By this, he meant not only my children, but also all my family.

He said, "If you see someone in need of that dollar in your hand, give it; someone will always put another dollar in your hand. Remember you cannot take it to the next world; do not be stingy." This practice I have followed throughout my own life. If family needs help I always try to share in whatever way I can. If I know of other people who need help, I will offer it.

I was so angry with Darryl for putting me through such a stressful time that I did not enjoy myself. I was waiting for the day I could get home. I vowed that the next time I would go on a trip, I would go because I wanted to go and no more depending on someone else.

We got back to Edmonton, stayed overnight with Louise and the next day we boarded the plane for Inuvik and home. The first stop on our way was Yellowknife. We got bumped there too. A heck of a way to travel, cheap or not-I would rather pay then, I know I will get to my destination. The rest of the day, we stayed at the airport until the return flight and we were bound for Edmonton again. We could not stay overnight in Yellowknife because we did not have the money for accommodations. When we landed in Edmonton, I phoned my brother Michell and told him what happened. He invited us to stay overnight with them and came to pick us up. The next night at 11:00 pm., we boarded a direct flight to Inuvik. I said to myself, this time we are going to make it home. Three hours later, we landed at the airport. Thank God! We finally got home. It would be a long time before I would leave my home again I promised myself.

I had many discussions with Blair about alcohol. I was still drinking but I wanted a reason to quit. I wanted to learn more about it, understand the effect, and to teach my people the harm it caused. I wanted to work in this field. I would have to learn to live without it and search for other positive avenues. I prayed to my Holy Mother to help, as I did not know how to even begin. Someday I wanted to work amongst my people in this field. Blair said there was a place just outside of Edmonton that dealt with problems that arise from alcohol. If I wanted to try this out, he could begin making arrangements. I did not think I had a problem, but I was not going to tell him that. Blair said I could learn about the effects of alcohol in this place. Maybe then I could begin to think of helping my people. I agreed.

I was supposed to leave on July 4, 1972. I packed all my things and some I gave away. I moved out of my place a week before I was leaving after giving it a good cleaning. When the last of the cleaning was done,

I looked at where I had lived in for a year. I was proud; it looked like the day I moved in. It was so clean it sparkled. I had asked Andy, a friend from my hometown, if he could put us up for a few days. Andy said we could stay at his place until I left. He had a 5/12, and he lived alone so there was room for us. At the time, he was working for the Power Commission.

July 1st, Canada's birthday, is always celebrated in the small communities in the North. We looked forward as there was a variety of games, traditional foods, and competition in sports and fun for everyone to, an event. After breakfast, we all went uptown to where the events were taking place. While everyone was eating, I had prepared the two chickens I was going to roast for supper.

The morning of July 2 I woke up with stomach cramps. I thought it was just a stomach ache, but by evening I was writhing in pain so I went to the hospital. After taking my temperature and blood pressure, they admitted me. I had worked long enough in the hospital to know there was something seriously wrong with me. I must have a disease that was contagious because the nurses were wearing green smocks, shoes, and rubber gloves.

The day after I went to the hospital the doctor said they were still doing some tests they were not sure of the disease I had. I was too sick to care anyway. I thought I was having nightmares. That night I did not know where I was. I saw my door, but I did not know where it led. I tried to think but I could not do that either. Sometimes I thought I was awake; I saw my children come through the window. They said they wanted to see me, but the nurses would not let them come to my room. They had to put a ladder to my window and climb through. I was very happy to see them and asked them to be very quiet. The children said they would not sit on my bed, just in case. They would sit on the floor beside my bed until I was better, so we could all go home together. I said to them if the nurses came they could hide in my closet, if they could all fit in there!

I awoke and I looked by my bed for the children; just the nurse was sitting there. Since I was awake, she asked me how I felt. I said fine but very weak. The nurse told me I had been very sick for two days and that

I had been delirious with high fever. They did not think I was going to make it.

A doctor said I had a disease called salmonella, (a bug you get from eating bad food or drinking contaminated water). Since I was feeling better, they would continue the treatment I was on. They questioned me about the food that I ate before the time I was suddenly taken ill and the water that I drank. They said they had admitted the children and had put them under observation. So far, they had tested negative. They would keep them in the hospital just to make sure they did not get what I had. I did not want my children to go through what I did so I agreed.

We were all discharged on 28 July and boarded a plane for Edmonton. Louise met us and we stayed at her place overnight and the next day took a bus to Lethbridge where my sister Florence lived. I had written her in the spring and told her of my plans. She agreed to look after my children for a month while I took the Henwood program. Arriving in Lethbridge was terrifying. There was no one there to pick us up. What happened to Florence? She said she would meet me. I asked people about the address. They said it was a dairy farm just outside of the city. We hardly had any money, but decided to take a chance and go out to the farm in a taxi. We could not hang around the bus depot. Maybe we looked different because people were beginning to look at us funny (as if to say, you should not be doing that; it is not appropriate, you do not do this in the city).

When we arrived at the farm, there was no one around so we decided to wait. Finally, I saw someone coming. It was Jim, Florence's husband. He said my sister had taken off a week ago and he did not know where she was. This was the first meeting with Jim; he sure did not look too friendly. I was far away from home. I was afraid, but I was hoping to find a friendly face. There was none. Jim did not invite us to stay. He knew I had come from the far North and I was tired. My experience with the ways of the city was nil. This man could have been kinder. He was angry at Florence. This made him angry with her family also. I asked if he could call a cab from where he worked, as they did not have any phone at their house.

We went back to the city. I told the children that we were going to eat then we would think of what were going to do next. I placed a collect call to Louise in Edmonton and told her what had happened. She said for us to take the next bus back to Edmonton and we would go from there. After we ate, we went back to the bus depot, got our tickets and settled down to wait for the next bus that would take us back to Edmonton. We had no place else to wait. The children were well behaved and did not fuss. Usually when the children were tired they began bickering and became disagreeable, but they were behaving very well. My children became aware very quickly when a crisis happened in our lives. At times like this, they did not throw tantrums. They would become very loving and well behaved. I was fortunate.

By the time we arrived back in Edmonton, we were exhausted. At Louise we went right to bed; we would talk when I was well rested. Louise was single and had no children. She worked at a company called Celanese and at the time, she was working the night shift. She offered to take care of my children, but was worried about the nights when she was at work from 6:00 pm. to 7:00 am. She offered to ask her boyfriend Frank and he was more than willing. He was kind and good with the children. Even today, when the girls talk about their childhood days, they talk about "Uncle Frank."

CHAPTER 18

Seeking Knowledge at Henwood

Again, I turned to my Blessed Mother and asked her to protect my children and keep them safe. My cousin did all this for nothing. She did it because she was family. Money never entered our conversations. I promised someday I would do something nice for her, like purchase the best native tan moose hide and one large dark beaver pelt that would make her happy.

After a week of settling down and making sure my children were comfortable, I left for Henwood. I had to do this. I wanted a different life from what I saw around me, in my community and in the surrounding ones. I wanted a better understanding and a better life for my children. I wanted their lives to be more meaningful; I wanted them to have dreams which could be made possible with schools close to home and more activities in the schools which would keep them busy. I believe the children of today have too much free time in their lives; this leads to boredom, then to trouble. To me, Edmonton offered activities my children needed. Little did I know there were other things that could lead to problems?

In Henwood, I learned how alcohol could become a serious problem. I heard stories of how people lost their homes, jobs and families. Although I did not think I was an alcoholic, I was glad I was there as I was learning a lot. They had counselors who never had these experiences because I asked them, but they said they were there because they cared, and they studied in this field so they could help people. It must have been sociology, learning about people's behavior. (In my language we say, their work tells us what kind of person they are). Earlier in life when I could not understand the behavior of some people, it made me angry and frustrated. Here I began to notice and understand what was going on around me, to listen, to watch and learn, to read newspapers and to read books. I began to find out life could be more interesting. The counselors wanted to help in their own way to make it a better world. Thank God! I had a little knowledge of what harm alcohol can do to a person.

I am thankful to Dr. Shaffer and his lectures and information shared with me from Blair. He saw it was becoming a problem in my life and he wanted to help me, as he knew I was searching for a better life.

I learned about alcohol and the ways and reasons it is abused. If it is used to replace the void one feels, and to overcome shyness, it will become a problem because it is used as a replacement and it is addictive. It deteriorates you physically and drains you emotionally. Unless you admit you have a problem and seek the help you need, it will get worse.

I felt sad for some patients who had lost so much. I could identify with them in some ways; I had children that I might never see again but the children I had now with me, I would protect with my life. Although I had problems of my own, I always wanted to do something nice for someone else. As long as I put a smile on their face, and gave them hope, in this process I forgot about my own troubles. I was glad I was there to seek the knowledge I needed to help my people when I returned home.

A few days after my arrival, a school buddy friend of mine was admitted. She had a black eye and many bruises. She said her boyfriend did this to her. She was lucky there were people who could help her get away. I asked her why she stayed to take this abuse. She answered, "I stay because I love him."

"That type of man doesn't deserve to be loved," I replied. I told her she made herself a doormat. He could stomp on her when he wanted to and wipe his feet on her when he wanted to. We had been friends for a long time so we could talk to each other like this, and we did not stay angry over what the other said.

I made a good friend at the clinic. His name was Bert. He owned a business in Fields, Alberta, a little town east of Edmonton, and he had a pretty little wife who came to visit him weekly. When he introduced me to her and she found out where I was from, we had things to talk about. She had worked in Inuvik at one time, so she knew many people I knew. When Bert and Blondie asked me what I was going to do when I left the clinic I said I did not know. I had to start planning as the day I was to be discharged was fast approaching. The time came when Bert left and though I was sad to see him go, I wished him luck.

One day I was told I had visitors. I expected to see people from the North or my cousin Louise but it was not like her to just drop in without phoning. To my surprise, it was Bert and Blondie who had a proposal that they wanted me to think about. Their suggestion was that I come and work for them as a chambermaid at their motel in to Fields.

They had a house with a three-bedroom basement suite, which was not occupied. They lived upstairs with their two sons, ages 7 and 10. I did not have to think about it I said "Yes" right on the spot. They gave me a phone number to call as soon as I was discharged. They would pick me up and then go to Louise to fetch my children. We were only carrying our personal belongings and that was not much.

I told my good fortune to my friend Anna and because it was three bedrooms, she could come and live with us until she made some plans. We both could work and she would be company for us when Bert and Blondie traveled. She congratulated me but said she had to think about it. I wanted to tell her the only way things change is if we want to change them ourselves, get out of the environment that is harmful to us, but I said nothing. She was an adult, capable of making her own decisions. In the fall, Bert and Blondie decided to lease their business and move to Northern Alberta to establish another one. They invited me to come with them but by then, I was lonesome and did not want to move further from my brothers and my cousin Louise.

The friend who was leasing from them said I was more than welcome to stay. I was comfortable with Bert and Blondie because they had become like family. To live in the same house with a single person and a stranger I hardly knew did not appeal to me. I told Bert and Blondie

I would prefer going back to Edmonton and try to make it there. If I could not adjust or adapt there was my cousin Louise and my brothers to turn to. I would not feel too alone.

While in Edmonton, I would also search out a good ear and throat specialist for my daughter Marlene who had had ear infections since she was two years old. The doctors in Inuvik gave her antibiotics but then a few weeks later, the high fever would return and treatments began all over again. She often ended up in the hospital. I did not want my little girl to suffer all her life so would to do something about it while I had the chance. I phoned Louise who said I could stay with her and she would help me find a place to live. When I was ready, Bert and Blondie drove me back to Edmonton I would sure miss these good people who came into my life at a time when I needed friends.

Once back in Edmonton I began looking for an apartment. I was afraid of almost everything. I did not know how to travel by bus. I did not know that sometimes I had to change buses to get to a certain place, and most of the time I got lost. I was so thankful for pay phones; they helped me get me back to where I wanted to go. Louise tried to help as much as she could, but she had to work. I felt very lost but I was not going to give up. There was always more to learn in the city but I did not want the girls to know how afraid I was. They depended on me; I had to be strong for their sake.

Finally I found a two bedroom furnished apartment. In those days, rents were not as high as they are now. The damage deposit and the rent were reasonable. We had money left over so we bought groceries and a few other things that we needed. Louise also contributed household items that she knew we needed and she did not use. The elementary school was across the street so the girls did not have to walk too far.

When we had free time, we walked downtown as it seemed every time we took the bus we got lost. It was easier and safer to walk! Oh, how important CN was in those days - it was our guide. I knew that it marked the downtown area. When we first walked downtown, I marked the streets that we passed. I tried to remember certain business names, mostly eating places, so that when we were returning home we would not get lost. This was not too hard as out on the land one takes the time to read the land and memorize the hills, trees and shapes so that you will not forget in the future. I thought of our explorations in this sense.

Through Louise I found Arctic Arts and met Hedi, the owner. I made beaded necklaces with polar bear designs on them and Heidi bought them. I did not have any sewing materials except for beads, so I made earrings as well as necklaces. The money bought us groceries but not very much. Finally, I told my cousin about my predicament and she contacted other people who helped me as well. I appreciated that she had done a lot for us since we came to the city; I could not depend on her forever.

I met a lady named Gina at the Native Friendship Center. She had worked there for many years. I have the greatest admiration for the lady who has contributed a lifetime of work to her community. Every time Native Friendship is mentioned, Gina comes to my mind. The many unselfish hours she has given to her fellow men will never be repaid in this lifetime, but she has paved the road for her entry to the next world.

I met many good people through this center. It was here that my name was given to Eric Shirt who called to say he was giving a drug and alcohol course at the University of Alberta early in the spring. Would I be interested in attending? I jumped at the chance. When I said "yes" he wanted to know why I was interested. He must have been satisfied with my answer because a few weeks later he called to tell me I was accepted. Never once did I think of how limited my education was. Nothing was going to stop me. I thought I will know when I try if I can or cannot make it.

There were students from several outlying reserves attending the course that spring. I met many good people through this course, especially Mary and her husband Jerry. We learned how to identify the problems in our communities, how to approach the problem, what course of action to take and all about intervention and solutions. We learned what organizations would help us and why it was so important at the time to take this course.

In June when we all graduated a feast, dance and sweat, ceremony took place at Doug's acreage outside of Edmonton. I heard he was a great architect whose work was recognized all over the world. Doug was very nice and we all had a good time.

It was my first introduction to the sweat lodge. I had a touch of bronchitis and was on antibiotics; when I came out of the sweat lodge, I was very well. Even now going to sweats when I feel I need help makes me feel cleansed of all doubt and fear so I can continue my journey in this life.

The customs of the native people in the South were rather different from ours in the far North but I wanted to learn all there was to learn. I was completely interested in all their spiritual ceremonies and in the people.

I will never forget the summer of 1973. Our instructor and co-coordinator Eric is one of a kind. When I think of him, I always think how hard it would be for anyone to fill his shoes. However, later on when I met his brother Pat, I thought the same thing. They were cut from the same cloth, both caring people.

The admiration I had for these two young men was immense. They were of aboriginal Cree Nation from the far South and I was an aboriginal Gwich'in ancestry from North of 60 and they spoke a different language, but the vision they had was the similar to what I wanted for my people.

They had the education to back them. This made Eric a very confident young man who worked wherever they needed him to deliver the message of the harm alcohol and drugs can do to us. It was the cause of many problems on our reserves and in our communities.

Eric always made others feel like they belonged. The love and patience that Eric had for his people and his employees was admirable. We would have never survived without a person like Eric. He shared his dream with us and kept it alive until it became our dream also. After we graduated from our course, Eric said there would be no pay as there was no money. He was seeking funding from different agencies and organizations with no success thus far.

It was up to us to begin working towards a goal that was going to be reality someday. We were to be trained in every rehabilitation center in Edmonton and Reserves in the surrounding areas. Sometime in the future, we would be able to earn a wage. How could we refuse? Eric was a born leader and a motivator. He was our co-coordinator and we were the first group work alongside him. There was Mike, Ben, Gordon, Joe and I.

Eric knew that alcohol was a major problem amongst the Native people. Each of us came from a different part of the country, but in his eyes, we were equal. We were all here for a cause. He made us feel that each of us held a piece of material to help put this foundation together. If we were successful this Native rehabilitation center would be named, Pound maker's Lodge. Because Eric made us feel part of the team, we gave it our best. I never forgot the fellows I worked with. Dear Mike, who had a sense of humor that cheered you up fast when you were feeling low? Ben was quiet but strong and always tried to do his best. Gordon, who was from Saskatchewan and the youngest of the group, was easy going. The task assigned to him, he did with the best of his ability, Joe who was older than us, had a peaceful nature and just minded his own business.

Sometime during the summer, the Alberta Drug and Alcohol Commission offered to pay us a small wage. We were pleased about this news. It was definitely a step forward. By this time, a young man also joined the group. Eric's brother Pat just drifted in as if he was always there. Next came our secretary Peggy. She was a woman who had left a steady job to join the group. The Native Friendship Center offered Eric a space, which he could use as an office.

We all met there when we finished our assignments. At this place, Peggy first began her secretarial work. I saw her as a little flower; she was so innocent. She was taught her values of life very well. She was polite and she had respect for all her co-workers.

I did not talk the language of these people, which was Cree but their attitude and actions made me feel I was a part of the team. At times, people forget this important principle, which then leads one to think, "Maybe I don't belong here." This group knew the importance of treating others with respect wherever they went. I felt good around them. It was I learned one of the first lessons in how unity plays an important part in the work environment.

The summer was filled with training in other rehabilitation centers, two weeks here, two weeks there. Mike and I were sent to Meadow Lake in Saskatchewan for a week. I enjoyed this very much as I presented a few lectures on my own. The clients and staff treated us well and the week went fast. In no time, it was Friday, and it was time to go home. I was sad to go as I had met some nice people. When I left Inuvik the year before, Darryl had stayed behind but as I was leaving, he said he would join me if I ever needed him.

When I knew I would be taking the course at the University of Alberta in the spring, I asked him to come to be with us. Because of his help, I did not have to worry about the children when I went out of the city. When we finished training Eric said we now needed a house. We were to go to people to ask for donations money, pots and pans, blankets, towels, anything they wanted to donate.

I remember one incident very clearly. It was a hot summer day when we received our assignment; it was a list of places to go and ask for donations. On my list was a place. I knew this about because I had gone to bingo there at one time. I thought all the people of Edmonton must be there, there were so many. In addition, the jackpot was so big! Well, I thought, this organization must have some money. I also knew they had a kitchen. Maybe they did not need some old cooking pots. There was no harm in asking. I went to the front door and knocked, no answer, so I tried the side door. No answer there either. I was just leaving when I heard someone opening the door. I told the person who I was and why I was there. He listened; then when I finished he said "Sorry we haven't got anything". For goodness sake, how can he say that? These people rake in thousands of dollars with their bingo I was sure. I would be glad to accept anything I told him, even a pot to boil water. Remember I was still very green about the ways of city people. I was a cook back home so I knew that there were unused pots and pans, packed in boxes and stored. This also was another reason I could not understand the response. How naive I was.

The Alberta Drug and Alcohol Commission offered us a house at 99 Avenue and 106 Street. They had used it as a residence for clients but they had relocated. We were so grateful and the joy we felt was overwhelming. After struggling the whole summer this was like winning the lottery. It was furnished with blankets, pots and pans, and towels. You name it, it was there. Everything needed for housekeeping was in this place. I could not believe our good fortune. What a giant step forward!

I became the cook. I had been in Henwood during the summer for two weeks learning to prepare meals for clients with special dietary needs and was well prepared for the cooking tasks assigned to me.

Occasionally when the counselors were busy I would be asked to help. It did not take too long for Pound maker's Lodge to begin admitting clients. Our days were full just getting things in order. Eric's vision was that this would be a rehabilitation center for aboriginal people with programs that would meet their needs. He had to use good judgment to pave the way and inspired us his employees to share in his dream. He shared all his information with us whether it was good or bad and kept the dream alive every day.

The hardships were not dwelled upon. We just kept going and every step forward was a triumph to us all. Eric was a true leader who had unending patience and understanding. Pat too was kind and caring.

These two brothers should go around the world teaching true and effective leadership. Many years had passed since but I have never forgotten the example they set.

Everything was fine until one late October morning when I awoke with abdominal cramps. I did not think it was anything too serious, so I went to work. I was sent home by noon by then I felt worse.

I phoned my doctor and he suggested I come see him right away. Dr. McGovern, a dedicated and kind man, said it was just stomach flu and two days later, I was back at work.

That weekend the same thing occurred and I was admitted to hospital. Anything I ate or drank I vomited. The pain was like nothing I had never experienced before. Needles for pain every four hours helped little. Blood was taken from me every hour and X-rays were done. Nothing was told to me.

Then Dr. McGovern, Dr. Link, the specialist, and other doctors came. Dr. Link had kind, gentle eyes. When Dr. McGovern asked how I felt and I replied "rotten, "he said, I was a very sick woman.

Dr. Link told me I was to have surgery that evening at 7:00. He said I had an obstruction in my bowels, which was causing the pain. Because I was five-months pregnant, they could not tell me what the results would be. I had a 50-50 chance of surviving. If they could not save me, they would at least try to save the baby.

I asked the nurse to call Darryl for me and when he came, I made him promise he would take care of my children if anything happened to me. I asked him to write a letter for me and I signed it and had a nurse sign it also. Then I asked him to take my children to Saddle Lake to my sister Lizzy. She could take care of them for the time being. I did not want to die while they were close by. If anything happened to me, I wanted them to remember me as I was.

When I asked him to leave as soon as possible, Darryl did as I bid and left. I have to give him a lot of credit; he never refused me when I asked him for a favor.

I thought about my children I had always treated them like babies, never thinking that I might never see them grow up. I wanted to cry but there was no time. I began praying to my Blessed Mother, and then to my Dadda and Mamma. I said, "Dadda you know how difficult it was to bring up children, you who took over the care of my brothers and sisters who had became fatherless and motherless early in their young life, but not once did you complain."

I did not want my children to grow up motherless like I did. I asked Dadda and my Blessed Mother to plead to the Lord for me. When I asked Darryl to take care of my children, I made him promise me that he would sacrifice his own needs for them and that he would always put them first in his life. He promised.

I was praying before they wheeled me to the operating room. Dr. Link asked if I was able to take care of things. I said I had done the best I could under the circumstances. He told me that they would do their best too. As sick as I was, I looked at this kind elderly man and said, "Dr. Link I know you'll bring me back through these doors alive." We were just entering the operating doors and I really believed what I said.

I did not remember anything until two days later. Sometimes I thought I heard voices but they sounded so far away. When I came to, I thought it was the day after the operation. I woke up to Peggy, our secretary holding my hand and all around my bed were my co-workers. I wondered why they were crying. Then I realized, I was back in my room, and I was okay; I was alive.

When Peggy said, "Terry, we love you," I squeezed her hand and tried to smile. These people loved me dearly as they were like family. She pointed to something; I looked and there was a vase with beautiful red roses and a card with all their signatures.

I loved them all. This and other gestures of love over the years have never been forgotten. People who showed me love throughout my life became my people. It did not matter if they were of different nationalities or strangers I had just met. Our paths had crossed and we understood one another and held respect for each other.

I had complications after the operation, so it was six weeks before I left the hospital, having been told not to go back to work. I knew that my baby was probably fine but with the many X-rays that were taken, only time would tell.

The diet they gave me to follow were foods that could easily be digested. The doctors said I had adhesions growing in my stomach from the operation I had had in 1970.

They said I would have to live with this discomfort for the rest of my life. I had to be very careful and follow all the instructions given to me because they would think twice before they ever give me another surgery; operations in the area of my abdomen would just speed the growth of more adhesions.

The doctor said my baby seemed to have survived well. Once she was born, I had to bring her in every week. I had to do this until she was two. Francie was born February 21, 1974. The doctor said she seemed healthy but we just have to watch her closely.

Four- and -a-half months later the same thing occurred. I was fine one minute and the next they were speeding me to a hospital in an ambulance. I spent some days in the hospital because the doctors were trying to correct the problem without surgery. Finally, I was sent home. A few days at home then back to the hospital to go on the stomach pump.

As long as the pain did not worsen, they followed this treatment. They were hoping the adhesions would untwist themselves.

For the next two months, I was very sick, in the hospital, back home. I had almost no nourishment, just a few drops of ginger ale. Nevertheless, I was stubborn too. I knew I was going down fast but I kept hoping and believing I would get better, and praying. At home, I carried the hot water bottle with me almost everywhere. It seemed to lessen the pain when I held it against my abdomen. Since then, I have always used a hot water bottle for pain.

Now it was August. I had not eaten since June when I first became sick. My specialist Dr. Link was going for his holidays and told me his assistant Dr. Hackett would look after me while he was gone.

Dr. Hackett was just as nice, kind and caring as Dr. Link. I feel that Doctors' work so hard. They are constantly on the go. The generous care they give their patients helps in the recovery. I know because Dr. Hackett and others visited me early in the mornings just to ask how I feeling was and how was my night. They made these rounds before leaving for their clinic. They made me want to get better.

I visited my specialist every Monday when I was not in the hospital. This visit to Dr. Hackett was different. He said because I had no food intake during the weeks that I had been sick I was weakening very fast. He had decided to operate while there was still some strength left in me. On Thursday and Friday, some X-rays would be taken. Sunday afternoon I should be admitted and Monday, I would be operated on. He asked what I thought about his decision. I said I was tired of pain; he could do whatever he thought was best for me. I had faith and I trusted in him. Anything was better than living like this.

The Friday after the last X-rays were taken, I began to get nervous as the time of my operation drew near. I tried to clean my house with some help from my girls. I got them to do the laundry and by supervising them, they did a splendid job. For a fleeting moment, I wanted to cry, scream, and just fall somewhere away from everyone and cry as much as I wanted. However, there were the children and I could not do this. I asked them to pray for me and hope that the surgery would go well.

Saturday afternoon as the children and I were waiting to catch a bus to the hospital I noticed that the pain did not seem so severe. In previous months the pain that I had would go away for a couple of minutes, then gain strength until it made me double over. This time it felt different so I told the girls we should wait; we could go to the hospital later.

At home, I felt positive there was now only a dull constant pain. This I did not mind one bit. I was also hungry! I was going to try some food, so I made some chicken soup. After taking, a teaspoonful of broth I waited for it to come up and nothing happened. By supper time, I had eaten a whole bowl of soup. I was so excited! I called Dr. Hackett to tell him the good news. I had a number to call night and day if there was an emergency. This was not an emergency, but I just had to share my news with him. The doctor said, "Terry, maybe you just needed a little scare. Let me know how everything is going tomorrow. Maybe you won't need surgery after all."

When I was ill there were times I was so hungry but I knew I could not eat. I made a promise to myself that if I ever got through this, I would eat anything and everything. I would never be choosy about food again. In the days that followed, I was progressing nicely. I began eating a little more each day regaining my strength.

A few weeks later, everything fell apart again. I felt sick, cold, and hot and my joints were aching. Oh my goodness, what am I coming down with now, I thought that maybe I had a flu bug. That is all I need. The next morning, I was admitted to hospital with double pneumonia and hooked up to oxygen. It is a wonder I lived through that also. I spent almost four weeks in the hospital at that time. Initially I was brought to the Royal Alex, but since I had a history of tuberculosis, they thought it best to send me to the Aberhardt Hospital.

Once more, I was home, and I was determined to stay home. I would watch what I ate and what type of weather I should wait for to go out for fresh air. With everything I did, I was going to be very careful, and if that did not work, I was going to resign myself to fate whatever that might be.

The spring of the following year I began to feel listless; I was always tired with no energy. On one of my monthly visits to Dr. McGovern's office, I mentioned how I felt. He suggested some X-rays as he suspected an ulcer flare-up. He gave me something to help the heartburn and a diet to follow. That helped, but not for long. I felt I was feeling worse as time went on. By this time, I felt like a complainer; there was always something wrong with me, so I went to see the doctor again. He just told me to stick to my diet. As months went by, I knew I was not well. Something was wrong. Everything gave me heartburn, so I was afraid to eat anything. One day I woke up feeling fine, but by 11:00 a.m., they were taking me to hospital. After a few days with a test for this and a test for that, they told me I had a gall bladder attack. Since I felt better, they were going to send me home. They said, "At the present time we will not operate on you, but the next time you have an attack like this, we will consider it." I was very tired but I had to fight to stay alive. Only those who have been sick for a length of time in their lives can understand the depression one goes through.

CHAPTER 19

My Troubled Children

By this time, my children had become friends with some Native kids who lived in the area. I was unaware of the fact that they were sneaking out at night after everyone was in bed. One night, I went to the bathroom. I do not know what made me check their room. They were not in their beds. My God, they were only 11 and 12 years old. Where were they? Where did they go and who? I woke up Darryl and we went out into the night and walked the neighborhoods but found nothing. I was sick with worry. There were sick people out there who could harm them. I wanted to take care of my children right, but why should I do this? I thought. At this very young age, their behavior showed ungratefulness. Why shouldn't I just die and hurt them as they had hurt me. Then what would happen to Marie and my baby June? There was no one to take care of them.

I had to think rationally, to make sense of the continuing crisis in my life. The only way I had been able to deal with things that really hurt me was to get very angry. I could survive. I could change the situation. I was not six feet under; I would do something. I lived through hell those years, but not once did I ever give up.

Right now, I was not going to dwell on what might happen with my health. I would take care of my children the best I knew how. I sat up and prayed that they were safe, wherever they were. I waited for them and let them slip back into their room before I confronted them. They said they were just playing with other kids from the same area. I was glad they were okay, but I warned them the next time it happened they were in for a willow spanking. I did not want them out there. Anything could happen.

Though I was very sick at times, I did not want my children to know I was seriously ill. The stress of this incident however may have caused the second attack. I was fine one minute; the next I was back in the hospital. This time I asked my doctor if I could have surgery but they were hesitant to perform it. He said if it occurred again, they would do the surgery if there were no other alternatives. A few months later, I was back in the hospital. This time it took a lot longer to recuperate. The doctor said they would let me go home for a month, so I could find someone to look after the children and put other important things in order, then the surgery would be done. I was afraid to have the operation but I was discouraged with feeling sick too.

Though they said it would be just a simple routine surgery and I would be home within a few days if there were no complications it was nineteen long days later that I finally was discharged. Now that I had the gallstone removed, I thought it would not be long before I would come down with something else. Illness rather took me for a friend; it would not leave me alone.

I wanted to think positively. I knew I had to do away with negative thoughts or I would not survive. I had today with my children, let tomorrow take care of itself. There were times when the two oldest ran away again. It did not matter how much I talked to them about the danger of what they were doing, they just did not listen. The kids they were traveling with were Darlene, Lorna, and Rhonda. Those were the only girlfriends that I knew they had at the time. I knew very little about them, or their families. They stood outside of the wall and whistled when they thought everyone was asleep in the house. I watched my children like a hawk watch its prey but somehow they slipped out into the night when I slept. Sometimes after being grounded, they asked to go to the store. I wanted to trust them to come home; sometimes they did come home and other times they did not. I shed many tears and went through many heartbreaks those years, but I would be damned if I was going to give up on them. I began to hear the girls were hanging around downtown. This caused great pain to my heart and spirit. Why would they do this? I asked myself. Prior to moving to this part of the city the girls were involved in school activities, went to a Saturday matinee and went to MacDonald's for fries with friends, I had girls who were happy to go to do simple fun things. Now they had met these girls in the new neighborhood things were totally turned upside-down. At first, I thought they were just being mischievous but when I heard they were downtown, I was furious. I took their latest school photos, went downtown, and showed them to people. I said they were my little girls; they are babies, please if you see them phone me at this number.

During my search, I prayed. I asked my Blessed Mother to please take care of my children, because I cannot, I do not know where they are. Sometimes my brother went with Darryl and sometimes with me, however, most of the time I went alone. Sometimes I found them; other times I did not.

I was more angry with the people I thought should care enough to help Social Services, the police and me. The police said there must be a reason why the girls were running away from home, Of course! They did not want to follow the rules I had for them. Simple rules: homework after supper, bedtime at 9 pm., up at 7 am. Eat breakfast, get ready for school, come home right after school as your chores have to be done; when this is finished, you can play until supper time at 5:30 or 6:00. How can parents enforce these simple rules of the home if we cannot get support from outside of the home, but nowadays parents are at fault, they are blamed instead? Now one may wander why I have such great faith, prayers, God and The Mother of Jesus, my mother and the Angels.

The social workers wanted to know if I drank. I thought, you try to be a good parent but they blame you the parent when children take off. The people, who were supposed to be there to help, made me feel I was the one who was in the wrong. They cause more harm sometimes. We cannot discipline our children anymore; if we do, we are charged with abuse. We cannot win no matter how we try. Some children do tell the truth, but some lie because they do not want to follow the rules that their parents set for them.

At one time grandparents had rules, the parents followed, and parents had rules the children followed, but not anymore. In my opinion, The Charter of Rights has blown this way out of proportion.

There are too many rights; it has removed the values and principles of society until there is little control. The few parents who try to instill values are called old fashioned. No wonder we are all in a state of confusion. Social services and police should team up with all parents who care enough for their children, those who guide and advise them, giving them responsibilities. Isn't this the way you prepare your children to become good adults? This training is not old -fashioned; it is the only way of the past, present and future. God and values, core beliefs and practices have been left behind. To me this means serious trouble in the future.

I began to know people downtown, some felt sorry for me be cause of the tears when I asked them if they had seen my children. I felt so sad for the people there; some had tried hard to better their lives, but it was so hard to get out. Many people asked for my phone number so they could call me if they happened to see my girls.

Once I received a call from a man who said Arlene and another girl, Rhonda, had taken off to Calgary. My God, those girls were only 13 years old. What did she think she was trying to prove? The person said that if I was going to Calgary to let him know. He was going to leave a number, and I could phone if I needed help. Again, I asked Darryl to look after the youngest children, and I left for Calgary. I had nothing with me except a tote bag with a few personal belongings. Arriving in Calgary, I did not know where to start looking, so I went to the police station. I told them who I was and told them about my daughter and another girl named Rhonda who was not much older than Arlene was. The police said they would keep an eye out for them, but that is all they could do.

Out there by myself, and scared to death, thinking about the many bad stories about what happens to women, I held onto my beliefs and prayed with all my heart. I do think it is my ultimate faith and my genuine love for people that protects me.

I have always asked my Blessed Mother to take care of me; this time I was fighting against evil, and there has to be someone up there to take care of me.

I took a taxi. The driver was a friendly person, so he was making small talk. He said, "Lady I am not being nosy, but are you from out of town?" When I told him I was he said "None of my business but why do you want to go to the drag area? You don't seem to be the type who would hang around places like that." I told him where I was from and what I was doing there. I said I did not know where to start looking, but because of where they hung out in Edmonton, they may head for the drag area in Calgary. He said that maybe he and his wife could be of help. He would book off his taxi, and take me home to meet his wife. He seemed so concerned that I felt I was able to trust him.

I remember them today as people who cared about their fellow man. In times of crisis in my life, people I do not even know help me out. I call them my angels, as I know God uses people to help. After I had a wash and ate, the three of us went downtown to the drag area. On the way, I checked at the police station, but there was no news. I gave them the phone number of the people just in case they did find my daughter, and we went on our way.

During the time we were parked downtown, I kept checking with the police. About 2:00 a.m., we saw the girls. We all gave chase but the only one we caught was Rhonda.

We drove back to the house and questioned Rhonda. I asked her where they were staying. She said no place. My God, my daughter was out there in a strange city with no place to stay. Any parent who went through the same thing as I did, chasing their children, praying to God to keep them safe and at the same time feeling so hopeless and helpless, can understand the heartbreak and the tears one goes through.

The wife told Rhonda to have a shower and then to eat, then gave her a bed to sleep. The husband and I went downtown again. We checked at the police station. We told them that we had the one girl, but my daughter was still out there. We stayed downtown until morning, but we did not see her again. We checked with the police but there was still no news of my daughter. I grilled Rhonda with questions. Where would

Arlene go? Rhonda said they had no place to stay; they were just walking around. I asked what in hell they were trying to prove. Little did I know some of the things that went on in these areas? I had no more money, so Herbie the taxi driver offered to take us back to Edmonton. I cried all the way back to Edmonton. I thought I had lost my little girl for sure, but I did not know what else to do.

I made one more trip to the police station and told them I was going home, and if they had any news to please phone me. A few days later, I found out that as soon as we caught Rhonda, Arlene ran to the police station and told them her mother was drunk and was going to beat her up. When she asked if they could help her, they put her at a crises unit until they were able to send her back to Edmonton.

A social worker phoned me and told me all this. She also suggested that if they looked after her for a while it might teach her a lesson. I said it was fine with me; I could not do anything with her. If they could help her, I would be so grateful. Arlene was angry. She did not want to talk to me. So what, I said! I could talk until I was blue in the face but it did not seem to matter. Therefore, I could be deaf too.

It did not take long before she was phoning, asking me to take her out of the girl's juvenile home. She promised with her whole heart that she was not ever going to do this again. She had learned her lesson, so I took her home. Because I lost my parents when I was very young, I had always told people who had their parents, that they were so lucky. I could not understand why my children kept running away. As sick as I was, I would not give up. I had a reason to stay alive; I had a job to do. Every time they took off from home, I went after them and when I found them, I brought them home.

I cried many tears especially when it was raining and cold, just wondering if they were warm, or if they had something to eat, if they were okay. Every time there was a body found, I went looking for them, praying that all the while it was not one of them. By this time, people began to see me often enough to know I was a mother who cared. These girls were never kicked out. The stories they gave other people were not true, so people I met and bought coffee for, were the people who kept me informed of their whereabouts. This made it easier for me to find them.

Usually my brother helped. He went along with me for company, or he would check around for me when I was too tired or too sick to continue. If I gave up, I felt it would be the end. I had to keep trying. I had to try while there was strength left in me.

I thank Darryl for his patience, for all the baby-sitting that he did for me and for all the times that I got home and there was hot soup and coffee ready. This continued before my gall stone surgery and afterwards. Whenever the girls came home on their own, I was happy they were home safe. I made sure they had a bath, and then I would put a meal in front of them. Then I would talk to them. In the later years, Marlene asked me why I did not spank them. The answer was, "What good would spanking do, except make you afraid. You would not learn anything, but talking to you might help. Maybe you won't listen today, but later on you will remember my words."

I felt like I was treading on thin ice. I was never able to rest. When they played outside or went to the store, I wondered if they would come home. I did not know when the urge to take off would hit them again. I lived in constant worry and fear. Trying to trust them was a strain on my health. At the beginning, when they began running away, I turned once more to my Blessed Mother and asked her to protect my girls out there. I could not, so she had to do it for me. Many times, I did not have a bus fare so I walked. I walked many miles. At times, I was very sick, but to find my children was all that mattered. The drag in Edmonton as they called it was not a safe place to be, especially at night, but I had faith in the divine power.

I was trying to find my children. I would be darned if I would let evil win. I was alone in my sorrow. Only a mother who loves her children unconditionally knows how painful it is not to know where your child is or if she is alive.

When I hear of a body found, I always say a prayer for the person and the family. The fear of this happening is constantly with you. Darryl was supportive and stood by me those years. He always offered his help. He never tries to discourage me. In addition, the strength that he gave me just by being there was important. He was there to talk to, to hear me cry if I wanted to. If I did not do this, I would go insane.

In the spring of 1978, I suspected I was pregnant, I prayed I was not because I was 42 years old. Who said after you turn 40, you cannot conceive? I heard this comment made when I was a teenager. I went to see my family doctor that verified my suspicion. Now they had to decide my fate. Because I was older and I had all these growths in my abdomen, they did not think I could make it through this pregnancy. They advised abortion because I had all these other health problems; if I decided to have my baby, I would sign my own death sentence. They said to think about it. What did I have to think about? My baby had the right to life. Abortion was against one of God's commandments, "Thou shalt not kill."

I decided to have my baby; I was going home to die where I was born. I was not going to be buried amongst strangers. I wanted to die in familiar surroundings and be buried beside Dadda and Mamma. With all the fresh white fish in the river and caribou, my children would not starve, they would survive. I was more afraid to go against God's commandment than to die.

When I told Darryl, he was happy but he was sad in addition, because of what the doctors had said and what decision I had made. I am not sorry today. First, I am still here and the joy that my son Jerry has given me! No money in the world would bring me more. He is very precious to me.

Darryl went to see some people he knew from the North who offered him a job. They were to fly him up to Inuvik where he would go to work for the Mackenzie Hotel. As soon as we could, we would follow. I told Darryl to put in an application for a house, soon after his arrival in Inuvik. Because there were always, several other applications it took months to get a place to live.

Fredrick, my oldest son, called me one day. He was the son that I had left with Lee. He said he was at Pound maker's Lodge. He was drinking a lot, so someone suggested he should go to a clinic to get help. He agreed. He did not want to quit drinking; he just wanted them off his back. Fredrick was 20 years old. He drank too much for a young man his age. He said he wanted to live hard and fast like his father, Lee. I said to Fredrick, "I am going to say this just once. Living in a fast lane of alcohol is not the only option one has in order to have a full life. To live to the fullest and to enjoy every minute of the life you live, to know all that has happened in one's life is what you call living." He answered, "My dad lived hard; he drinks to his heart's content, and he is still alive so I am going to do the same." I felt very sad for my son. If I had a part in any way in the way he was thinking, God forgive me. I was preparing to leave for Inuvik. Fredrick decided to go back to Fort Destiny.

At this time, I learned that Lee, the father of my oldest children, had taught the children to hate me. He made the children believe he was the good "guy". I was a bad mother because I had abandoned them. Fredrick said he remembered me enough to know it was not true, it did not affect the love he had for me, but his younger brother believed his dad and hated me.   Gene believed everything his dad told him. He said, "Gene hates you." It hurt very much, but only my Creator knows what happened.

I despised this person more with each hurt he caused me since the first day I met him. He did not stop at anything. He never thought of the pain it caused me to leave my children behind. He put a knife into my heart for using the children to feed the hatred he had for me.

Had he not done enough? For this reason, the children I had with me never knew much about my first marriage. I was not going to contribute, or be an accessory to hate. There was already too much of it. If they ever found out the truth, it would be from other sources, not me. I am against people who hold their children as a hostage when their relationships break-up. Arguments, fights over children and with each other, and children get very hurt, because it makes them feel, maybe they are the cause.

Children are victims because at the time of the break-up, they are caught between those they love. They are children, they cannot understand as adults do. This leads to confusion and they always feel that they are somewhat to blame. My oldest daughter Meg also felt the same way about me as Gene did.

She was still in Charles Camsell Hospital when I left Fort Destiny. Soon after my arrival in Inuvik, I wrote a letter to the hospital informing them of my move, asking them to send my daughter to Inuvik when her treatment was finished. They wrote back and said, "She was sent from Fort Destiny and Fort Destiny is where she was returning to". Not long after Meg returned to Fort Destiny, Lee was going to let her be adopted. When I heard about this, I got in contact with him and asked him to send Meg to me in Inuvik. Rather than let me have her, he decided to keep her. Because of my relationship with Lee, and how much pain it had caused me, the children and I became very independent. I never asked Lee for a dime. I knew he would refuse, and if the children heard me ask him and they knew he had refused they would feel unwanted. Therefore, it was up to me to be the sole support of my family.

Not once did I ever mention what was going on in my life to Dadda. Later when I moved back to Arctic Red River, he once mentioned he knew what I went through. Because I did not ask for his help, he never said anything or did anything. Thank goodness for this. If Lee had ever suspected that I said anything to my Dadda, I would have been beaten for it, anything not to set off this man. I used to pray that he could become a cripple so he would experience the feeling of hopelessness and helplessness and the pain that he had caused.

I am still bitter and deathly afraid of him. If I was alone with him, I think I would kill him and ask questions later. That is how much I am afraid of him still. The only therapy I could think of to rid myself of this hate is to write my life story. If I could help, some women get out of an abusive relationship, not only for themselves, but also for their children, that would make my effort worthwhile. Children are the most important part of our lives. They look to us for protection, love, and we as adults should make decisions to protect our children always. I do not want hatred in someone's life, as if it was in mine. It happened so long ago and yet the memories are still here with me. If I see someone being beaten up, I have to try to stop him or her even though I am just shaking, and I do not stop shaking for a long time afterwards.

I told the girls we were going back to Inuvik, so I expected them to stay home. I did not want to go looking for them when it was time to leave. June was four years old. I could not take her bottle away. She used it at night when she went to bed. When we were preparing to leave, I said to her that if she did not get rid of her bottle, she could not come.

She went right out to the garbage and threw her bottle away. That night she cried for it. June used to make her own sandwiches when she got hungry. She would get the peanut butter, ketchup, and mustard; she would spread all of these ingredients between two pieces of bread and called it her yummy sandwich. The girls told her it was gross, but every snack time out came all the ingredients for her yummy sandwich.

CHAPTER 21

Home to Inuvik

We left for Inuvik at the end of May. I was happy to be heading for home. Little did I know it would be the beginning of another nightmare? In those nine months, we were kicked here and there; people got drunk and pushed us out. I learned too how much little children meant to some people.

If they were mad at you, they did not care if children were involved. They thought only of their feelings at the time, and their words hurt because they said them in front of the children.

The teachings of our Elders were not brought forth to this present generation. I thought of all my Elders who were gone and those still alive with us. At one time, our elders were our role models. The elders of today should remember this and take back that control they had at one time by showing good behavior and caring. What would those Elders say the ones who are gone- if they see and hear all what is said and done today? They must be very sad to see their grandchildren acting in this manner. We can adjust to any environment we choose. The important thing is how our behavior and attitude is presented wherever we go. It makes adjustment a lot easier. I can understand if strangers in a strange country treated me in this manner, but people who I grew up with and worked with, this behavior puzzled me.

We stayed in a motel for a few days; then a friend of mine, Perry, gave me a job, and we moved to the ground floor of his house. Being back around my friends it was easy to join in a couple drinks now and then. Not too long after our arrival, my son Fredrick phoned. He wanted to know if there were any jobs in Inuvik. He wanted to spend the summer with us. I asked around and I found him a job hauling gravel for the summer. He went to work soon after his arrival. Fredrick still drank, and he loved to dance. On Saturday, after he finished work, he got all dressed to go out in the evening. A couple of times I drank and quit again. He always insisted I go with him for an evening of dancing. Sometimes I went with him but just for a short time. I never wanted to stay for long. Fredrick always wanted to dance the first dance with the most beautiful woman in the world, "his mother." When I think of him, I recall those words and the good times he always had. Fall came and the job closed for the season. Fredrick left for Fort Destiny.

I was no longer working at my job so I moved out of the house. Janitorial work was difficult for me. This was in August; from then on, my children and I went from place to place. I was going to have my baby in December. At the beginning of December, Florence and Dave offered us the basement suite of their house. I went to the social services to see if they could help us. They were able to give me one month's rent, but they told me not to expect this assistance to continue. At least we were going to have a roof over our heads. I was expecting any day now and I had to have a place to live. I worried what I was going to do at the end of the month.

My son Jerry was born December 6, 1978. He was very special. I was told I could not carry him full term and that there might be some complications. Except for two days of hard labor, he was fine. Christmas was coming and we had nothing. I told the children we were all together and healthy. That was all that was important. There were beds in the house and a couch but no blankets. We were happy, and we were alone at last. I knew it was not for long, but we were going to enjoy our peace for now.

When Christmas came, God bless my Marie. She got a good size paper and set down to do one of her drawings. Then she hung it where we said our Christmas tree would be if we had one. It was a picture of a tree with all the decorations on it. My little girl was so positive in the way she looked at things. We all went to church for midnight Mass. We had just returned when there was a knock at the door. There stood Darryl, Dave and Elaine, the staff from the Mackenzie Hotel. The box they carried was so big. I thanked them, and while I was serving coffee, the children were opening the box. There was a present for each of them. There was also a turkey for our Christmas dinner. What a lovely surprise!

At the end of the month, we went back into the street. One can imagine how cold the weather is at that time of year. A woman I knew said I could stay at their place. It did not last long. Too much drinking was going on and my children and I never had a decent sleep, so we moved out to someone else I knew from my hometown.

I did not mind if people drank, but I hated the arguments. I wished they would go to bed when they came home, but no, they continued. I knew how this woman drank, but I thought if I did my best and took care of the children, maybe it would make a difference. This woman had six children and there were three of mine. My oldest girls stayed with friends, so I did not have to worry about them. There were many mouths to feed, and there was never enough food to go around. I went to see Nellie at the Co-op and she gave me musk-ox meat. With this, I made soups and stews. It was good. I was so grateful and I thanked Nellie for her kindness. In the time that I stayed at this woman's house, not once did she thank me for what I did. I took care of her children, cooked for them, did their laundry; I had five children of hers and three of my own.

When she drank and was mad at her boyfriend, she also would look for an argument with me. The children and I stayed in one bedroom. When we heard attempts made to come into our room, we used to pile stuff against the door so she would not be able to enter. I do not know why we did this, because when we locked her out, she got angrier we had to open the door just to shut her up.

My emotional state was whirling from hurts and tears, I would never wish this upon anyone, I was not important to anyone, just my babies. As long as I did what I was told like a slave I was treated like one. Why should I waste my energy and time trying to make them understand? All I was trying to do in my own silent way was to put a message across on how important children are to one's life; how important it is to care about one another, and to try and recapture the close relationship once held by our people.

How can cultural beliefs go so wrong in such a short time? There was no more respect for values. The people, who were taught by their grandparents and parents, just as I was taught, did not seem to remember their teachings. I remembered mine.

There was no more meaning to the words of caring, sharing, and respect amongst my people. Everything had a price tag. I did have other friends, but they had no room and most of them had their families living with them. There were friends of mine like Lorna and Mike and many other Inuit people, but I was staying with a person who was from my own community. I could not justify their behavior.

Dadda went hunting many times when the town did not have any meat, and he always got his moose. He did not bring the moose to our house. No! He went to the Chief's house and told the chief exactly where the moose, he had killed. He asked the chief to get the boys to hitch up their dog team, bring the meat to town, and drop it off at the Chief's door. Then the chief would distribute the meat amongst his people in the community. If he was fishing, he gave fresh fish to people who were not fishing. When we were very young, Dadda ordered groceries through the Hudson's Bay Company. We the children always had lots to eat. Our clothes were very poor but we never went hungry. Sunday after church, Dadda always packed a bag with a few oranges, apples, and a dozen eggs to bring to the Elders in the community. Sometimes when the weather was good, we went to fishing camps, which were located not far from the community and brought them tobacco and apples. I remember one Sunday after church when Dadda said to me "Therese, get ready. We are going to visit the old people - Old Modeste and his wife Macreena". They lived down the Mackenzie River. They had not been to town for quite some time. We packed up some eggs, oranges, apples, and tobacco. I never forgot these acts of kindness my Dadda taught. To my disappointment, when we got down the hill, Dadda said, "We will take our small canoe and we will paddle down." I tried to tell him that it might take two hours, but he had made up his mind that we were going to paddle. When the water is calm on the mighty Mackenzie it is a beautiful sight to see, the calmness brings peacefulness to us, and Dadda used to love paddling it to capture the serenity.

He not only gave to old people, but he also shared with people who had nothing and to people with many children. Darryl came and went as he pleased. I knew he drank because his breath told me so, but as long as there was no argument, I did not care what he did.

Once the woman I was staying with came home from the bar. She was upset and ready to argue with anyone who would even look at her. I was very tired and did not want to listen to any bickering. As soon as she walked in that door, I knew we were in for a rough evening. I decided to go somewhere for the night. It was 50 below zero, a real cold winter night. My baby Jerry had a very bad cold, but I wrapped him well, took Marie and June, and left the house. We went a short distance to where a couple of Elders were living, and I asked them if they could put us up for the night. The old woman said we could stay but they had no spare blanket. I said it was okay. I would just wrap the children well in our coats. The old man had had a stroke some years before which had left him disabled. His wife and a 40 -year- old daughter cared him for. The Elders also had a son who was partially disabled. The old lady had her hands full.

The grocery store was still open so I sent Marie to get some bologna, jam, peanut butter, and bread the few other things I needed to fix us something to eat. My heart was heavy, and I had a lump in my throat. I wanted to cry. I wondered about the future and did it held for me. I asked myself what I have to do in order to have a decent life.

At times in my life, my morale has been very low, and this was one of those times. It would have been very easy to give up, but my children looked to me for protection so I could not. I was going to do something; I just did not know what. I knew I had better start thinking. I had always disliked bullies, ever since my school days. I fought against people like that. I did not agree with them using other people for their gain, and I am still against people who want to control and do anything to gain at the expense of other people.

I had heard some talk that the people drank, but I never believed this. These were Elders, and Elders did not do this. At least not the Elders I used to know. Sometime after supper, the daughter left. She came back a little later with a paper bag, which she took to her mother's bedroom. I did not think more about it. They were both making trips to the bedroom during the course of the evening. Now they were acting funny and talking much more. I realized what the trips were for. I could not even get one night of rest and old people at that! Our Elders in my childhood days always showed respectable behavior. How can Elders get respect when they do this? We went upstairs early. I cleaned the room as best I could and we settled down. Later I heard argument, crying, and singing all night. I said to my children that things would be different from now on. No more of this wandering from place to place. I would not care if it were an old shack as long as we had a place of our own.

I spent a sleepless night, planning what I was going to do, who I was going to see, what I was going to say. I shed tears, just thinking of what had been happening to me since I came back North. I wished I had a log cabin out in the bush alone with my children, away from all this, and lived with the Creator's nature and the wild. They would never hurt you if they sensed the respect you had for them. In fact, they will take care of you. People could not see me as a mother who just wanted a roof over her head for her and her children. I only wanted a little place in the world without being kicked in the teeth from those who had the power to say "No." I cried holding my children for the little things in life we didn't have, a roof and some food. Because of my life and what I had to do to survive, I understand how under-privileged children feel. I know what it feels like when other people use you. I know what it feels like when one feels so alone in a world full of people.

This makes you wonder if it is worth it, to continue. Throughout my life, I will not stand by and see bullies and power-grabbers people, abuse others. This is the reason why I always speak on justice and fair-ness. I keep hoping and searching for the harmony that my people held at one time. I want to try to create awareness of what values mean in our life. Respect for others would create better relationships in society. This would create a good future for our children and grandchildren. For me that night in 1979 all my dreams for my children's future were fading before my eyes. All I saw was evil through drinking, abuse, power, and control. The innocence of the years when I was growing up was gone. No one knew what kindness meant anymore. If someone did a deed, they wanted something in return, or they would say you owe me one. Why not just do the good deeds because we want to. The caring for one's fellow man was gone. To try to stay sober in the midst of all this was tough, but there were my children; they were precious to me. To be sober did not help me in any way. I was still getting verbal abuse. I was told, "Who the hell do you think you are? You used to drink too. Now you think you're something." What the hell?

They should be glad someone is living a sober life. Maybe if I drank, they would accept me. I could not justify their behavior. If there was just me, I could take it, but there were my children. I wanted to hurt all the people who had hurt me all my life

Nevertheless, there was a reason I lived through all the life and death situations. It was up to me to find out what it was. I asked my Blessed Mother to come to my aid and make me strong. I dozed off for a few minutes and woke up to my baby crying. I felt him; he was hot. This meant he had a temperature. At 5:00 a.m., I woke Marie up. I asked my little girl to walk up to the Eskimo Inn, and ask Darryl for some money to take Jerry to the hospital. His cold seemed to have worsened as he had this fever.

When Marie got back, I was ready to leave and we all went to the hospital. Jerry was admitted with a slight touch of pneumonia. When I told my story to the doctor and the nurse they asked if we wanted to clean up and gave us a ward that was not being used so the children and I could have a bath and wash our hair. We had no change of clothing, but this was a start. After we finished, they took us to the staff cafeteria to have a good breakfast. A bath and a good meal was something we had not had for a few days.

When you lose faith in humanity, and you do not think there are any caring people left on earth, you let yourself get into a deep depression.

Sometimes you cannot get out by yourself. Kindness from a fellow human is like food for your body and soul. I know; I have been there a few times in my life.

After we had a good meal, we went to the front entrance of the hospital. I phoned Richard and Cindy, who I have known for many years and considered them friends. Richard answered the phone. I told him in a few short words what was happening to me and what I had planned to do. Richard said, "Terry, just wait right there, I will come and pick you and the children". Within a few minutes, he was there. He took us to his house and said, "Before you do anything, I want to say, you are more than welcome to stay until you find a place. Cindy is down South going to school, at the moment no one is using this part of the living quarters." Dick said he stayed in the research part of the house. I was welcome.

Nevertheless, I did not want to cause any embarrassment through my behavior while living in their home. I was going to find a place before the day was over. I was not to going to take this type of treatment lying down. I was going to put up a good fight for my children's sake. We washed our clothes, and ate a good lunch. Richard said he wanted to help and accompanied me to the agency I had on my list. I had made a list of agencies, that were supposed to be there to help and we went to see them. We received the same answer. "We have a long list of people who are waiting for a house. We haven't got any vacancies at the moment." However, had I applied in June 1978, and this was February 1979. Richard asked what the real problem was. I had told him of some vacant houses that were pointed out to me by other people, so we asked about them. Some answered; some did not, and some just shrugged, what deadbeats! I saw all these people working, and none showed any emotions or concern. Why should they? They were going home to a nice cozy warm house later, so why should they care. They were just doing their job. They were there for the pay cheque and that was all they were there for.

I remember the years that I worked in the hospitals. I worked for only a few dollars, but my job in pleasing the patients meant more to me than anything. When I had my hour off, I went to the Hudson's Bay Company to buy a few things the patients needed. I always did this because I wanted to see the smile on their faces. This made me happy, this was a job well done.

The housing department said they would see what they could do. The Social Services suggested I go back to Arctic Red River and live with friends or relatives. They would pay for our transportation and the people who accommodated us. Forget it. I was not living at anyone else's house again if I could help it. I did not want people to abuse me again.

My children and I would set up a tent in the yard of the Housing Association Building. We would live there until we got a place. This was what we planned to do anyway. I had already got in touch with a few friends. They offered to get the spruce boughs for the flooring and they would get some wood. People donated, Caribou meat and I would cook great amounts of caribou stew to feed everyone who came. Continuous drumming would be done. We would live in this tent and no one would move us.

I had followed the procedures of applying. I had done everything the peaceful way. Now I would have to use some white man's strategy. Maybe they would understand that! If I was arrested and they put me in jail, my friends and children would continue.

If it came to this type of treatment, this would just add more fuel to the fire. I would go to every media outlet I knew and I would give my story. My children and I had suffered enough. I was not going to hesitate anymore and sit to wait for an answer. As young as my children were, they would stand by me. They knew what we went through. When you teach your children the values and principles that were taught to you and always remind them of these teachings, they support you.

Treat people like you want to be treated; never take anything that doesn't belong to you, not even a penny; never let me catch you destroying other people's property; listen to your teachers because they take the place of your parents while you are at school. These behaviors I stressed everyday. I told them, "I never spanked you children but this will give me a reason to get a willow".

I tried to teach to my children all of the values I have been taught, as a young child. I felt the isolation and the rejection from many things, especially the sense of belonging and the many things that people and families enjoy and take for granted. The sense of belonging to something, somewhere, was what I missed. Although Dadda loved me very much, he did not interfere much in anyway. Dadda used to make me upset at times because I felt he should say something when he knew my feelings were hurt. Dadda said that he was there to give me strength, but the battles had to be fought by me.

As I recall the words of my Dadda "Therese, you are an orphan, many things in life will hurt you. People will hurt you; do not cry over little things. When adults hurt you, they really intend to hurt you for their own gain and vindictive reason. Then you will really feel the hurt. The hurt you feel now is nothing to what you are going to feel later on. Then you will cry for a reason. As grown adults, they should know better, but some of us never grow up. They know how to get to a certain point and then they act like children. All that we have taught you, your Mamma and I, we did because we wanted you to grow into a strong adult. We wanted you to be a good person. Many things you will not understand now when they occur, but if you take the time and energy to understand, you will gain wisdom. When you have done this, you will store it in its place; it will be useful sometime during your life. You will also teach your children well because of these experiences. In addition, in all your life, do not forget these experiences, whether they are good or bad. In your generation, you will know many people with different cultures. When I was your age there was no interference with our parent's and grandparent's teachings, so children were taught our way of life without being distracted by other destructive forces which will harm our people.

Therese, if you do not forget my words, you will not be lost in the great confusion that our people will face tomorrow. My people and a few non-native people I have dealt with during my lifetime. I have never had a bad friend. Everyone is my friend, my child, these are my people. I have taught you the traditional ways of our Elders, now you go and learn the culture of the white man so that you can sit across from them and look them straight in the eye.

You will feel equal to the white man and you will feel equal amongst your people because you will understand both cultures. Do not forget who you are, or your people, your community, or your neighbor. Offer your help. This gives the sense of belonging. Each achievement accomplished gives us joy because we know we are part of whatever happens. Because you are an orphan, you should understand what I would say next. Make people around you feel they are wanted. Give the sense of belonging. Be good to people and respect them and they will respect you in return."

Those were the words of my Dadda. It all made sense only in later years, but I never forgot them. Teaching my children to be caring persons was important. It was how I was taught. The people in the community were teaching my children to see things differently. My children always called people like this "mean people." They were right. I had always said to them, be a caring person. When you see that someone needs help, offer it. It does not matter what nationality. We are all equal in the eyes of our Creator. These were the words of my Dadda and Mamma.

How would I explain my actions to my children at the time? I told them that sometimes we might have to step on some toes to help them remember. At the time I thought, this is the only option I have, to make noise and if need be to make more noise.

These were the strategies I used to help them take notice: Day 1: Richard and I went to agencies I thought were in the position to help. The response we got was not too hopeful. That afternoon I phoned Darryl at the Hotel. He had responsibilities, if not to me at least to the children. He got a room for us at the hotel only for a couple of days because he did not have the money to pay for more.

Day 2: Richard had asked me to hold off on whatever plans I had. I had to give these people some time to put something together. I would put off setting up the tent. However, speaking on the unfairness and the injustice was my priority. I wanted to create awareness, to show how things were done. I wanted people to be aware of how some people were being ignored. We had to have input in our communities so we could bring our concern to the people who had influence to help make it a better place to live.

We had not had anything to eat at all by late afternoon, so I borrowed $5.00 from Richard I bought French fries from the hotel, which the children ate. I gave my portion of the food to the children.

Day 3: Through the grapevine, I heard that the Housing Association might have a house for us, but I pretended I had not heard this. I kept doing what I had to do, talking to people. The plan was to set the tent up in six days from the day I had begun my campaign against unfairness and injustice. To me, great injustice was done because these people knew me. I had worked and lived in Inuvik most of my life and so I was no stranger to them. Later in the afternoon, there was a message for me at the desk. It was a phone number. The number looked familiar, but I did not have time to worry. I was on the warpath. I called the number. It was the Housing Association, saying that public housing unit number 12 was ready to be moved into. The board had agreed to let me and my children rent the place. I could pick up the keys and move in whenever. "Oh my God, thank you." When I told the children, they all jumped for joy. They asked, "When can we move in?" I said, "As soon as I pick up the key."

With this latest experience, I learned what power could do. I would use it sometime in my life when I needed to, but never at the expense of others. I would use power to help people.

I had applied for a job at the Sewing Center, and they had given me a call. My friend Lorna was the supervisor at the center and she knew I sewed well. They did not have to teach me much except how to handle the industrial sewing machine. I knew this would not take long. There were at least 15 girls and women working at this place. It was like a small factory where each individual was assigned a certain task. Skilled women who knew the art did the delta braiding. Everyone had to be skilled in order to bring forth a quality product that was marketed to different countries all over the world. The wages were not much, but we had fun. The girls who worked at the Sewing Center were a bunch of great people and so was our manager.

I was a board member for the Drug and Alcohol Association. I recently had been chosen by the board to be the chairperson. Because of what was going on my life, I was not involved as much as I would like to be. We had no director for our Drug and Alcohol Rehabilitation center, called the Delta House. Most of the work fell on the board members and our secretary, Pat.

Although the position was advertised and applicants were interviewed, either the applicant found the weather too cold, or there was not enough to do in a small town such as ours. Consequently, Pat, our secretary at the Delta House, was kept busy. The board helped as much as it could, but most of the workload fell on her. There was no complaint from this little girl. She just went along and did her job. Under her care, the center functioned well during those months. There were good people on the board; they did not mind the extra work when someone was needed.

Teamwork made our tasks easier. Although my doctors told me how my adhesions would affect me in the future, I was doing fine. I could keep it under control as long as I took care of myself and followed their orders. I continued the prescribed diet and limited physical work from my job as much as it was possible.

Now that I had a home there was no reason for my girls to stay away, but they were too busy running around and partying with friends. They did work though, so I did not say anything. Darryl stayed away and came home whenever he pleased.

At times when he came home with the smell of alcohol on his breath, I did not like this and it caused an argument. He frequently stayed at the hotel. It made our relationship more distant. I felt that if he wanted to stay at the house to be close to the children, he had to follow the rules of the home and they were to contribute financially and to abstain from alcohol. Either this, or move out. His behavior and the girls not listening to me and not helping caused a lot of stress. I felt I was carrying the full load of trying to keep the family together. I felt so sorry for Marie, who was only 11 years old, yet she took jobs to contribute to the family income. I depended on her for babysitting, and she tried to take some of the workload from me. God bless this child. All through her young life, she worked hard and she cared.

Darryl was physically abusive a couple of times. The rest of the time when he drank it was verbal abuse, but it hurt as much. If I knew he was drinking, I dreaded the thought of him coming home. He used to say to me, "Terry, you're nothing but an old bag and you think you are so smart. If I walk out on you, you will never find another man who will listen to your bullshit. No one will want you. You are mouthy. Take a good look at yourself, you're nothing." He was a good man when he did not drink, but like many who drank over the limit, he became abusive. At the time, I did not care if I had any man around. I was doing just fine. If he wanted to walk out, that was okay with me too. At least there would be peace.

Sometimes people came to town and had no place to stay. Whenever they came to ask if they could camp at my place, I said yes. I never turned anyone away. If they were drinking, I made sure they did not bother anyone. They had to be quiet and go to sleep. Otherwise, if they were noisy, they had to leave. I took in young people whose parents had kicked them out. They stayed at my place, but in return, they had to respect rules. Whenever they needed a place to stay, they could always come back. I believed in my heart they were good young people and somebody had to show them caring and kindness. They just needed someone to listen to what they were saying.

LATE SUMMER SEASON

WINTER SEASON

2005/03/26

FOUR DEMPSTER SCENES

I never did worry about food. We did not have much, but everyone ate. I understood these young people, their anger and frustration and how they took it out any way; they could because they felt they were given a raw deal. I too felt anger because of rejection. However, I had a wise person who cared about me. With Dadda's guidance, love and wisdom, I learned to do something else rather than surrender to my anger. Dadda always said, "Therese, don't waste your knowledge and strength on anger. Let people say whatever they want. They only hurt themselves. They are building your trail to the Creator's heaven. When you die, you do not have to do much to enter the gate to the home of our Creator, this path will be prepared for you by other people. Take care of your true friends; show kindness, and it will be returned. If for some reason, they meet with unfortunate accidents and you lose that friend, you will never find another who will replace them. Each friend is unique in his or her own way. Use the knowledge I gave you to do good things, kind things. Even though no one knows, it will bring you peace within yourself." Today I treasure friends who respect me. I try my best for them. And I have a lot of them.

CHAPTER 22

I Am Too Young To
Have a Heart Attack

One morning at the end of May 1980, I woke up with a pain in my abdomen. It felt like hunger pain. I got up and had something to eat. Later the pain was still there, the food I ate did not help any, but now there was a tightening in my chest. Still I did not pay too much attention. It seemed to get steadily worse as the hours ticked by. It was Saturday, and I had laundry and house cleaning to do.

By supper, it felt worse. Every time the pain came, I felt weak and dizzy. I could not stand it any longer. I told the children to get dressed, I bundled my baby, and we walked to the Eskimo Inn where Darryl was working. I left the children with him and went to the hospital. The doctor came and examined me and he admitted me. He did not say what was wrong. All he said was they had to do some tests and I would be better off in the hospital.

By this time, the pain was unbearable. It began in my abdomen and moved to my lungs. This made breathing difficult. Then it would move through my arms to my fingernails. I honestly felt the pain in my fingernails. I was so sick that night I did not sleep. The nurses were giving me Tylenol 3 tablets for pain every four hours, but it still did not help. In fact my pain seemed to worsen every time they gave me these tablets.

The nurses had their orders and I could not see a doctor until Monday morning, if I am still be alive by then.

A lady I knew worked at the hospital. Her name was Mary Venelsti Decker. When she saw how sick I was, she came to see me when her shift was done. I was barely speaking by then. I was very weak from all the pain. She asked if I wanted her to pray. I said "yes." I remember her prayers very well: "Dear Lord, spare Terry, take her pain away and make her well; her children need her. Terry is kindhearted and a joy to have around. Please Lord Jesus Christ hear me a poor servant, make Terry better. She has suffered a great deal in her life."

While she was praying, she was rubbing my arms. The massage felt good; it seemed to ease the pain a little. Evening came and I felt the same, not any better and not any worse. I asked the nurse to phone the doctor who had admitted me and asked if I could have a needle for my pain rather than pills. They said I had to wait until the next morning when he made his rounds. By this time, I began feeling much worse; I felt each pain might be my last. I could not stand it any longer, so I made my way to a pay phone in the hallway and phoned Darryl. I asked him if he could phone Doctor Heinz, my regular doctor, and tell him what was happening with me. He should tell them I could not take certain pain pills because of my illness in 1973 and that I was able to take only needles for severe pain, and that I was very sick, so please hurry. I knew this would make me have some sleep even if it was just for a few minutes. I was crying, so Darryl promised he would phone Doctor Heinz. At around 10:00pm, a nurse came and gave me a needle. Shortly afterwards, I fell asleep.

I woke at 3:00 a.m., and I rang for the nurse to ask for another needle. By this time, the pain seemed to have lessened. I went right back to sleep. Although the pain was still there, it was not as intense as it was the day before. I awoke to Doctor Heinz standing beside my bed calling my name. He asked how I felt. I said much better after I had had some sleep. The pain was still there but not as intense.

He listened to my chest with his stethoscope. Then everything began happening. Nurses wheeled me down to where a machine was located.

It was a cardiograph machine. A test was taken; then they took me back to my room.

A heart attack was the furthest thing from my mind. Even if the symptoms were similar to what I had read in books, it just did not seem possible. I was too young to have a heart attack. They gave me a needle; then the nurse gave me a little pill to put under my tongue. They also gave me extra pills and told me to follow the same procedure when the pain re-occurred. Later when the doctor came back to see me to give me the results of the test, he said I had, had a slight heart attack. He would know after more tests how much damage had been done to my heart. I had to be very careful because this was just a warning. If I had another, it might be my last. (He must be kidding). They were going to keep me in the hospital for at least a couple of weeks just to monitor my recovery.

When they finally discharged me it did not take me, long to go back to work. I was still in denial; I kept telling myself I was only 44. I was just too young for a heart attack. I could not die, I had never even begun to live, and my life would be over. I tried to recall if I had ever achieved or accomplished any of my dreams. I had not. I was always too busy just trying to survive with my children. The dreams I had as a young girl had been forgotten somewhere in my young years. I had lived for my children and to please others, never myself. My son was just two years old. Who would take care of him? Would Marie and June do it? They were just little. It would not be the two oldest girls; they were too self-ish. They only cared about themselves. It would not be Darryl either; he did not know what responsibility was. Once again, I turned to my Blessed Mother. She was the only one who could help. I prayed with all the faith I had.

Holy Mary Mother of God are you are tired of me always asking for my life, but I never ask for myself, I ask for my children's sake, the old-est ones because they have not found you, and the younger ones because they need me. Please ask your son Jesus to spare me once more and if it's his will, and I will get better, I will tell people about you and our Lord and all you have done for me. I will devote the time I have left to work for my Creator so people will believe in his goodness and in his love. I will tell people about you, Blessed Mother, that to love you and have a devotion to you is the greatest thing one can do in this troubled world. I will work with young people, children, old people, and the poor. With this prayer, I gave her all my dreams that I had and I prayed with all the faith I had in me.

Every day after this heart attack, things that I had been putting off all my life were constantly on my mind. The dreams and goals that I had at one time and kept telling myself I will attend to when the children leave home and in my old age had to become a priority. I had to start doing something.

The chest pain continued. Nitro pills helped when the pain got worse. My blood pressure continued to be dangerously high. The prescription they had given me did not stabilize it. My doctor said I had to quit working but, I said, the therapy that I needed at that time was to continue work. I did not want to think about it. To feel like an invalid would cause me to worry and I did not want that.

Every month that I got through safely, I patted myself on the back. In September 1980, Dr. Heinz said I needed open-heart surgery. I was constantly on nitro pills and now another heart pill, Isordill, because the Nitro could not do the work alone. I did not want to have the heart surgery, but the doctor said this was the only way to live a somewhat normal life. I did not want to believe him. I was working for the Gwich'in band as an outreach worker. I loved my job. I was still the Drug and Alcohol chairperson. I wondered how I could walk away from all this. I loved working with the people. There was a lot of work to do in this field. I just could not resign at this time. I never told my co-workers any of my health problems. I am sure if they known, they would have told me to resign.

The doctor said the hospital would make all the arrangements. They would set up the appointment for me with the best heart specialist in Canada, Dr. Frazer at the University Hospital in Edmonton. I did not want to go; I had had enough of hospitals. I was frustrated with my illnesses but I pretended there was nothing wrong with me.

My doctor said he had a patient who a few years previously had the same condition as I did. However, he had had the heart surgery, and today he lived a normal life; he could even join in a good square dance. Dr.

Heinz said if I wanted to talk with Bill and hear his story he could set up a meeting with him. I met Bill, who told me he was glad he had listened to his doctor because he now lived a healthier life.

I listened and thought, why not; maybe I can live a healthier life than I have now. I said fine when I can go. They sure did not waste any time. I was to leave December 12, 1980. I was afraid; I prayed with all my heart and faith to ask God to spare me and to ask my Blessed Mother to make a miracle that I would not need the surgery. I had had too many surgeries in my life. I just did not have the strength to go through a major one. My doctor said they had wasted enough precious time. He hoped I had accepted the surgery; it was for my own good. Dear Doctor Heinz, he had a severe heart attack later on, and he died quickly.

Little did I know then that I would outlive my physician? He was always concerned about one's health and one's spirituality. He walked with and believed in God.

December 12 came too soon. I boarded the flight to Edmonton. At the University Hospital, I began my tests the day after I arrived. The fourth day was the day that the doctor would tell me my fate. They would let me go home for a few days before my surgery to prepare my family. The day came. There was the doctor I dreaded to see. He said, "Terry, the damage done to your heart was minor. You won't need surgery after all, but you need treatment because the heart attack you had was caused by stress."

He suggested a stress program. The University Hospital had a six-month stress program. It was available to patients who in some way had their health affected by the stress in their life. He felt the program would benefit me. I did not know stress could cause a heart attack. He took me for a tour through the University Heart Unit and pointed out how many patients were there because of a heart attack caused by stress.

I believed him then. They were so young. He would let me go home, but I had to be back by January 4, 1981 when this program began. He wanted me to prepare my family. He would send a letter to my doctor in Inuvik, and to the regional head of the Department of Social Services agency to help my family if needed. If I wanted to live, I had to make some sacrifices. I had to resign from my job, and live away from my family for six months. They would provide the home for me. They would see to it I had no stressful situations. If I made this commitment, I would have to do what I was told. If I wanted to live a few more years, this was what I had to do.

How could he suggest living away from my family? They were my heartbeat. I said nothing; I just listened. Nevertheless, I had my prayers answered. I would not have the surgery after all. Now it was up to me to make some sacrifices and leave everything up to my Creator. I thanked him for this miracle. Many times when I was told I could not survive or was given a 50/50 chance, I never dwelt on the thought of dying. Yes, during those crises, I thought of my children. I asked my Blessed Mother to let me live and I prayed for my children's safety, but I never actually thought of dying.

CHAPTER 22

Chairperson for the Drug
& Alcohol Association

I left for home feeling sad. I decided to have a good talk with my doctor to tell him I did not want to enter the program in January. I would promise, however, to enter the next one on June 4, 1981. As a chairperson for the Drug and Alcohol association, our board had planned an Alcohol Awareness Week. It would begin January 9, 1981. With the hard work that we did to prepare for it, I did not want to miss this. It was important for me to be there. We had everyone in the community involved, the elementary and high schools, police, businesses, oil companies, the hospital and the clergy. I wanted to monitor the interest that was shown and to see if it would be a success. Then we could make it a yearly event.

Moira and Vaal was dedicated people who worked very hard alongside me to make the awareness week a success. I could never have done it without them. They were the key players. When I did not know what to do, we all got together and brainstormed. They gave me confidence. The Sir John Alexander Elementary School was given a one-week project, what was alcohol, what it was doing, and to suggest solutions. Because they were very young students, we asked them to express it through drawing. There were prizes to be given first, second, and third. The Samuel

Hearn High were also given similar task, it was more intense as they had to write a short story, saying if they thought it was a problem, each then to present a solution which they thought would be effective. There were prizes also for the students who presented the best recommendation.

Each morning we had someone from AA go on the local radio station to speak on the effects of alcohol and drugs. Others were involved in other projects, through speaking, showing films, and to make sure that materials and posters were left with interested parties. The project was a success with everyone involved, which made me very pleased.

To resign from my job was something else. As an outreach worker, I had many people who had become dear to me and many children whom I had met and cared for. To leave this behind meant I had to make a choice. It was to be able to live with my children just a bit longer or just to continue doing what I was doing and hope for the best. I chose my children because there was only me to care for them.

I was going to work as long as I could and in June, I would leave for Edmonton to take the stress program. I resigned from the Drug and Alcohol chair not long after the awareness week, but continued to work until March. I knew I had to quit. On one of my trips to Yellowknife, to attend a meeting, I ended up in hospital. When it happened the second time, I was finished.

The stress program in Edmonton came quickly; I left Inuvik on June 2, registered at the hospital on the third and began on the fourth. Each morning I left at 7:00 am. So I could be at the hospital for 8:00 and we finished at 4:00. This was my pattern every day, five days a week, for six months.

Although the hospital had arranged for me to stay at the Bonaventure Hotel, I had a generous offer from my cousin Agnes. She had just finished her second year at Grant Mac Ewan Community College and would be leaving for Whitehorse within a few days. She said if I wanted to take her apartment over, she would leave the damage deposit and would let the management know.

Darryl had refused help from Social Services. This was because of the letter written to them by the doctor from Edmonton about my case. They had said there were to be no worries, and they would provide for

231

my children would be well during the program so it would not interfere with the therapy. Darryl had promised he would take care of the children and I thought they would be better off in familiar surroundings. Nevertheless, they were phoning me every night, sometimes twice a day. Marie said they had nothing to eat, so I phoned Michael and Lorna and asked them to give them some meat if they had any, and some fish.

Darryl did not keep his promise. Most of the time, the children were alone all night with just Marie taking care of them. When they phoned in such distress, I did not know what to do. I wanted to complete this program. I wanted to be able to get better, but it was not going to happen if it was going to be like this.

I was crying one day after the kids phoned. I was torn between staying and just heading home. When Agnes asked what was wrong I told her all that was going on and that I did not know what to do. She offered to help so we decided to pool our money and get plane tickets for the children. Agnes had to leave for Whitehorse but before she, left she bought groceries for the children. I phoned Darryl, explained the situation and asked him to take the children to the airport.

When they arrived, although they looked pitiful, they were happy they had come to join me. This would not have been possible without the help of Agnes. I came alive as soon as I saw their smiling little faces.

We had no furniture, but the rug was thick so we were comfortable. We had no dishes so we bought tin foil plates, which were just as good and plastic spoons, forks and knives. We did not think we were poor. We were together, that was all that mattered.

The Health and Welfare Department in Yellowknife was supposed to send me a cheque for my expenses but I did not know when it would come. I told my doctors and therapist about my children's arrival and why. They did not agree with the decision I had made, but there was no other way. I explained to them that my children were my life; I could not breathe without my family. I had to have them with me. They were the reason I wanted to live. We could go through many hardships, but as long as we were, altogether we would be just fine.

The doctors finally saw my point and said they would assign a worker from their social services department who could help me through our difficult times. I agreed. Deep down, I was worried. What if the pills, did not work sometime? What would happen to my children if I just dropped dead? To have someone around my children I could learn to trust was fine with me.

Donna was the worker who came into our lives. She was a wonderful and understanding person who brought sunshine to our days. She became our friend and helped a great deal in my recovery. She was there when I was worried about things, or when I had to make a decision. She offered suggestions and this helped a lot. She was a person who thought positively and had a laugh to go with it. This was good medicine for me.

Mary was a woman assigned to my case. Her job was to take the children out to the park once a week or just spend that couple of hours with us. I owe my life to these good people of Alberta.

Every day I asked God for his mercy and asked his Mother Mary to intercede to take care of us, and she did. Because of the many unexplained incidents and happenings in my life, I have a very strong belief in the existence of my Creator. He has put people along my life journey to help me. Through people, I meet everyday of my life; I have begun to live positively and spiritually. There is no room for negativity. All this has made me realize that there is hope even when everything is hopeless. One has to have faith.

My children and I bought miscellaneous items at garage sales, and we picked up bottles. Every occasionally we treated ourselves to French fries and these had to be shared.

There were about 40 patients in the Stress Program. Within a few weeks, I made good friends. We were all there for health reasons and we had to change our lifestyle. Our health depended on how much we wanted to change. The therapists were there to help us, but we had to do the work. The longer I was there the fewer heart pills I was taking. I am no doctor but I believe very strongly that stress is a major factor in all heart attacks. All Stress and no exercise! To live and think positively is hard to do but to be aware of it makes life more challenging. I had to learn to live a stress-free life. If I wanted to regain my health, I had to follow the doctor's orders. When I left Inuvik, the older girls were not told where I was going to stay in Edmonton. The doctor said it was better this way; I did not need the worry about them too. That did not stop them; Arlene found me and then Marlene came soon afterwards.

In October, the family was called so the doctors and therapists could discuss my case with them. Darryl came from Inuvik. My family was told the cause of my heart attack, the progress I was making, and that it was imperative that this progress continued. Now it was up to them, my family, to do their part. Darryl had to begin to take his responsibilities seriously and the girls were told if they could not follow the rules their mother had set for them, they should not live at home. They should begin to live their own lives.

Two days later Darryl left for Inuvik. I was glad; I did not need the stress he caused me. The family's positive behavior and participation was essential for my recovery and he was not doing his part.

The program ended in December, but the patients had to do volunteer work for a month before then. I was to go to the Charles Camsell Hospital where on my first day they assigned me to the fourth floor. I was to help feed stroke patients and assist the nurses with little things that needed to be done. Being on that floor bothered me. I looked at the patients and thought that if I had a stroke, I might end up like this. I went to the volunteer supervisor and asked to be reassigned. She then had me accompany patients going to other hospitals by ambulance to get their treatments and tests. I was more comfortable with this type of work

Finally, it was our last day and we all had to go our own way but we promised each other we would keep in touch. I was happy it was over. I wanted to go home, but my doctor said in order to live a healthier life it had to be a quiet one. He had asked me how living in Edmonton was before moving back to Inuvik. I said it was very quiet, so he wrote a letter to the doctors telling them that it was better for me to live outside the northern community because prolonged stress would probably prove fatal.

I will be forever grateful to these dedicated people who have helped me livelong enough to see my Marie mature and give me three beautiful grandchildren. Millie married and is the mother of three children.

Moreover, June finished high school, found a good job and is married, Jerry, is going to high school, finishing his education. Not all this would have been possible without these good people, the help of my Blessed Mother and the Creator's mercy. Every evening I thank them for the day; every morning I thank them for my waking up and keeping us safe through the night. Sometimes when I am alone, I cannot believe that I have made it this far!

CHAPTER 25

Native Crafts

I began thinking of what could I do. What type of work could be available to someone who was partially disabled? There had to be something. I had already written an entrance test to Grant Mac Ewan Community College and had been accepted. My doctors did not believe this would be good for me because of the stress involved and the frustration it would cause. The continued growth of the adhesions in my abdomen prevented me from any type of physical work. I was a wreck in body but I had a healthy mind. I decided I could put this to work in the form of Native Arts and Crafts.

Although I have never considered my crafts as a money making source, I began to look at this in a different light. I knew how to draw and cut patterns, design, embroidery and bead. I could create my own work, as well as teach other people who would produce gift items for shops throughout Canada and possibly other countries in the future. Disabled people who were good with their hands could be taught this skill. We would create the best handmade quality crafts ever. Although people in the North looked to me as one of the best Native Crafts artisan I never considered myself in this way. However, they thought it so I had better get used to it.

I had never been involved in business before; how should I begin? I brainstormed and the best idea that I had was first to do research. If

I wanted to write a proposal for money to research the field of Native Crafts, because of my disability, I would not be eligible.

I would do this on my own time, where do I go. I visited the retail craft shops that were in the city. What were the wholesale price and retail prices? To find this out, I had to see what type of craft they purchased and sold. When I talked to people, I eased the topic of Native crafts into the conversation. I told them I was very interested in producing crafts which had market potential if it was done carefully. I only had work experience, no formal education. The research I set out to do was time consuming and complicated and the process slow. Quality work catches my attention; this is an advantage I had. I was proud of my work; it was done with meticulous attention to detail.

I did not get discouraged even though there is a huge difference when one tried to do such work with no money. It helps to have money to work with, as it brings you from point A to point B much faster.

I thought of all the people who were partially disabled through no fault of their own, who wanted to keep busy. If they had the use of their hands, it was still possible for them to be employed. It was not only the craft shop that I hounded, it was any store. The ideas and designs just kept coming to me. How could I change a certain design to fit the occasion? I really wanted to have a wholesale company with one exclusive shop, which would only provide custom-made orders. A big dream, but it was possible.

I spoke to people I felt could enlighten me in my search for answers. Some had negative responses. There is no money in the Native Arts & Crafts industry. No one wants to invest in the Native crafts project. Very few were positive. If the person was interested in hearing about the background knowledge, materials that were used, leather, fur, design and cutting the pattern, it gave me hope.

In the fall of 1982, the phone rang and June who was 8 years old at the time answered it. I knew from her answer and her facial expression that it was her father. She handed me the phone. Sure enough, it was Darryl. He was in Whitehorse and stranded. I was annoyed with him because he had upset June. I had always told him that no matter how much disagreement we had, do not upset the children, I knew what I was getting into, but my big heart took over. I told him to give me a call back in an hour. I would see what I could do because I do not believe in adults making their children a part of the war they created between themselves. I always dealt with my children's welfare the best I knew how. This meant not having their real father involved unless he asked. I do not, and I cannot stress this enough, I do not ever want children to feel unwanted. I am dead set against this type of treatment, not only to my own children but also to all children. I am a mother and a grandmother who cares what happens to them.

I phoned my cousin in Whitehorse and asked if it was possible to put Darryl up for a couple of days. When I explained why she said, no problem. He was Jerry's and June's father. I just could not see him stranded.

My bank statement told me I had over a hundred dollars and I was slowly working on a beaded moccasin. I knew where I could sell this product so I could come up with the rest of the money needed for a plane ticket. The fare was almost two hundred dollars and taxi fare was fifty dollars; I knew I would have to borrow a little. When Darryl phoned later, I told him Agnes was expecting him and his ticket would be there the next day; we would expect him on the afternoon flight.

All my life I always cared about people no matter who they were. If I knew I could help, I did. If June has ever blamed me for the break-up with her father, I would remind her that it takes two.

This incident was just one of the many things I did to try to keep a stable friendship with their father, for the children's sake. Although I did not need the stress, I would try my best not to let things worry me. At least now they did not have to worry about their father being stranded somewhere.

Some women would have told him, "I don't have any way to help you; get here on your own." I could never be that malicious with someone I know. Darryl had never beaten me up; he had only mistreated me. He slapped me a few times, verbally abused me, but that was because he had been drinking. I had to keep the relationship as peaceful as possible, but if he began taking advantage of me, I would do something about it. If he put pressure on me, he would have to go.

Darryl arrived and from the beginning, there was no communication between us. I had no trust in him; he had forgotten the doctor's words. If he cared, he would have remembered. Donna suggested counseling, but this did not help. He drank whenever he wanted, then he would pick an argument with me. I was too depressed over the decision I had made. Nevertheless, someway, somehow, I had to get myself motivated again. The spring of 1983, Darryl found a new friend. She drank as much as he did so they deserved each other. He moved in with her shortly afterwards. I knew June was hurt. Jerry was too young to understand. He had his mom by his side; he could not care less.

I began to take an interest in my crafts again. I had done the basic work but what to do next? I would have to market my crafts. Well, to whom? People of course! Nevertheless, how? First, I had to promote Terry's Products. To do this I needed finished items. One producer could not do all the work that is involved. I pitched the idea I had to my daughters and asked for their help. It would teach them the value of Native crafts. They did know how to do crafts, but not well enough. I said I would teach them all I knew so they could do crafts of their own. If they had to sew, I wanted them to feel confident.

Their interest in producing crafts did not come instantly. I felt it was important that they enjoy it. Creating and designing takes time so to take up sewing, first it had to be a hobby. Pride in creating a piece will follow. I had to continuously remind them that this would benefit them someday. I worried about my children. I was still on Nitro and Isordill pills. There was less pain, but once in awhile chest pains and dizziness did come without warning. I took the nitro, then I would relax for about 10 to 15 minutes and continue what I was doing. I began to get headaches, unbearable headaches, after these attacks.

One day I sent the children to school and began to do my morning chores. My cup of coffee was at the kitchen table and I was by my couch. I always carried my pills even just to cross the room because if a pain hit me suddenly, I would never be able to get them.I felt discomfort in my chest, warning me that the pain would follow. I opened my container to take a pill and leaned back on the couch until I was able to breathe normally and the weakness began to disappear.

Usually after a few minutes, I would be able to continue but not this time. When I tried to get up to get my coffee, the pain hit me again. I took the pills again (Nitro could be taken every 15 minutes, Isordill, every four hours) and lay back in the same position. After what seemed like hours, I saw that only an hour- and- a- half had passed. I had no phone either and since I was recuperating well, Donna only came twice a month to check in and make a report on my progress. Many things went through my mind. What if my children came home and found me dead? Their father was gone and I knew it would hurt them very much.

I could not think like this. I got up slowly. No pain. I took a step forward; again, no pain. I was still holding the pills in my hand. I went to get my coffee to refill the cup and put on my jacket. It was a nice spring day. I was going to sit outside. At least if something did happen, someone would find me and report it. They would take me away before the children came home.

I tried to stay calm as I sat outside. There I wrote the number to call and who should look after the children. It was at that time I began to think about finding a father for my children. It had to be someone with a kind heart. He would take care of the children if something happened to me.

I decided to talk to Darryl and try to persuade him to come home for the children's sake. We were adults, I told him. We had to think of the children. He had to give up his girlfriend. He said she was not going to let him go. He wanted to live at our house but also keep on seeing her. I did not agree with this and was very angry about his decision. I could not believe he would choose her over his children. He came and stayed a couple of days, but when he went to pick up his clothes, he never came back. I was past hating. He had all the chances I was going to give him. If this was his choice, it was his loss.

SAMPLES OF TERRYS CRAFTS

CHAPTER 25

Mother's Greatest Sorrow

It was the spring of 1984 and although I did not drink, sometimes I would go to the Cecil Hotel bar on Jasper Avenue. All the Northerners went there when they came to the city. If I happened to meet someone from the North, I would sit down with them and have a cup of coffee. One day as I walked in and looked around, I heard someone call my name. It was Debbie, Lee's youngest daughter from his first marriage. She came over to me and began to cry. I knew something had happened to one of the family, maybe her father. After she calmed down a bit, she said Lee was trying to get reach me; it was bad news. Debbie said they had asked the police to help them locate me. Thank God, I had come to the hotel.

It was my son Fredrick. He had taken a number of prescription pills with alcohol as a chaser. He was brought to the hospital but they could not save him. I wanted to scream; I wanted to cry; I felt so much anger. I wanted to destroy something, anything. It lasted only for a moment; then tears began to trickle down my cheeks, but no sound came.

I told Debbie to phone her dad and give him the number, and then I went home. I grieved for my son. I remembered everything about him, his first little parka that I made for him.

Why had this happened? I blamed myself; then I blamed Lee. I hated him more for causing so much pain. Lee phoned and he wanted me to go to Fort Destiny for my son's funeral. He said he would pay for my ticket both ways and would send money to pay for a baby sitter while I made the trip.

I asked him why now? Couldn't he have offered his help while Fredrick was alive? I said I did not want to attend Fredrick's funeral. I did not want to see him put six feet under the ground. I wanted to remember my son alive somewhere, laughing and enjoying life, as if he was with, the young people his age. He had so much to live for.

I remember once when Fredrick told me his father controlled his life. The children had to do what their father told them to do. This was one reason Fredrick could not stay long whenever he came for a visit. I remember my own life with Lee. He wanted to control me too. He wanted me to be his property and to do everything his way. If I did not, I would be kicked, slapped, and punched. How can a person be so mean and yet remain alive?

During this sad time, I talked to my second son Gene. It was the first time I had a good talked to him in years. It surprised me when he called me Mom. After we had talked about Fredrick he said, "Mom, I am sorry for everything, for hating you because Dad said you left us. He said you were a bitch and a slut. He said many bad things about you. However, Fredrick told me different. He said you were one of the nicest persons he had met. He knew you loved us, because he remembered you a little. Lately I asked people who knew you. Before I did not want to know because I believed what my Dad had said. However, since Fredrick is gone, and I remember what he had said, I began to ask questions. The people here talk very highly of you. They told me you are a nice person, loving, kind and a hard worker. Mom, after all these years, I want to say I am sorry for everything. I wish things could have been different, but since it is this way I guess we will have to get to know one another in the future."

I thanked my son for what he had said; then I told him I have loved him and will always love him no matter what, and not to blame himself for what adults do and say. I told him just to concentrate on his life. I was his mother and I would be there for him always, whether he stayed with his Dad or wherever he chose to be. I do not believe in the parents making the children choose. Parents should always be thankful for their children's well being. I told Gene I wished he could visit us, as I wanted to see him. He promised he would come. We were both very sad about Fredrick but l did not suspect that anything else was wrong. For the first time we talked and we were able to share our grief. Fredrick would have been very happy. He would have wanted it this way.

A few weeks later, I received another phone call. This time it was about Gene. He had followed his brother. When Lee called he said, "Why did this have to happen to me? I loved my sons very much. Why?" This time I was angrier. I wanted to say it was for all the hurts you caused, our boys paid the price. Nevertheless, I said nothing. All I did was to listen.

Maybe some people thought it was mean of me not to attend my boys' funerals but I believe very strongly in life after death. When it is my turn, I will meet them again. In the meantime, I liked to think they were traveling freely wherever they wanted to with the wind and feeling at peace. My Creator gave them to me for such a short time; now he wanted them back. It was his will.

I began to watch my son Jerry constantly. I had to be everywhere he was. I even took him out of school for a short time and when he went back to school I would sit outside the school until it was time to take him home. I did not know what I was going to prevent, but nothing was going to happen to him if I could help it.

A friend finally told me it was not good for him. Jerry did not understand why suddenly I had become so possessive. I had to get a grip on myself. I turned to prayer. I said my Rosary every day for my sons Fredrick and Gene, and I asked my Blessed Mother to protect my son Jerry from all harm.

When I see young people, I think of my boys and what they would be doing if they were still alive. If I had gone back to Lee when he wanted me to, I know what would have happened when he drank. Maybe things would have end tragically; it was best for me to stay away. By leaving, I thought there was always a chance that someday I would have the money to take my children. Dear God, it never happened.

I wanted to write my story because the hatred I had for Lee ruled my life. I could never say I forgave him for what he did to me, emotionally, verbally, as well as physically. The words he had flung in my face had broken my spirit into a million pieces and it may take a lifetime to heal. My anger surface when something reminds me of him. I hope telling my story will let me go foreword in peace.

Thanks to my husband, Tom, for his patience and understanding, I began to believe I could be a good person and try to live a peaceful life. I grieved for my sons who were too young but praying for them, made me learn to accept the will of Our Creator.

There were many setbacks in my craft research, but I continued doing my work at my own pace and on my own time. I began designing jewelry. It was all I could do for the time being. Then I met Bobbi. She was working for Alberta Native Arts and Crafts. Bobbi said there were grants available for skilled artisans. I told her a little about my illness and made her swear that she would never repeat what I told her. As Native people, we have so many strikes against us. This happens especially when we apply for jobs. If anyone knew of my health condition, I would never be hired.

Bobbi obtained some part-time work for me, telling elementary school children stories about my Native culture, and traditional crafts. I told Bobbi I did not want people feeling sorry for me. I wanted them to treat me normally. If they wanted me to do a job, it was because they believed in my skills and that I would do the job well. Determination and challenges were the best qualities I had. I THOUGHT.

The challenge was to produce no matter what stood in my way. Many times, I said to my children, when I say I am sick, it is because I am very sick. Otherwise, I would be working on crafts and other things until I go to bed at night. There is no time to lie down because there is so much to do. The most I sleep at night is five hours. When I die, I will forever sleep. Today I am not going to waste my precious time.

That fall I met Tom who was to become my future husband. He had lost his wife in 1980; they had no children. He became our friend; he was lonely by himself and making friends with my family was easy. Because of the children's upbringing, they made friends easily. They notice people with good attitudes instantly. Tom was working out of town, so we have to see him when he got back to the city.

Now that I had finished many small gift products, where would I begin to market them? Again, Bobbi came to my rescue. (God bless her, she was always there when needed, and she passed on to a better world a few years later May she rest in peace). She phoned me when people wanted some Native crafts for a show, and I went. This helped me to promote my crafts, and it made me meet people. I loved this. I met people from all over the world. My youngest children came with me and they enjoyed themselves too. Bobbi helped to keep my dream alive. I knew I had to promote my crafts to people throughout Canada. I knew I had to learn about what people wanted, exactly what they were looking for. I had to get to know crafts of all the aboriginal people, from the East to the West and the North to the South. I have to know many craft producers, to make it more interesting.

It was necessary to know the climate, the type of clothing, and the materials they used in making their products. If we had to serve the people internationally, we had to know what products would serve the people best in what country. Accumulating supplies was what I did, a bit at a time but it was worth it. Keeping emotionally active was the best therapy for my recovery. To participate in a craft show was part of my dream. To be able to have enough finished products was another? To write my story and document Gwich'in culture was yet another.

My daughters began participating in the selling of the crafts and began to design their own jewelry. When we were called to do a craft sale at Heritage Days for the Native Friendship Center we were excited. I had taught my children that their knowledge of a finished product is very important. This would give them confidence in answering people's questions. Their attitude was also important, as was their personality. They had to think of this as "introducing your Nation to other Nations." This would open doors of communication and build relationships. Attitude and behavior play a major role in how successful one gets in the business world. It is a win or lose situation. Now my children have a good knowledge of crafts, especially Marlene and Marie. They could be craft instructors if they were on their own, and they could teach people to become producers. I have never given up hope in the Arts and Crafts being part of the Aboriginal economic industry.

The girls' enthusiasm was short-lived as there was no income. The money we made went to buying more supplies. Purchasing supplies at retail cost did not buy us much. I continued in 1987. By now, people were becoming aware of our crafts. If they wanted finished products in quantity, I could not do it. Still I felt it was a major progress when my girls gave this much of their time. In today's generation, where youth seem to feel they have worked if they pushed a button, my daughters giving that much of their time was considered a success.

As they learned later, hard work and the feeling of achievement is a very positive experience. We met people from all over the world; it was interesting and fun. The long hours it took to make certain products were forgotten. I cannot describe the sense of pride this gave me to be able to meet people from all over the world and from all walks of life. It was a joy to me. The slow process I believed now was lack of education and lack of confidence to pursue a business. I had the knowledge and the talent; I just did not know how to begin.

My friend Tom used to go out drinking once a month. This made me very uncomfortable. I did not see the fun in drinking; I thought it was a waste of time. He was never mean; he just acted stupid. I told him if he wanted a serious relationship, he had to make a decision about his drinking because I was not going to put up with the drinking from anyone. He said he was going to quit because he could not see his future without my family. I thought to myself, this I have to see before I believe it. I was in no hurry. However, he did it.

Since our relationship had become serious, the children had to be consulted, especially the younger ones. This was their home. What they had to say had to be taken into consideration.

During this year, I had taken Nitro pills only about twice. I did have shortness of breath and felt dizzy periodically, but this was because I had high blood pressure. I had to keep my direction as positive as I could. I knew how it was to live with chest pains never knowing if you can make it through this one. I was not going to jeopardize the major progress I had made.

247

Darryl did see the children once in awhile. I always brought the children to him for a short visit. When he and his girlfriend drank, they would phone and tell me I was an unfit mother. She would say she had a lot of money and that she could hire a lawyer to take the children away from me. I was fed up with this threat, so I went to the Family Social Services and asked for custody of the children. I wanted to put an end to this harassment. I told the family court I wanted custody of the children but I would grant permission to Darryl for visiting rights at least one day a month. There was no problem, and it was done.

Now he had no excuse not to show up. He had to obey the courts. He was given the first weekend of each month from 10:00 a.m., Saturday to 7:00 pm. Sunday night. He was also told clearly, that the phone calls should stop.

One Saturday, I brought the children to the Bay downtown to meet their dad. We had coffee. He did not look too well, so I asked if he was ill. He said not really but his back and his legs were giving him problems. He had made an appointment with his doctor for later on during the coming week. I knew this person. I knew the harassing phone calls were not his idea. I thought our friendship was good and that we had the children's interest at heart. Even though I felt he did not do enough, I understood that he was in no position to do so. However, he cared in his own way.

On January 14, 1988, after we had finished supper I asked Tom to sit with the children while I went to bingo. I did not have much money so I walked to the closest bingo hall. I always phoned home if I went out. When I phoned during the intermission, Tom said he had some bad news. Instantly I thought of the girls, but he said it was Darryl. He had had a severe heart attack and they had taken him to the University Hospital. His girlfriend had phoned to tell us this. I knew he was not well but this news was a shock. It was during a break so I went outside and walked around praying he would be all right. I went back into the hall to finish the game, and then I walked home. I wanted that time to myself so I could think.

When I got home, I knew something was wrong by just looking at Tom. He said, "Terry I am sorry. They were able to revive Darryl for a few minutes, but his heart stopped again after he was brought to the University Hospital. He is dead".

My God, I was not ready to hear news like this. June was not asleep so when she heard me come in, she came downstairs. She took one look at me and began to cry. She said, "Mom tells me my dad is going to be okay." I could not answer her. I was in shock too. All I could do was hold her. After a while, I told her about her dad and that he died painlessly. He had had a hard life. If he could not look after them, it was because he could not. It was not because he did not want to.

Jerry was too young. He did not understand what was going on. For the next few days June was devastated, and tormented with grief. She cried a lot. She kept saying, "I didn't have a chance to tell my daddy how much I loved him." I told my little girl to tell her dad because he could hear her, and that he was more in a position to help her. To see my girl grieving was hard to take. You want to say something to ease the pain, but there is nothing you can say; you can only be there. Darryl's sister and her husband came from Calgary to attend his funeral. His girlfriend was there too. I was able to tell her I was sorry.

It took a long time for June to get over her father's death. My poor baby had to endure this. Sometimes I used to catch her crying, and I knew why. All I could do was being there for her. It took some time before I got over Darryl's death too. This cannot be helped if you have known a person well. I prayed that he went to our Creator for the peace that he had longed for. Although he was the only son, he felt he was never part of his family. They had looked down on him because he was never successful like the sisters he had. I was glad he did not have to suffer.

CHAPTER 25

My Uncle Amos

In March, my cousin Louise phoned to say my Uncle Amos and her sister Elsie were coming out to Edmonton because her father was very sick. He had a bad cold and although he was put on medication, his coughing continued. We all thought it might be tuberculosis. Some tests were taken at the Inuvik hospital and there was a spot showing on his lung, so they were sending him to Edmonton for more tests.

The evening they were to arrive, I went to Charles Camsell Hospital to greet them. My uncle did not look well but he was happy just to see me. I did the interpreting for him in my Gwich'in language for his admission.

After he went through this process, we wheeled him to the ward. My uncle always thought the world of me especially towards the end. He saw me as the only person who understood the Elders. I was the only link between the old ways and the new because I understood both worlds.

Many times my uncle said, "Therese, I trust you because what I say will be repeated as I say it. Because our young people do not understand our language, what we say in our language is that sometimes interpreted wrong or exaggerated. You, Therese, understand us well." Amos was my mom's stepbrother. When I lived in Inuvik, he stayed with me every time he came to town. Louise worked nights and slept days so she could not entertain her dad when he was there. This job fell to me and I did not mind a bit, I loved it because he told me stories.

My uncle drank his beer and told stories of his young days, when he traveled the land, when he was single, and later as a married man with some young children. I never got tired of his stories. I was my uncle's interpreter while he was in the hospital. The doctors said they suspected cancer. I had to take him to Cross Cancer Clinic for many tests. The results did show that he had cancer and it had advanced too far. He might have three to four months to live. There was nothing more possible to do. He could leave for home whenever he wished to. Later, when the pain worsened, they would provide him with pain pills, which would make him, sleep most of the time. I felt sad. To me he was the only link to the Arctic Red River history and the histories of the Remi's and the Ritchie's. He knew the old ways of how the kinfolks related to one another. I knew enough, but I wanted someone to help me know more. The help from an older person would have been more inspirational. Now he was leaving us and I could not do anything. I felt so helpless. Although I was not his daughter, I felt closer because I was the oldest of the family. He said it was my turn to take over as head of the family. He did not mention his sister or his adopted brother. He named me as head of the Remi's and the Ritchie's clan.

He said, "Therese, no one takes the time to know the true knowledge and culture of our people. You know the true culture of our people. You have kept the ways of our people. You have lived in both worlds. One you had to live in because you had to work to feed your children; it was something that had to be done, but you have not swayed from your culture. You speak our language well and you have the understanding of our culture. You will outlive me; now it is your turn to take over as head of the family."

Those were the words of my uncle. Our people followed these patterns not so many years ago. I was brought up with the beliefs and teachings of my culture, but when we lost him, some of it went with him and I am one of the last ones to hold the true culture of my Gwich'in people.

My uncle and I understood this pattern, but it was not the ways of our young people anymore. They were taught by the white society. This makes their culture European. They do not know enough of either side so it confuses them. They do not know respect. When the clan elder dies, the power he has held is passed on to the next Elder of the clan, but sometimes he makes an exception and gives it to someone of his choice. My grandfather Dadda gave me his blessings before he died, but for my uncle to give me his, this was a real privilege. Before my Uncle went home, I explained to him all that the doctors had said. He wanted me to go back to Arctic Red River with him but it was impossible.

I promised him someday soon I might have the opportunity to visit. He was pleased by this promise. After he had gone back to his community, his health deteriorated quickly. In May, his daughters Louise and Elsie phoned. They said their dad was failing fast and they did not think he had much time left. He had kept asking for me so if it was possible, could I go to see him? Financially I could not make it. I was barely surviving. They offered to pay my way, as it was Uncle's wish. I said I would go.

Now I had to make plans. I was not going to travel without my children; they were my strength. We decided to rent a car from Rent a Wreck as none of my daughters had a car then. "Rent a Wreck" has some very good reliable cars to rent. My daughter Marie would do the driving with some help from her cousin Liz. My oldest daughter's boyfriend rented the car for us on his Visa card. Arlene's boyfriend Don gave us some money for the insurance.

These people helped to make this trip possible. If we were very careful, we would have enough money for gas to Arctic Red River and for food on the way. There were my daughters Arlene, Marie, and June, my son Jerry, my two-year-old granddaughter Christina, my niece Liz and her son Robert.

The weekend we were to leave, I got a call from my cousin Elsie. She asked if I could hurry, as her dad was very ill. He kept asking when I was going to arrive. On June 11, 1988, we left Edmonton. The first evening we traveled as far as Dawson Creek and slept at a motel.

Early the next morning we arrived in Whitehorse. We went over to my Cousin Agnes's home and went to sleep for a few hours. We had a good shower and breakfast and were on our way again by noon. We

252

arrived at the Junction by late afternoon. This is where the highway separates, with the Alaska Highway straight North and the Dempster Highway, East. The highway sign said it was 371 km to the next gas station and rest stop at Eagle Plains Lodge.

We were somewhere between Junction and Eagle Plains at about 11:00 pm. Marie was driving and I noticed she slowed down, as the car seemed to swerve a little.   She said, "Mom I think we have a flat tire." We were in a valley with mountains on both sides. We had the midnight sun so we were not worried. We all missed the midnight sun so to have the sun all night, who wanted to sleep. The girls were having fun taking pictures. We could change tires with no problem. We all got out; stretched, and walked around before we went to work. When we started lifting the car, our jack handle broke. By this time, the other tire had also gone flat. Now we only had three good tires for the car, and two bad ones. It was close to midnight and on Highway, there is very little traffic at this time. The Mackenzie River ferry and the Peel River ferry had just begun to operate and they had shut down at 12.30am, and so the traffic on the Dempster highway would be slow at this time of the year.

CAMBELL LAKE INUVIK AREA

TSIIGEHTCHIC FERRY & CAMP

ONE OF MANY UNUSUAL ROCK
FORMATIONS

FOOTHILLS OF MOUNTAINS

FOUR DEMPSTER PICTURES

254

We were stranded for the night. I said to the girls that we had to do the best we could. I did not think there was a chance of going anywhere until the next day. I told the girls that the land was grizzly bear country and if we saw one we should make sure, we did not disturb it. If it did come over to the car, they must do exactly what I told them to do. Grizzly bears do not harm anyone if respect is shown to them. The only time they become easily angered is when they have a cub. Because we had children, we had to be responsible for our actions.

The mosquitoes were terrible at this time of the year and we had no insect spray. After our talk, I walked along the road praying silently to my Blessed Mother for help. I took my Rosary out of my pocket. I asked her to send some help as we had small children. It was our first visit on the Dempster Highway. We did not know how far we were from Eagle Plains, a place halfway between The Junction and Fort McPherson. There it had a hotel a restaurant, lounge, rooms and a gas station.

Just as I finished my rosary, I thought I heard a vehicle. I was not sure though, so I listened again. Then I heard it again, very faint but I was sure I heard something.

Everyone was in the car, in order to get away from the mosquitoes. Towards Eagle Plains, I could see the road coming down to the valley. I saw a truck appear, then another. I was excited. From the Junction, another truck was coming. This was too good to be true. Silently I thanked my blessed Mother. I made a sign to the girls pointing in both directions. Excitedly, they got out of the car. I felt happy for them because they were not used to being stranded out in the middle of nowhere. The oldest ones could handle it, but the little ones were my concern.

All the big semi-trailer trucks arrived at the same time. The drivers got out and asked if we had some problems. Did we ever! Our jack was broken and we had two flat tires. They asked where we were going.

I told them my uncle was very sick and he was asking for me, so we were on our way to Arctic Red River. We were coming from Edmonton. Then they asked if we had mosquito dope. We said "NO;" Axe. "No." Everything they asked if we had, we said no.

They said if you are Northerners why you aren't traveling like real Northerners. You should be well prepared; you should have all the supplies you need to travel the North Country. The two trucks going to the junction took the girls with the two flat tires. The truck that was going to Eagle Plains took the children and. The children and I went with the truck that was heading west. Once we got to Eagle Plains, I was to wait there for the girls. I was very tired, so as soon as we were on our way, I fell asleep. The next thing I heard June calling me. She said we were at Eagle Plains. I gave the girls all the money I had, so now I had to phone Louise. Her husband Jim got us a room on his visa. This gave us a chance to have a good shower and sleep while we waited for the girls.

It was about 9:00 a.m. in the morning when they arrived. I felt sorry for my poor daughters. They were all very tired as they had been busy right through the night. They all had a shower, and then we left for Arctic Red River. The gravel road was slow to travel. There was not enough traffic at that time of the season and after the spring thaw, the road needed padding. We were afraid to have another flat so we were very careful. We arrived in Arctic Red River at about 4:00 pm. Everyone was waiting for us; Elsie was looking after her dad at her house so his apartment was made ready for us.

My Uncle Amos was very happy to see the children and I had made it safely, but he wanted to know why it took us so long to get to Arctic Red River. I said we drove; it is a long way from Edmonton. Uncle talked a lot when he felt better. Because he was very sick, he took pain pills, which made him, sleep a lot. I was glad he was not suffering too much. He kept saying he had a bad cold, but deep down he knew he had an illness, which was terminal.

The girls stayed overnight and rested. The next day they were off to Inuvik to visit with friends. My little granddaughter, Ann, June Jerry, and I stayed behind. A few days later, I asked my Uncle if I could go to Inuvik and visit with my friends, as I wanted to see them all before I left. He said sure, but not to be gone too long. I was in Inuvik for only two days. The trapper's dance was held the evening of my arrival. I was able to see everyone there.

A few days later after a good visit with friends, I was back in Arctic Red River. We stayed until the end of June, and then I told Uncle Amos that it was time for me to leave for Edmonton. He did not answer me. I kept bringing it up in our conversation but he did not answer.

I could not leave until he gave me his blessing. One day without me bringing it up, he began to talk as soon as I got to his room. He said, "Therese, I don't want to be selfish, I know you have a life of your own and other commitments, but when you are here I feel very comfortable. I should be grateful, you had a long way to come and see me. Now you can go back to your home. I wanted to see you once more, and now my wish has been granted. I am pleased. Take good care of your children and yourself, and do not forget our Creator in whatever you do. He is still the boss".

I phoned the girls in Inuvik and told them to come and pick me up. I wanted to make a trip to Inuvik just to get a few things we needed for the trip home. This done, we were on our way. When I went in to my uncle to say goodbye to him and give him a hug, he said "Therese, why do you want to go back to Edmonton? There is nothing there but rocks." He meant it was a big city with many people, but one might as well live alone in the middle of nowhere as it has too many people. So it did not matter how many people there were, you were still alone.

The trip back to Edmonton was long and tiring, but with no problems and we arrived without a flat tire. A few days later, I received a phone call at 2:00 am. My uncle had passed away. I was very sad. I felt another part of me had been taken away. I did not go back to sleep the rest of the night. I recalled how my uncle had been so much part of my life. I felt that slowly with each Elder passing, the old ways of thinking, and our traditional culture was slipping away, and I couldn't hang on to it. I had the teachings and the stories, but I wanted some Elders with me so I could tell the stories as if they told it.

I knew I had to let uncle go as he was very tired and he wanted peace and rest. I said goodbye. I promised him I would do my best in my lifetime for all my Elders who had gone before me. Their histories should have been documented. I felt with the passing of each elder, a part of our history is forever gone. So would their teachings and stories. Their language would be recorded for their great-grandchildren

As each one of my Elders pass on, I felt great sorrow. Slowly our stories, our history was disappearing. Each one held a story of the past, the historical stories of the Gwich'in Nation. I know stories from elders were being gathered, but yet many other stories are untold.

CHAPTER 27

Ben Calf Robe Junior
High School 1989

I was involved with the Native Parents Advisory Board and with Trevor who was the Native Education Co-coordinator for the Separate School Board. I was interested in the education of our children and why so many drop out each year. Somehow, I wanted to help these children to stay in school.

During one of our meetings, we were discussing ways to keep the native children in school and I brought up the police as a subject. I had taught my children to have great respect for the police because they were our protectors as were the firefighters. They help save lives, they do not think of their personal safety, but always of others. I told my children, when you see them, greet them with a hello and wish them a good day. Police are not to be feared if you do not do anything against the law.

I felt our young children should have a program where the police came to the schools and build a trust with the police. St Charles school was located close to where the city Police had their office. I met Kevin who was the police officer for this community. Trevor spoke to him about a project the students could do; they had native crafts project in mind. Kevin asked if I would be able to help him draft a proposal for this project. We got our grant and the project was to begin in September.

The students at Ben Safe Robe junior high loved and became friends with Kevin, and this was one-step forward and a joy for me.

During this time, I received a call from Chief Peter from Arctic Red River. He wanted to know if I was interested in acting as a delegate for the Arctic Red River band when the Dene had their assembly in Yellowknife, NWT in July. This meeting had to do with Land Claims. I agreed to go.

Jerry, my son, and I left for Yellowknife by Greyhound Bus. When we arrived in Yellowknife, we had to go out of town about 20 miles to Detta. Many people from the Northern communities were attending the assembly. It was fun visiting and meeting everyone. Each day the assembly began at 9 a.m. and continued all day. If we were not finished, what was on the agenda for that day the meeting went late into the night. No matter how tired everyone was, a drum dance followed.

When community concern was on the agenda, it was what I had waited for, as I wanted to address an important issue that I had thought about for quite some time. I addressed my concern to the assembly.

"For many years now, the Northwest Territories have used Alberta hospitals facilities. As a child, I recall the Charles Camsell Hospital was used for TB patients who needed further treatment. This could not be done in the North so the patients and their families were sent south to this hospital.

At present, the University Hospital and the Misericordia Hospital are used also in some cases. I feel that persons who are familiar with the North and its people should establish a support program. More concern is needed for persons such as relatives of patients who passed on. There are phone calls to be made in support of someone who has lost a husband, wife, or a child.

This should be looked at seriously. Our patients then could feel there was someone they could identify with. Students who come down South to further their education for the first time have difficulties experiencing city life. The loneliness and the frustrations they go through trying to adjust and adapt to a completely new and different lifestyle are frightening.

We want these students to finish their studies. We need them, when Land Claims are negotiated and signed. I would rather see graduates and money invested successfully than have students quit in the middle of the year because of loneliness or not adapting to city life. There is much discrimination amongst people in the city who are not familiar with people from isolated communities of the North. For some, it is hard to handle. Our native people have to have helped to regain the self-confidence that they have lost during the assimilation process.

Having a lack of confidence brings many tears and hurts. For example, speaking and writing English is difficult and many cannot express themselves as well as their fellow students. Non-native children never accept you into their group because there is lack of understanding. This makes young children become more withdrawn and then angry. When applying for a job once they see what nationality you are, excuses are made.

Applying for a house to rent, once they see you are a native, they say, "Sorry the suite has been rented." Your children are always watched. They have already made up their mind about what kind of person you are as soon as they see you are an aboriginal person. Statements made by European society go back in history because the government with no association with the rest of society has kept the native people in the closet so long.

I believe our culture and our way of life were not properly introduced. A few aboriginal persons do break away from their own tribe and then go on his or her own. These brave souls face many problems. Their own tribes exclude them because they have chosen to work and live a different lifestyle. Your people look at you as a traitor; you have left them. It never enters their mind that you have to work in order for your family to survive. The dominant society is saying to you, go and stay on your reserve. All this negativity touches all native people especially throughout this last century. This is particularly true in the case of Aboriginal woman and their children. When an Aboriginal woman marries a non native person, her status is taken away and also her children's. An Aboriginal man marries a non native woman and instantly becomes a status and all the children from the marriage, my opinion on the subject, big time discrimination, against aboriginal women.

I feel that the governments have to compensate the native people for all the damage that has been done, physically, emotionally, and spiritually. Their spirit has been broken by oppression by the so-called organizations set up to represent the government. Support is needed in all areas for those among our people who have taken a step forward. They need strength so they can lead our people into the Canadian society where they have belonged since the beginning of colonization. We have to support our people who strive for education so they can help pave the way for our people to become independent".

I addressed this presentation to the Dene Assembly. It was at this Assembly that the Gwich'in walked out, as they felt the land claim negotiations had dragged on long enough. Despite the many dollars spent, they were no further ahead. I understood this. The part I did not understand was why they had walked out. This, I thought was very childish. To sit across from the people from each region and explain to them why you want to pursue land claims by region, because you thought the process was too slow, would have been more appropriate. Maybe this would speed up the process. This would let each region that thought there was more work to done decline from the signing until they felt comfortable, and the regions that were ready could go ahead and make their claim agreement with the Federal government.

Certain clauses in the claim agreement, which needed more work, could have been studied, before being accepted by the people and the government. If it was done in this manner, there would be no bad feelings and everyone would have understood.

I had abstained from this vote not because I was a traitor nor went against my people wishes but because my belief was to sit there and try to work out our misunderstanding. I believed then and now that Aboriginal people have to go forward in unity, striving for independence, having the future of our children in mind and asking Our Creator daily to give them a well thought out agreement for now and into the future.

Now my chief from Tsiigehtchic was not going to pay my bus fare back to Edmonton. It was not my intention to create a barrier I just wanted adult behavior. Because of this now, I am on the other side of the fence. I do not feel guilty for my actions then, and I still do not today. I approached the Dene Nation Chief who found some money to pay my transportation back to Edmonton. Delegates were being paid an honorarium, plus accommodation and meals.

I was a delegate too but they did not pay me like the rest of the delegates. This I felt was the injustice and unfairness done by some of my people. To go through an experience like this made me a stronger person although it hurt me terribly, this act of rejection. I learned to give it to my Creator to deal with because I did not know how. I had a good visit with my nieces, nephews, sister, friends, and joined in the drum dances and feasts until I left for Edmonton.

September came and I went to work for Ben Calf Robe Junior High. I did not know what to expect from the youth. I was from another tribe, and I did not speak their language. I felt great love for my students as I began to know them. I looked at them as my children. I loved teaching them to sew, teaching them to go out to the markets and sell their own crafts to the public and not to be shy but to be polite to people they met. The police officer, Kevin, made friends with the children easily as he was very good with the youth. They respected him, and he was good to work with. I loved my job and the young people.

In March, the chest pains reoccurred. Finally, in April, I could not take it any longer. I went to see Dr. Mac Govern. My blood pressure was high, and I was no longer fit to work. I was very sad; I would miss the children whom I had grown close to. Now I could work at my own pace. If I got tired, I rested until I could continue again. In the stress of rushing, my heart had been disagreeing. Someday I told myself, when I have my own craft place, these young people will work for me. I would teach at my own pace, on my own time, with my own money. In the meantime, I was back to the same routine, taking it easy and seeing the doctor every two weeks just to monitor my recovery.

CHAPTER 27

Who Am I?

In January, Chief, phoned me from Arctic Red River telling me about the craft shop they would like to open in the community and asking if I was interested. I said I was very interested but since my children were in school until the end of June, I was not able to leave. June was in grade XI at Archbishop O'Leary High, and Jerry was in grade VI at St. Matthews.

In May, my chief from Arctic Red River once again phoned, this time to ask if I was interested in a job translating the Gwich'in Land Claim Agreement to the Elders in our Gwich'in language. I thought this work is up my ally, just read and talk, sure I am interested. As soon as Jerry was finished school we would take the Greyhound bus to Whitehorse, and Marie who was in Arctic Red River would meet us there to take us the rest of the way.

It was nice to be home again. A few days passed and no one mentioned the job to me. I finally approached the Chief and asked. He said he was going to check it out, and then he would let me know. I had to inquire twice more before I was hired.

If it were I who asked someone to come back and live in the community to work, I would have the job ready and a place for them to live. I found this very disturbing. There were no preparations made, no travel expenses and all my personal belongings were left behind. No one should be expected to move 1100 air miles (3000km by road) with without any preparations made for him or her. I made that sacrifice at the time and because of it I lost everything; my furniture, everything. I would never do this again.

Individuals who have lived out of the community are very resourceful people. They are used to punching a clock. They have the knowledge of how the world operates on the outside. They would be much help to their community in this time of change especially when they are speaking of self-government.

The Gwich'in Assembly was to be held in Arctic Red River with Gwich'in people from all the communities in the region attending. The group had to deal with various issues concerning the Land Claim Agreement. People in the community were glad that I was back. Jerry and I stayed with my adopted Mom, Joanne who was the community's Elder. She was a widow; she lived alone in a one-bedroom apartment. She was glad of our company.

The next few days I spent catching up on news and studying the Claim Agreement. Of course, I visited the people and listened to stories. It was good to be home, to eat fresh whitefish, cooked on an open fire. I missed this lifestyle a lot, especially my food.

When I am in the other world, I live that lifestyle. I eat the same food that other people do. I tolerate the everyday pressure and the fast pace out of respect for a different environment and culture. Nevertheless, back in my hometown, I could dress in whichever way I felt comfortable. I could just wash and brush my hair and go wherever I pleased. I had none of those hectic moments trying to keep up and constantly being on the go, demands made from every which way, money for food, rent, heat, light, phone, with never enough to go around.

Here in my hometown I could set a net in the river and catch many whitefish, prepare them myself, and have a delicious meal. I would go out on the land and set some rabbit snares and the next day have rabbit soup or rabbit stew. The only thing I needed money for was tea, sugar, coffee, milk, and my cigarettes. I could charge this at the community store, and when I was paid, I would settle the account whatever the amount.

Rose and her husband Dale had a big house. It was built for them from territorial housing so the little shack they had lived in before their new house was empty. Rose said I could rent this place from her for the time being, and the rent was cheap. There was no running water and I had to burn wood for heat. Physically I was in no shape to cut wood. I had not done this for many years. Nevertheless, Jerry and I managed. The town children were glad there was a new kid in town. Jerry did not know too much about their lifestyle except what I had told him. He was young; he could learn.He was on the land of his grandfathers. If he learned the skills of the land and his culture, he could adapt anywhere easily with the full understanding of the people and their environment wherever he chose to live later on.

Gwich'in people from the surrounding communities began arriving for the assembly. Everyone had prepared the accommodations and the food to look after the visitors. (A decision was made many months before to have the assembly at Tsiigehtchic, so caribou meat was stored in the band freezer for this occasion.)

Now the Chief had to choose people to assist him and have everyone involved in the preparations. Who was going to accommodate how many people, who were delegates and who were visitors? How many of the women were to do the cooking and of course who were to do the security.

Monday was the traveling day and the assembly began on Tuesday. All the important issues to be discussed were listed on the agenda. If we did not finish by Friday, we would continue into the weekend. Meetings began in the morning usually at 9:00 and continued all day. There was a break for lunch, supper, and short ones for coffee. Sometimes the meetings continued again after supper until the issue discussed was dealt with. Then there was a dance, which lasted most of the night. The little shack I rented was filled with people's laughter every evening. Funny stories were told and stories of long ago by the Elders. Staying up most of the night did not bother me because we had the midnight sun and there was a lot of excitement.

This was joyous for me because I had missed the gathering of my people when they told stories. It was a waste of time if we slept. I do

266

not even think the birds slept because they were singing their little hearts out whatever time it was. Maybe they were on shift, as they had to sing around the clock to the midnight sun, which was 24 hours a day. I could not be involved as much as I liked to be. There was much to read in the Claim Agreement, which I could not cover in the short time that I had. There was much to learn. The best I could do was to observe and listen. Hyacinth Andre, former chief for 35 years, spoke to the people on the third day of the assembly. He talked about me. This was our people's traditional way of, the pattern they followed. He spoke in a way I remember our chiefs and Elders spoke when I was a child.

Chief Hyacinth said "Therese, Remi's granddaughter and the daughter of John and Liza Remi, has come back to us. Let us celebrate. Remi was a respected man around our people and so was his son John Remi. John had begun to assume his father's role, but he had been taken early in his young life because the Creator needed him more than we did. They have gone before us to prepare the way for their people. We are to follow the footsteps of our ancestors, the footsteps of these good people. These two people showed us the ways of our people during the time they were here with us. Their generous heart and their concern were always for their people as was the unselfishness in the way they have treated people. Today we have the granddaughter of Remi, the daughter of John Remi with us. She has the old language of our people. She understands our culture because her grandparents raised her. She assumes their role; she is very much respected by her people. She has the interest of her people at heart"

I sat and listened. I heard every word that was spoken by my Elder, my former chief. Forty years ago, my people would have sat silently; even the children would have been very quiet because an Elder was speaking. Everyone would have understood the spoken words of the Elder. The word was taken with great respect, and these words would be repeated down through the history of our people. The young and old took the words of the Elders seriously. Thirty years back, people would have listened and understood what the chief was saying, but they would not fully realize why it was being said. What was told was history being told the way of our ancestral, verbally? Twenty years before, people would

267

have heard what was said but would not understand, but it would make them think. This was how it was not so long ago but it did not belong in the world they now know. Today only, the Elders listen and took this seriously; the others talked amongst themselves. Kids were busy playing.

To me, bringing the culture back means teaching the values and the way of our ancestors, but many do not understand the whole aspect of their own culture. I observed the expressions on faces and I realized then how many of my people are caught in between their own culture which they knew little of and the western culture which they also knew very little of.

Values and principles that were taught to us as children were forgotten and left behind, just as our language and way of life. It was a very sad day for me because of this realization. The rest of the assembly went well.

The closing of the assembly was celebrated with a feast and a dance. The town was quiet once again when everyone left. Alcohol was not allowed and everyone tried to respect this wish. There was only one incident where they had a small problem, but the Chief dealt it with immediately.

CHAPTER 28

The Gwich'in Land
Claim Agreement

I began reading the Agreement in Principle, AIP. Therefore, I would understand the document before going to my elders to translate and explain why the Gwich'in leaders were making an agreement with the Federal Government. This had to be done before the referendum vote, which was set for September of 1991.

I visited he Elders and those who could not read very well to explain the document over a cup of tea. It was difficult to translate the document as it was written, but this was what I had committed myself to when I accepted the translator's job. I did the work as was expected but I did not agree with rushing. I thought the Claim Agreement should be gone over thoroughly; I felt we could have waited another year. To me the written document should have been examined more carefully and received input from those who did not agree or understand certain statements. I do not think of myself in this matter, I think of our future generations and their well being. For example: Eligibility: The passage should have said that the Gwich'in people who have Gwich'in ancestry, Status, Non-status, (Métis) are eligible and are to be accepted as members of the Land Claim Agreement. It did not matter where they lived, when they came back to their community, they would participate and be involved in their community affairs.

When the Land Claim Agreement issues have to be dealt with, they could have a say if they wished to do so. As Gwich'in members, they could participate in the community and regional affairs as long as they were residing in the region.

Gwich'in members, no matter where in the world they lived, would vote any major land claim issues on. This was the way of our people from time immemorial. They never excluded their own people for material reasons.

My Elders of long ago always said that when an injustice had been committed, then the person who was guilty of committing the crime and the children of this person or family would never have a good life. An injustice committed against one's own people was a serious crime. It was a wrong committed against our tribal law.

Respect: My people's way of dealing with this matter was by banning the person from the group or village or by terminating their life. The clause should have said that people with Gwich'in ancestry should all enroll for membership. My Dadda and Mamma is the root of the Gwichya Gwich'in people, (fiat land people) I am what the government call 100% Indian, so my grandchildren are third generation yet my grandchildren are not allowed their status.

My opinion is that all Gwich'in members that voted for the Claim Agreement should become without question as well as their children and grandchildren. The discriminatory clause in the Indian Act is troubling to this day. Although the government has said, it had amended this act, it remains racist.

When an Indian man marries a non-Indian woman, his wife and children are granted full status, but this is not applied when an Indian woman marries a non-native man. Although the act has been amended and we Aboriginal woman have been re-instated our status we are treated as unequal to the status we held previous to our marriage to non-native men.

The government who says children are a priority has done great injustice to women and their children and the so -called clause that should better our lives and our children's lives has remained unjust and unfair.

Education: One important component of the claim if we want to self-govern and become an independent nation. Post-secondary education is valuable. Educated individuals will help guide, plan, and access funds needed for those students who have committed themselves to further their studies. This will give them a better understanding of the world out there in order to lead their people in good constructive planning and will build a closer relationship with other nations to accomplish and achieve success.

Support and sponsorship are important. Leaders and chiefs should do their utmost to keep the spirits up by thoughtful consideration for students far away from home. For example, with a card or a phone call just to ask, how are you? This type of gesture will be very much appreciated by the student who at the time is amongst strangers and a different lifestyle. It also makes the student feel he is appreciated for trying and being recognized for the hard work, he \she is doing. It is a big sacrifice that a student makes to leave his\her home, community to live elsewhere. Encouragement is very much needed during this time.

Leaders and chiefs have power and have access to education monies for their people. If aggressively and strongly demanded, additional funds could be found. Our people who have lived elsewhere because of their work and the knowledge gained and the skills they have acquired from other societies could bring this back to the community. This would help develop the community's goals. All this of course has to be accepted by the community.

Our leaders should support those individuals who commit themselves to post-secondary education so they can work for their people more effectively.

When the federal government established the government in the Northwest Territories, they did not establish this on "peanuts." Offices and buildings had to be built. Residences had to be built for their employees. Personal belongings were shipped at the government's expense; the government paid traveling allowances. Billions of dollars were spent relocating this government to the Northwest Territories, and then establishing many government agencies in other communities to give public services to isolated communities throughout the North West Territories.

I remember the houses that were built in Inuvik, and preparing the houses for the arrival of the government employees with new colonial type furniture and appliances. How much more money was spent in salaries, isolation pay, etc?

Now that self-government is to be moved to communities, the same pattern should be followed. Even if our own people in the communities want to hire their own people with skills and other professional people, there are no accommodations.

Poor living facilities are a major factor for our people returning to their communities. People with technical skills and vision are needed to set and succeed in future goals. The government and the dominant society have committed oppression ever since they set foot in the North because the government labeled the native people wards of the government and not part of the Canadian society. No one was interested in learning about our culture. They took and took from us from the beginning. They did not treat us as humans. They treated their pets better than they did the natives.

Free education as I remember was "a fat cat sat on a mat." The baby class it was referred to in the days I went to school. The big class was geography and arithmetic. The Bible was taught in big class. So much for free education! This they told us was to the level of grade 5.

Just recently, some brave native people pursued higher education. They said education should be available to them as much as the rest of society. Only then did the doors begin to open to higher grades, colleges, and universities.

With health, tuberculosis was an active disease amongst the native people at one time. The government took charge. The light cases were left in the regional hospitals if the region had one, other patients with more severe cases were sent to hospitals down South. Many of these patients died far away from home. Families were informed, some months later that their relative had passed away.

Burial sites of relatives to many are unknown. Much injustice has been committed and is still committed today. This is not going to go away because we wish it to do so. My Dadda told me so many times that if a big problem happens, it is for a reason. It is because of the many little ones that led to the one big problem.

Begin by attacking and straightening out all the little ones and soon the big problems will disappear. This makes sense. There are human rights agencies but whom do they represent? As of today, the government and Canadian society has to acknowledge that the aboriginal people should be accepted into the Canadian society.

I would like to establish friendship with other nations, learn from history, and take the good and the experiences learned into the future so that mistakes will not be repeated again.

To be able to go forward together with all nations: To offer our help and knowledge, to plan the future in partnership, with respect for one another so no conflict arises. Money from all governments should be in place for environmental groups who are concerned about the environment. This is my dream.

I feel the mills and other mining companies will eventually pollute the Northern Rivers and its fish, which are part of our daily diet. Our wildlife in the North will be affected by pollution fallout that settles over the Arctic. Wild meat will no longer be edible. Because of permafrost, we cannot grow our own vegetables. Our land is harsh. Our livelihood depends on the wildlife of the Arctic.

Will our children be compensated for the destruction of our environment if it happens through no fault of their own? For them to be compensated for the unexpected crises during their lifetime is essential. Because of greed and the quest for power, the land is being stripped of her protective clothing (ozone layer). She has suffered at the hands of humanity through greed and if we do not stop and change our direction, heat will dry the earth. No vegetation, will grow, fires will destroy. Destruction will come because no one cared to say: it is time to stop, and start having the respect once more for, The Earth.

Greed, power, and control were never part of my people's lives. Control used wisely under Our Law of Respect is good. The teachings start when a child begins to talk and understand a "no" and a "yes." Elders and parents have to return to teachings of values and guide with wisdom and knowledge. The Native Law of Respect should be legislated and adopted as a law to be followed and taught. There is too much freedom in society today. Nothing is respected anymore especially the commandments of the Creator. As a believer in faith, this should be a part of our everyday life. To address my concerns and opinion would have been met with deaf ears; instead, I chose to write. Why, because someone always said, "don't rock the boat Terry" or "Don't make waves."

I try to understand the changes from life on the land to where we have to earn a wage to survive, and to see a full picture of the present situation.

To envision ten, fifteen, fifty, years is important. The decisions we make today will affect our generations of tomorrow. Young people that I have spoken with know how much I am concerned about their future, as my Dadda was for mine. He wanted me to enjoy the life that he himself had enjoyed. This is the way my Elders prepared their younger generation for the future

The solutions to our problems are very simple, but because we see everything in dollars and cents, in this time of history, it becomes complicated.

To build close relationships over the border is crucial. It is important to develop relationships with neighboring communities, and become partners in an economy, which will succeed so nations can survive. Many times, I used to hear my Elders say in the past, help other people and they in turn will help you. Show respect and teach them that will then create understanding and harmony. Work together; it is the only way.

Our Law of Respect is also forgotten, This Law unifies everything in the universe so they can work with one another in harmony. Each has their assignment under the guidance of our Creator. The assignment given to mankind through his word should also never change. We have no right to change it, no matter how much history changes. In the history of the Gwich'in culture, it did not change much as it was based on

The Law of the Land: "RESPECT". If the Elders saw or suspected negative behaviors or attitude changes, they spoke with harsh stern words,
which brought back stability and balance. Today voicing one's opinion
is called complaining.

I was confused, because everything was going so fast for me. I wanted
to say to them, let us wait. This will give us time to study the content.
It will give us more understanding. However, I was not someone important; I was just someone to vote for my leaders, and just a number to the
government with hardly any education.

I did not stand a chance. The Gwich'in tribal council spoke on mod-
ern treaty for old treaty, once we have made the land claim agreement
with the federal government, there would be job creation through community development, and we would eventually become an independent
nation through self-government.

My daughter Marie and her husband Robert and my granddaughter Didi'ghoo (Christina) had gone to Arctic Red River (Tsiigehtchic)
a few weeks before I had. Marie had left her little car "Betsy" with me
in Edmonton. When I left Edmonton, Betsy was parked in my parking
space. Tom, my friend, was in charge of my place. I did not know if I
was going to stay or just work for the summer. First, my health could
not take the harsh winter weather in the North. I knew I would be fine
during the summer months. Nevertheless, coming home made me feel
so great; I did not want to leave.

I decided I would try for one winter to see how my health could take
it. After about two weeks, I phoned Tom and told him I was staying.
Whatever happened I would drift with the flow. I asked him if he could
possibly pack everything with the help of my girls and put it all in stor-
age. He agreed, and I thanked him.

In the meantime, Marie and I both pooled our money and got
enough cash together to pay for her plane ticket to Edmonton to pick up
"Betsy." She would bring "Betsy" back North.

Marlene my oldest daughter phoned and said Tom had decided to
come north so he might be catching a ride with Marie. I did not believe
this as several times in the past, I had urged Tom to visit my hometown,
but he was afraid to go north.

I think he had an idea that the people in the North still lived in a primitive way. To him the North was unknown and going to an unknown country was not something he had in mind.

The day came and Marie left for Edmonton. By then all my furniture was stored, the house cleaned and the keys turned in. All Marie had to do was pick up "Betsy." Two days after her arrival in Edmonton, Marie and Tom headed back North. It took them several days to arrive in Arctic Red River as they had a washout somewhere along the Dempster Highway and they had to wait until the road was repaired. Little "Betsy" made it all the way to Arctic Red River with no problem. The car was a 1984 Ford Acadian, 4 doors, and 6 cylinders. She was loaded, but she had a good trip. Marie made it in time before the ferry shut down for the night; this was about midnight.

I was surprised at Tom for coming after us. I began to think that maybe he did love me after all. Jerry and I were glad to see him. A few days later, he asked me to marry him. He said since he had followed me to the ends of the earth, he deserved an answer. I thought about it for a few days; then I said "yes."

The date was set for two weeks after his arrival in Arctic Red River, August 23, 1991. He made friends with the people in no time and soon became part of the community. We got married on a rainy day and the people had a reception for us at the Community Hall. My father, Dadda, and Mamma are all buried side by side in the cemetery. I hoped they were glad for me.

It was back to work a few days later. By this time, Tom had a job taking care of the gym. We were all busy preparing for the referendum vote, which was fast approaching. I translated what was written in the Claim Agreement. I did not say anything otherwise. I felt sad. I prayed to the Creator and the Spirit of our ancestors to ask for protection for all our children. I hoped the preparation for their future by the leaders would be as good as their ancestors had been when they passed on to the next generation.

Whenever there was a band council meeting, I attended. I could not miss out any important issues. The referendum vote went well, but now it was up to the government to accept. I wanted the time off during freeze up, as Jerry and I wanted to ice fish. People were busy setting nets a few days after the Arctic Red River froze. I asked Dale if he could set our net for us, as he was the only person in town who had a jigger. It took him just a few minutes to do the job.

Every day after school, Jerry and I went to see our net and we caught about forty - fifty whitefish. Jerry was having fun learning the traditional skills. We also had a rabbit snare line, which he visited every day with his dog. He kept himself busy and he had no time to be bored.

I had to be a resident for a year in my own hometown before I was allowed to vote. This regulation I was not able to understand. All this because of a policy set up by the Indian Affairs, which all band councils of each community had to follow. I read this policy differently and it was the non-Gwich'in people who could not vote. They had to be resident of the community for a year. My children are band members, so the number of dollars given to the band was on our behalf too, but we were always working outside of our community. We never have been able to use the Band services.

Counting us and the rest of the band members, our money pays their expenses, wages and services. They willingly take my family's money, but when I come back to my community, I am treated as a stranger. What about the people who reside in the community for years and are registered with other bands but use our band money while theirs is going to other communities? It is not fair. If our band excludes their band members, it creates conflicts and discontentment amongst people.

Although our funds were given to the band, we seemed to have no say in how the dollar was spent. When we try to address our concern, it is ignored and it makes us feel rejected. Some of us during recent years have gone from our community to work elsewhere. We have had to move out of our community to where we can find work so our family can survive. Because we have learned to punch the clock from early morning until late afternoon, we have learned to be active all our lives. We cannot sit idle all day and have no job. The only way to support our family is through work we have done and learned. Therefore, we go wherever we can get this. For this, some of our people in our community disown us. We cannot win either way. Damn if you do, Damn if you don't. The system has not been fair to us and it pierces our hearts when we get this treatment from our own people.

There was one meeting that I went to I would never forget. All the band councilors were men including the Chief. I had addressed a concern of mine and one of the band councilors said, "Terry, where were you these forty years while we developed Arctic Red River? Now all at once you come back and you talk about changes."

Another band councilor said, "Shut up Terry, you have a big mouth. You want to talk about everything." This got me fuming. I said to the chief and council, "The people in the community do not come to the meetings because if they address an issue that concerns them, this is the way they get treated. This makes them feel that their time is wasted. Nobody likes to be ignored. They come to meetings to participate, and if they are not listened to they don't want to come anymore".

But not me; you won't get rid of me that easily, I did not want my time wasted and if I was concerned about an issue, I had every right to address it to the chief and band council. I wanted to answer William's comment.

"Yes, I was gone for many years, but when I had a holiday and I could afford it, I came home. I had to live elsewhere in order to work for my family. You people developed this community. How? As far as I know, the government developed it. The government brought the materials and when you could not build the houses, they brought other people to do it for you. I remember the days when our people used to build their own houses with logs that they cut, and then rafts were made which they floated down the river to town and then brought them up the hill to the location where they chose to build their house. The NWT boat delivered doors and windows, which were paid from the individual's pocket. This money was part of their fur money that they had saved. That is what I call development. I have been away from the community for many years but when I work, the government takes income tax, pension and UIC. The money for these services is deducted from my cheque. My God, I have helped to develop the Northwest Territories. I have helped to develop your town; paid into your education fund and medical funds and you tell me I did not help develop? Think again! I did more than all of you sitting there, so don't tell me I did not help develop".

No one had anything to say to me or even answer me. All the chief had to say was, we are sorry; it was a misunderstanding. There was a chief and band council election on December 9. My name was given for nomination, and the leaders who said they followed the Indian Act Policy did not accept it. They said again I had to be a resident of the community for a year before I ran for an election. It really disappointed me because I believed I could have done a good job with the experience that I had.

Fall came and Chief asked me if I would like to make some crafts for the Fashion Show that was to be held in Inuvik at the end of November. I said I would. There was to be Arts and Crafts show held at the same time. I said I would do both. I had a month to prepare.

The day of the fashion show I was up very early and did all the last minute things that needed to be done. I phoned to Inuvik to send a cab for me. The fare for this cab was $160.00 one way and $320.00 return. This is puzzlement. When someone is trying very hard to promote products or a place to gain recognition, the community should help pay expenses. This is good business. Advertising agencies are paid for advertising, merchandise, businesses, Places'

Why not help in my expenses? I felt the band could have offered a ride, but I had to get my own cab and pay for it with my own money. I was not working at the time so I did not have much but I knew I was going to sell at least some of my products so I was not afraid to charter a taxi.

We were supposed to turn in all the clothing for the fashion show at Imago Hall at 11:00 am. I just made it. I had a good sale and orders that I had to do before Christmas. A woman who was getting married on February 14, 1992 ordered nine fully beaded adult slippers and two children's. I told her I was going to do the other orders first, and then I would do hers in January. A week before Christmas I said to my husband we should go to Inuvik to deliver the crafts that I had made for these people and at the same time get a few things we needed for Christmas.

Since Tom had come to Arctic Red River, he had been to Inuvik once. I finally got him to agree, and off we went. I had to bring two beaver pelts, some duffel, and a piece of moose hide. There was still a pair of beaver skin mitts ordered that I had not finished.

We were going to stay at my friend Sarah and Bob's place so I was going to finish it that night. I could deliver it before I left the next day. We arrived late so we just did a little shopping. That night some committee was having a big bingo in Inuvik, and we went. They played about 12 to 15 games and the bingo finished close to midnight. We got home, and I told Sarah I was going to begin sewing the mitts. I might have to stay up all night. Sure enough, I stayed up and finished at 11:00 the next morning. I phoned the customer to tell her mitts were finished. As soon as she picked them up, I had a wash and took off to Stanton wholesale. This is a wholesale grocery warehouse. We purchased all our grocery supplies, and we left for home.

It was my first Christmas at home in many years, and I did not know what to expect. When I had lived away from my home community during Christmas, I thought of home with great sadness and loneliness. However, I remember how joyful it was. After midnight Mass, people went around visiting one another, shaking each other's hand and wishing a "Merry Christmas."

Sometimes people made goodies before church so you would stop there and there and have snacks. In those days, people were so lively. Today people are tired with a dragged out look. They are too tired to have fun and have a good time. They seem to wake up some when they have a drink; then they get sick afterwards.

I always kid around and have a lot of fun. I think this world needs more people who love life and live it to have a good time. I always try my best to have a good time, whether I am down or not. I feel life is too short to walk around dragging one's face. For this, I am told to act my age. I act too immature to be an Elder. You cannot win either way. In those days, the young people would be preparing for a dance and we would dance until maybe 6:00 or 7:00 in the morning. The church would be open; as it was never locked. We would go visit the Baby Jesus anytime we wanted to. Today, there is no celebration like that one. To me it was like spending Christmas in a strange land where you did not know anyone, but went to church and then home to bed. Where was the celebration of this joyous occasion? Sadly it was gone like everything else.

In January of, of 1992, violet, said we had work in the community of Arctic Red River. This first project was enrollment and then later on self-government. The Gwich'in nation initialed the claim agreement which was ratified by an election September 16 to 20. 1991 the Gwich'in people were just waiting for the claim to be accepted by the government of Canada and the territorial government. If the both parties agree, the land claim agreement would be formally signed. The legislated settlement would then become law; this would make the agreement legal and binding.

The first objective of the agreement was the enrollment process, and then began structuring the platform for self-government. Violet would be our coordinator and she was to hire 2 field workers, Jim and I. The first assignment was to put out questions to the people of the community. Who would be eligible and who was not? This process took a lot of time as we had to have everyone's input. These reports were then sent to the Gwich'in tribal council for evaluation. The next question on our agenda was how would they like to see their self-government platform structured? Jim visited the younger generation and I visited the elders as I can speak with them in our language I can translate the question. I told them what the question was asking of them and what self government meant, self sufficiency and independence. This will give the right to our Gwich'in tribal council to be Gwich'in tribal government. This means they will be the one's to give the monies to our communities to deliver services to their people and to seek and strive for our own economic independence. Indian affairs had been delivering these services because the government had labeled the aboriginal people children of the crown in the year 1763. With Self GOVERNMENT we would be able to take back our independence and responsibilities. These responsibilities include:

Health
Education & Training
Social Services
Drug and Alcohol Programs
Enhancement of our traditional culture and language so
Recreation
Housing infrastructure
Renewable Resources
Economic Development & Tourism
Justice

The elders whom I had to go and visit were delightful as each one of their answers were the same except in different words. They set a hot cup of tea in front of me then answered to the question I asked. There was always a short story thrown in here and there, as it may relate to a story they remembered. Based on this, they felt the community should begin working together and our people should feel free to address their concern, without being told they are complaining. They did not want discrimination in their governing body; unity is what they would like to see. And this could be achieved only through listening to one another, with respect. Always be grateful to other people who offer their help, and always remember to be considerate to others. To my elders this was a major power point to good leadership. Respect creates and builds good working relationship and sometimes creates friendship for life. I was very pleased with their answers.

I was busy working during the day and in the evening after my supper dishes were done, I sat down to work on the beaded vamps. Rosa's wedding was on February 14, and she wanted the slippers to be delivered by Feb.12th finally the slippers were finish on the 13 and I went to Inuvik to deliver. My friend was very happy I had finished all her wedding shoes. What made me feel sad was that I had not finished the two children's shoes. She was going to try and find them from elsewhere.

The A.I.P was to be signed in Fort McPherson on April 22, 1992. Chief Peter said he wanted me to make some beaded slippers for this occasion, he wanted to buy a man and a woman's beaded slippers. He said this was special gift for Tom Siddon and his wife. Tom was the minister for Indian affairs. He was going to be present at the signing. So once more I was sewing late into the night. By April 20th

I had all the beaded vamps done. Now I had to cut out the moose hide then begin assembling. I had the twelve pairs to do so I did not go to work that day. By 10pm in the evening there were still six slippers to sew fur on and I was very tired. I asked Louise to come and help me. By the time we were going to give up for the night there were still 3 pairs not finish. I was up very early and began sewing. Almost all the town people were going to Fort McPherson; they began picking up people about 8.am. I was pack and ready, but no one came to pick me up. They must have forgotten me. By 10am I phone Louise, I ask her where Wayne was, she said he was out on the Mackenzie River, clearing the drifts. I said, Louise, they must have forgotten me I am still here. Try to get a hold of Wayne someway and tell him I need a ride, the ceremony will begin at 11am, I will be late. The Minister, Tom Sid don was to arrive at 11am and will be leaving at 2pm right after the signing. I was ready to panic. In few minutes a truck stop outside, Thank God! I grab my bag and left. Just as we were going down the hill, we met Margaret and Bob. Margi said her brother called her to check for me in Arctic Red, because they couldn't find me in town. Well of course they cannot find me because I was still in Arctic Red. We arrived in Fort McPherson and went directly to the Rec. Hall. As soon as I went in I gave the two pairs to the Chief. I was happy; Mr. Sid don and his wife will get their slippers. Within minutes the rest of the slippers were sold. The signing done and had many government speakers. Then a big feast was held followed by a drum dance. I was too tired so left I for home early.

At the end of May, I received a phone call from the language bureau in Yellowknife. They asked if I was interested in translating for the Legislative Assembly on June 15. I said I was working but I will ask my boss. I told Violet and she said I should go as it would be a good experience. The money was good plus all my expenses, how could I turn this down. The next day I called them to say I was going. I should have asked them to confirm this in a letter and fax it to me. Once again lack of Education, trust took over common sense. I grew up trusting in words

283

that are spoken. Today I still have a hard time getting use to letters that confirms whatever is said. I still believe very strongly in words that are spoken. Translating at the legislative level would give me experience. On June 14 my son Jerry and I boarded the plane to Yellowknife. On arrival we were escorted to Northern Lights Motel, here we were to stay for the next two weeks. The next morning I went to the Language Bureau office. The office was located at the Laming building, only a short distance from the Motel. There were papers to sign. The Legislative sitting would begin that afternoon; I had to learn how to use the equipment, which took over an hour. I had done numerous translating exercises in my life for people, hospital, meetings, but never for a government assembly. It was an experience.

During the time I was in Yellowknife, I came across a brochure. It was information on The Yellowknife Arctic College Campus. They were advertising fall courses. I saw one program on tourism I was always interested in Native Crafts and had a dream it would become one of the industry for the communities in the North, which can serve the tourist, what better way to introduce the NWT, Information, stories and traditional Crafts. I began to think. I wander if I could take this course. I wander if I could pass the entrance requirements. A grade 12 diploma or upgrading to the level of grade 12 was required. I could give it a try, what crazy thoughts. I was in Aklavik Residential School and went to grade 4, but did not finish because I was in the hospital for few months with tuberculosis. That was many decades ago, I thought what have I got to loose. I made an appointment with someone at the College for the next morning. I was supposed to take test which would give them an idea of what grade level I was. I was very nervous when I entered the college the next morning, but the people there were very nice which put me at ease. I thought; what if I didn't make it at least I tried. I followed the instruction given to me. I did the test. I gave it my best shot, now to wait. The College would contact me later. I had many working years behind me, it was the only tool I had. Acceptance was base on grade level... I sure didn't have any.

My son Jerry and I decided to visit my daughters in Edmonton, before returning to Arctic Red. My husband was also suppose to be in

Edmonton Alberta attending a Drug and Alcohol healing conference, we wanted to all have a good visit with our children. My brother Mitchell, who lived in Lesser Slave and who had not been home since the early fifties was going to drive us home by the Dempster highway. As soon as the Assembly was over Jerry and I boarded the greyhound bus to Edmonton. We had a good visit with the family. Tom was to fly back to Artic Red, and Jerry and I were taking the highway. I love traveling the highway. There are so many beautiful places where one could build a cabin and live forever.

My sister in law June came to pick us up. Lesser Slave Lake is about two hours drive North of Edmonton. We stayed overnight with them at Slave Lake and early the next morning we were on our way.

It took us two days to get home. The day of our arrival home, I had to attend a band meeting. I had Michell drop me off at the band office. Early the next morning I left to attend another meeting in Inuvik. I returned to Arctic Red the same day. I did not see my brother that morning because I left very early. When I finally got home, Tom said that Mitchell had left for home because one of his children was sick. I felt sad because I wanted him to have a good visit with everyone before he went back south. I was back at work as soon as I returned. Working with people, one needs a break once in a while. The Gwich'in Assembly was to be held in Fort McPherson close to the end of August. We were a community that had to prepare our presentations, concerns and recommendations. There was much work to be done.

Sometime in July, the Yellowknife College wrote and congratulated me on passing and asked if I would give them a call as soon as I received their letter. I phoned them without wasting time. They wanted a Phone interview. I was accepted Wow! I could not believe this was happening. They did not say we do not think you met the requirements needed in English or you may need to take some upgrading. They gave me a date for a phone interview. The day of the phone interview came and I was quite nervous. Once I was on the phone, I was fine. Too many hesitations on their part, I felt I might not make it.

Few days later the College called, they said they felt Tourism program was too intense for me because a large part of the program covered math.

They felt the course was beyond my capability. However, they suggested the Native Study Management program which closely identifies with the program that I wanted. This program specialized in Native History. It also relates to the work that I was doing at the time. I agreed. Going through the process of applying for a financial loan, then waiting to get it approved, it took some time. Once my funding was approved I began to make plans to leave for Yellowknife.

In the North fax machines are sure appreciated very much as correspondence can be done so quickly. My husband did not want to come to Yellowknife with us; he did not want to leave Arctic Red. This was his home. The people had made him feel welcome and he had a good job with the community Drug and Alcohol group. But my husband understood if I wanted to work more effectively, education would give me this chance.

Yearly the Gwich'in people have their assembly, this year their assembly was to be held in Fort McPherson, as one of the delegates I went. When it was over I went right home to Arctic Red. Sunday Morning I was up very early I had some fast packing to do. My son and I were leaving Monday morning. Golly, time flies. Monday morning, the Band Office phone to say, taxi was coming over from McPherson, bringing back some of the people and if I wanted to take this taxi to be ready. Yes, I will take it; it was a band charter so it will cost me nothing. FAT CHANCE!!!! I got to McPherson I had to pay. I should have asked my chief before I took the taxi if I had to pay. I had my son and I bus fare to get in Whitehorse, I needed to save my little earnings to get to my destination. I caught a ride with my friend Gladys and her father, my dear Gladys she also paid my son Jerry's fare to Yellowknife. I have so many friends from here and there through out Mackenzie, in our Delta Region through out Canada.

I am lucky to have them and grateful, and pray to my Creator to bless them each day. I was able to bring a few of our personal belonging and boxes that held our few housekeeping stuff. Pots and pans, beddings and things that we needed to set up housekeeping in Yellowknife. We had about ten boxes. The freight cost less than if I had to buy all this in Yellowknife, we left McPherson and Gladys father drove all night, some-

286

where on the road he had a nap then we got going again. Arriving in Whitehorse the next morning about 8am, we all went to Bess place, had a shower, then made sure all the boxes were securely packed, we went to the bus depot.

We checked in, paid for our freight, got our ticket and it was time to board the bus. It took us two days to get to Yellowknife. I am the kind of person who love vehicle ride. I am so busy in life that it is difficult for me to rest. So bus rides give me the time to think, and rest. I love when my son Jerry travels with me, he takes care of everything as young as he was. My coffee, and transfer to the right bus. My son never complains, if he finds things boring, he looks for something else to do, my son is good with his hands, and he does creative work, builds, and paints. He takes care of me. I am very pleased with the way my son is maturing. He has my Dadda and father's qualities. He loves the bush life. Maybe someday we can travel together by canoe up the Arctic Red River (Heritage River) and I can show him where his great, great, and his great grandfather had traveled. I would like to do this with all my children.

At the bus depot, we got our tickets. Alice paid for Jerry's bus fare. I didn't want her to do this but she insisted. She knew what it was like to be a student and always short of money. She wanted to help a little. She said not to deprive her of what little she could do to help. She was so young and already so wise. Afterwards, alone in the bus, I had tears in my eyes. I thought she was the only one who cared. I didn't ask; she just offered. Even though she was very young, she understood her culture very well. I will always remember her good deed and for being there when she was needed. I was feeling partly sad and partly angry, as no one wished me luck in my home town nor did my chief and anyone else offer help in any way. I felt very alone. Maybe if I did what they wanted and went to Inuvik and went to College there, they would have offered some help. My reason for wanting to go to Yellowknife Arctic College Campus was that it had many resources that could be beneficial: government, libraries, museum, archives and many other things I could use during my college year. And they had this Native Studies Management course which would help me to make future decisions. People from another community cared enough to make sure I was in Whitehorse to catch my bus, and each one that I saw there, both young and old, wished me the best. They said they were glad I was going back to school. And dear Gladys, I will never forget her. I heard my Elders many times while growing up, thanking me for bringing in wood for them or getting a pail of water or just visiting them. They used to say, "Old people like it when the children or young people visit them. This shows respect and a generous heart. We are thankful to the Creator, that we have young people and children who will carry on the ways of our people." This came to mind so many times while I was home that year in Arctic Red, my home community. All the young girls from Fort McPherson who came to Arctic Red came to visit me. It reminded me of when I was growing up, and how the young people of McPherson used to come over and go to Dadda's house to camp with him.

Once on my way I felt a tinge of fear. What am I doing? How did I get myself into this predicament? At my age, I must be nuts. My health was not too good; I must have gone completely mad! I should be embroidering or beading in a little log shack somewhere out at a good fishing lake. Why do I put myself through such a stressful, difficult situation? "Oh Terry, you are such a problem to yourself. You always think you can do something, you don't really know anything about..."

During orientation, we came to a classroom which had many computers. "Oh my goodness, I cannot touch those; I might break them" I thought. I did not know how to work them. They might as well be foreign objects. I would never touch those machines. I would play sick on computer day. Fat chance! Now I was really afraid, but I could not turn back. It was done, and now I would just have to learn to handle this situation as best I could. It was very difficult entering college at my age. First of all, I was much older than my classmates. Another thing, it was a different scene from the 1944 classroom to the nineties. I must be crazy, out of my head, completely gone mad. But without education, I could not achieve the goals I had set for myself. I thought that we all learn from trying.

Sometimes the experience we learn from taking a direction we set for ourselves is not good but we learn from these decisions. I wanted to write, to record and document my history, language, skills taught for

288

survival on the land, and the native crafts. Very few people are left who have these skills from my generation and even fewer in the next generation. The Traditional skills of our people are to be given to the younger generation to give them their identity. This would then strengthen the individual. It makes you proud. It was like my Dadda and Mama who taught and prepared me for when it was my turn to take over. I wanted to write and teach all the young generation through recorded documentation. But without an education, I would not be able to see these goals of mine achieved. Without an education I wouldn't know how to look for a Publisher, or even know how to search for one. I would need another person who would help me do this. They have to respect the way I think, the way I say what I want say, and understand what I am saying. He or she must recognize the process of my documentation. Myself, I must respect their point of view or opinions. I also want to find a person who will help my family pursue an Arts and Crafts business. My girls are able to teach, and we can teach people to be producers of the native crafts; then we can market to the rest of the country and eventually to the world.

I hope my children will carry on after I am gone, especially Marlene and Marie and June who have learned that the quality of a product is what sells. I see an industry here that nobody else seems to see. Maybe it is too much work. We would like to begin today if we could. Sixteen hours a day is nothing to me. If I see success at the end of the road and someone to carry on, this is all I care about. But having capital is a problem. Native people never had much money. When one works at labor jobs they barely make enough money to cover expenses. We work; we get paid; we spend it. Our money is spent on our family needs which make the dollar circulate. We never have a chance to hoard it as there is never enough to go around. Native people always have a difficult time getting where they want to go in business or pursuing other opportunities that are available and are taken for granted by society.

In the age of human rights, we are not looked at, as equal to the rest of Canadian society. I know we are making progress, and we have to be positive in all our actions and behavior. We have to learn to work with others so that our children will have a better future. I feel the history which was recorded in the last five hundred years was always done by non native, who observed, it should be left where it belongs, learn from our mistake, and prepared ourselves for a better future for the sake of our children. History is important where we come from and who we are.

The Gwich'in told their historical stories verbally, I felt, to be call a nation one has to have history otherwise we become extinct. I belief the government and the elected leaders have to make sure that whatever symbolizes Canada remains intact because it is Canadian. If I ever go to a function, where they asked their guess to dress formal, I am not going in there dress as an Indian in traditional wear. I am going to wear whatever the host wears because I have respect for the people who have invited me. There has to be some practices that represents Canada and out of respect for all those that are born in this country. There should be no argument about this, its common sense. We are a country with many cultures. My opinion is to have respect for our culture and other cultures, but we have to have certain events, holidays, and organizations which belong specifically to Canadian people as a whole. We are free to practice our culture in our environment. I think this is great. But as a Canadian, I would participate in whatever the Canadians do because I am a Canadian and my nationality is Gwich'in, from the far northern Arctic of the Northwest Territories.

I am very concerned about how the bureaucrats operate. Human rights are so blown out of proportion. There is no more law and order amongst society. Where parents had control of their children at one time, children seem to have taken that control over and the law says they have that right. At 12 and 13 years old, young children are telling their parents what to do and they say to the parent "It's my life, and I have to live it the way I want." Human rights is good for when wrongs are committed and there is no justification for those actions, but I feel it is not right where they intrude in family life. Already, there is a cry over so much corruption in humanity. Why? Because God is outlaw from the class room, respect is not taught. For generations this has not been taught because the parents involved now weren't taught this. Sometimes I sit alone and think about where we are going today and I don't blame the Creator if he gets angry and says this is it. I think of the story of Sodom and Gomorrah.

There is no respect for Law, Mother Earth, Family, Church, Our Creator and His Law. Everything taught is based on money, economy, greed and power and material gain. This makes me very sad. In this day and age of advanced technology, people still complain

About how much work they have to do. Hey, we have it so much easier than in the early 1900's. I have had to work two jobs, my family and my job outside the home, and sometimes three in the native crafts when extra money is needed. And now as far as my education goes I get up at 4:00am or 5:00am because I love the peace and quiet of the early morning. I thank my Blessed Mother and my Creator for a safe night and I plan my day. But if something not related to the plan had come up, I deal with it as best as I know how. Most mothers have two jobs, their work outside the home, community and family. So do most of the men. Their jobs, their community, sport activities and sometimes other volunteer work. These people are committed to helping their community function well and be healthy. The time they have to themselves is very limited, but they do it because they care.

The project that I would like to do needs people who are as interested as I am, to commit themselves to the history and crafts project. In the meantime, when success is achieved, they will also have played an important role for, our future generations. This is what I hope to achieve so education to me is a must. I cannot accomplish these goals without completing my studies and without my Creator. He has become so important in everything I set out to do.

My first month was spent getting used to the classroom activities, listening and observing. Oh! What emotional turmoil and stress I went through. On the surface, I may have looked fine, but inside my heart pounded like crazy. My stomach was churning and upset. I was afraid constantly. I think what saved me the first few months was always being able to participate in class discussions. Maybe this showed I was listening. Many issues were related to work that I had done so it was easy to get involved. This built my confidence, but I was very self conscious because I didn't think I had the education that the rest of my fellow students had.

They were all younger than me, but they showed respect which I was grateful for. They all had something to do with finishing my studies in June. Dennis, who I thought should mind his own business, always wanted to know if I had done my homework. Rather than saying no, and trying to explain why I didn't, because of his nagging I did my homework. Anthony, a young man who had so much potential, was a good carver and very intelligent. He could go so far if he had the determination to do so. Charlie was a friend who was searching to find a path to travel. If education it was, education it will be. He was also trying to find his spirituality. Once he finds this he will have found his inner peace and he will make a good leader. Georgina, who had the skills of making any type of clothing and a personality that can capture your heart, was another classmate. It didn't matter what; she was always ready to help. Maureen was non-native, but her thirst for the aboriginal knowledge was genuine, and she was always ready to offer her help. Last but not least was Norenda-kindhearted, sweet, bubbly and caring. She said anything she wanted which was refreshing as she reminded me of myself so much. She was lively, full of energy. With Norenda around, there was no time for idleness.

They all contributed in their own way to my finishing my year. Many a time I had the urge to quit, to go home, and to forget about my goals. Sometimes I thought it was too late. If ever I achieved my goals, the people who were involved in my life since the day I had begun would have all played a major role in my success. Many times I thought I would never make it. I failed the required marks to pass my computers and my accounting, but I challenged them again. I passed my accounting, but again failed my computers.

We were given a choice to apply to enter a university in Peterborough, Ontario for second year of Native Studies but I didn't want to travel too far from my home and my people. People from the North come to visit Edmonton and I always got a parcel of goodies like Dry fish and dry meat. Maybe someday I will just have to get myself a computer and practice and become an expert. I did the best I could.

I had applied to Grant Mac Ewan Community College in Edmonton, for my second year. I wanted to enter the General Arts and Science program. I was accepted but because of my late application, I was placed on standby. Applications that were sent earlier had taken all the space, but if someone dropped out, I would be given priority.

.Jane who was the chairperson for the Native Communications Program, she came to visit the college in Yellowknife. I met with her and from the information she gave me on what the Native Communications Program offered, I felt I could use some of the courses, especially the English language. I knew I had to improve in that field. By taking the course in the Fundamentals of Writing and the Journalism class, my English should improve. To enter another college with not much time wasted, I would not lose or forget what I had learned in the past year.

At the end of May, some people who co-ordinate Midnight Madness, an annual event, which was celebrated on the 20th of June phone me. They wanted to know if I was interested in having a table with my crafts. I said I was going to college till the 11th of June and I just didn't have the time to sew. I thanked them for asking me. Graduation was on the 11th of June and the graduating students all had a good time at the reception and dance held at the Explorer Hotel.

A few days later, the Tourism people phoned to ask if I would do some crafts for The Midnight Sun Festival held July 18th. I was just resting after my hard year; I was in no hurry to do anything for a week. Anyway, I asked for their phone number and promised to call them back. I phoned Georgina and asked if she was interested in assisting me as I could not make the many products needed to have a craft sale. Georgina said "yes." She would love to do this. So I returned the call to tourism and said Georgina, another lady, and I would jointly do this project. We began sewing. We sewed from early morning till late at night. In the meantime, Chief Grace from my community phoned to ask if I would like to translate for my community at the Gwich'in Assembly that was being held in Inuvik at the end of July. I said I would be glad to do this. I would have a table of crafts for the midnight festival.

When this finished, I would catch the plane the next day. I did just that. I did not have much to sell for the festival as the beading and embroidery part of the product usually takes time, but it was promoting my craft to people who didn't know me. Every craft show that I do gives me more experience, and I love the people who I meet through the shows that I do. I left for Inuvik two days before the assembly was to begin. There was someone to meet me at the Inuvik airport and they took me to where I was to stay during the Gwich'in Assembly. The Assembly lasted a week, and I was asked to go to Arctic Red to act as translator for the Native Women's Association who were holding their Assembly there. Off to Arctic Red I went. But I had such a bad cold, I wanted to go home. I hate to travel when I am sick. While in Arctic Red, my aunt Annie sent someone to get some plants for Indian Medicine. She made this and I had to drink this bitter stuff. I had a chest cold and it was difficult to breathe. I asked a nurse who was stationed there to ask the doctor in Inuvik if I could have antibiotics. She refused.

She said the doctors now do not want to prescribe antibiotics for little illnesses such as colds. I was very worried because I had such difficult time breathing, and I have had pneumonia several times in my life. I felt I was coming down with something very serious. I was staying at Violet but I moved down to my aunt's and asked her to take care of me. She did. In no time, I was Recovering. I wanted to go home. By then I was able to travel, so I left for home.

By then it was racing to the end of August I had to be in Edmonton soon so I got ready and in few days I left for Edmonton and College.

TO BE CONTINUED......

Author's Note

I began writing my story in 1994, and finished the manuscript in 1996. Maybe because many things had hurt me so deeply in life, I cried many tears during the writing of the story. This story could have been published, but when asked to review, correct, and take second look at the sentence structure, I was afraid to. The fear of being hurt all over again. Something else came into my life which made me decide to self publish the book. I was diagnosed with a terminal illness and I cannot wait a year for the story to be published.

The next story I will be working on has 125 pages, rough draft. The Title is SILENT TEARS, SILENT CRIES which is the story of my culture, teachings of our survival skills, our native spirituality. Our teachings, then comes my story, **LIVING IN TWO WORLDS BOOK 2**

I tried very hard to find words in the English language, to be as expressive as I can be. At this time of publishing my story, I was able to forgive my ex. He has passed on, but we were able to talk to one another. I also want to thank all the people who were there to encourage, support, me throughout my writing.